LACTATION AT WORK

In recent decades, as women entered the US workforce in increasing numbers, they faced the conundrum of how to maintain breastfeeding and hold down full-time jobs. In 2010, the Lactation at Work Law (an amendment to the US Fair Labor Standards Act) mandated accommodations for lactating women. This book examines the federal law and its state-level equivalent in Indiana, drawing on two waves of interviews with human resource personnel, supervising managers, and lactating workers. In many ways, this simple law – requiring break time and privacy for pumping – is a success story. Through advocacy by allies, education of managers, and employee initiative, many organizations created compliant accommodations. This book shows legal scholars how a successful civil rights law creates effective change; helps labor activists and management personnel understand how to approach new accommodations; and enables workers to understand the possibilities for amelioration of workplace problems through internal negotiations and legal reforms.

ELIZABETH A. HOFFMANN is Associate Professor of Sociology and Law & Society at Purdue University. Hoffmann studies how people's legal consciousness and organizational location shape their experience of the law in the workplace. Her research has been supported by the National Science Foundation and has won awards from the Labor and Employment Research Association, the Upjohn Institute for Employment Research, and the American Bar Foundation.

CAMBRIDGE STUDIES IN LAW AND SOCIETY

Founded in 1997, Cambridge Studies in Law and Society is a hub for leading scholarship in socio-legal studies. Located at the intersection of law, the humanities, and the social sciences, it publishes empirically innovative and theoretically sophisticated work on law's manifestations in everyday life: from discourses to practices, and from institutions to cultures. The series editors have longstanding expertise in the interdisciplinary study of law, and welcome contributions that place legal phenomena in national, comparative, or international perspective. Series authors come from a range of disciplines, including anthropology, history, law, literature, political science, and sociology.

Series Editors

CAMBRIDGE
STUDIES IN
LAW AND SOCIETY

LACTATION AT WORK

Expressed Milk, Expressing Beliefs, and the Expressive Value of Law

Elizabeth A. Hoffmann
Purdue University

CAMBRIDGE
UNIVERSITY PRESS

CAMBRIDGE
UNIVERSITY PRESS

University Printing House, Cambridge CB2 8BS, United Kingdom

One Liberty Plaza, 20th Floor, New York, NY 10006, USA

477 Williamstown Road, Port Melbourne, VIC 3207, Australia

314–321, 3rd Floor, Plot 3, Splendor Forum, Jasola District Centre, New Delhi – 110025, India

103 Penang Road, #05–06/07, Visioncrest Commercial, Singapore 238467

Cambridge University Press is part of the University of Cambridge.

It furthers the University's mission by disseminating knowledge in the pursuit of education, learning, and research at the highest international levels of excellence.

www.cambridge.org
Information on this title: www.cambridge.org/9781108488549
DOI: 10.1017/9781108770828

First published 2021

A catalogue record for this publication is available from the British Library.

ISBN 978-1-108-48854-9 Hardback

This book is dedicated to my mom, Milly Hoffmann, who is my constant Ally Already in everything. She nursed me as a child and continues to support me in all my endeavors.

CONTENTS

TABLES

ACKNOWLEDGMENTS

Special thanks are due to the many interviewees who participated in this study. This work would not be possible without them. Their voices are this project.

This project received support from several institutions, in addition to the resources given me by my home institution, Purdue University. It was jointly funded by the Innovation and Organizational Sciences Program and the Law and Social Sciences Program National Science Foundation, grant SES-0853534. I am also grateful for the feedback and support I received while a visiting scholar at Department of Management, London School of Economics and Political Science (LSE), and at the Center for the Study of Law and Society (CSLS), the University of California, Berkeley. While at LSE, this project was furthered by the ideas and suggestions of Alexandra Beauregard, Uta Bindl, Jonathan Booth, Richard Hyman, Pat McGovern, and Matt Vidal. While at CSLS, I particularly benefited from the advice and mentorship from KT Albiston, Tom Burke, Lauren Edelman, Bob Kagan, and Rachel Stern.

I would like to thank fellow panelists and participants at the annual meetings, including those of the Law & Society Association, and the American Sociological Association, and the biannual meeting of the Midwest Law & Society Retreat. I would also like to thank the reviewers and editors at *Law & Society Review*, which published a version of Chapter 5. Certain friends read and discussed various drafts, furthering and refining my analysis, including Jeannine Bell, Lynette Chua, Kathleen Hull, Mark Hurwitz, Val Jenness, Erin Kelly, Anna Kirkland, Ron Levi, George Lovell, Anna-Maria Marshall, and Elizabeth Nisbet. In particular, I would like to thank Howie Erlanger – a mentor since before I even began law school – who read numerous drafts and offered incredible advice and encouragement throughout this project.

Within Purdue University, I am very grateful for the support I received from Sociology department heads Ken Ferraro, Linda Renzulli, and Bert Useem. Many Purdue colleagues helped me develop my ideas and encouraged my work, especially Rosie Clawson, Rachel Einwohner, Scott Feld, Spencer Headworth, Alice Pawley, Carolyn Perrucci, Kevin Stainback, and Jill Suitor. I would like to thank my research assistants, both undergraduate and graduate students, who helped with the literature, interviews, and coding.

I would like to thank Purdue's College of Liberal Arts and Dean Reingold for awarding me an Engage Grant to fund the workshop for this book. The feedback from the book workshop was incredible. I am forever indebted to those brilliant participants: David Engel, Sandy Levitsky, Jeremy Reynolds, Robin Stryker, and Mark Suchman.

Finally, without the encouragement from friends and family, this book could never have developed. I would like to thank my mother, Milly Hoffmann, who has cheered me on throughout my academic career and has always been a source of great love and inspiration. I also would like to thank Mikaila Arthur, Jenny Bellehumeur, Scott Barclay, Elizabeth Boyle, Catherine Capellaro, Jane Collins, Joe Conti, Chuck Epp, Emily Hoffmann-Noll, Mona Lynch, Jenny Moss, LB Nielsen, Robert Noll, Becky Sandefur, Mitra Sharafi, Susan Silbey, David Witzling, Nancy Worcester, and Kathryne Young. Your advice and support at the various stages of this project made this book possible.

CHAPTER ONE

INTRODUCTION

When Margie* returned to her job as a sales analyst after her maternity leave in 2006, she was determined to continue breastfeeding her son, Nathan. She was aware that her milk supply would diminish if she didn't create a constant demand for that milk, so she resolved to pump breast milk for him at work. Not only would this maintain her body's production of milk; it would also provide expressed milk for her child-care provider to feed Nathan while Margie worked.

Because she worked in a cubicle, she needed to find a private place to pump. At first, an assistant vice president was away for two weeks, so Margie was allowed to use his office. But, once he returned, the best place she could find was the women's lavatory. "This was food for my son, so doing this [expressing milk] in a bathroom stall was gross," she said. "But it's all there was."

Similarly, Josie wanted to express milk at work when she returned to her position as a receptionist for the corporate office of an insurance company in 2007. However, her managers told her that she needed to spend her break time and lunch hour at the reception desk – as she had before her maternity leave – in case anyone might need her. She tried to negotiate for time away from her desk, or for one of the office secretaries to fill in for her while she was away pumping, but the company concluded that it would be too disruptive. She gave up on the idea of expressing milk during the work day and nursed her infant

* To protect the identities of study participants I use pseudonyms throughout.

before and after work, supplementing with formula during the day. After a few days, she started wearing thick sweaters and brought extra blouses and bras to work to hide when her milk leaked through the pads she wore. After she had been back at work four weeks, her body no longer produced any milk. This situation may have had a detrimental effect on her infant's health.

The American Academy of Pediatrics recommends that women breastfeed for at least twelve months, and the World Health Organization recommends at least twenty-four months (American Academy of Pediatrics 2015; World Health Organization 2002). Yet, with most US maternity leaves lasting six weeks (eight weeks post Caesarean section births), these goals are nearly impossible to reach without expressing milk during the work day (Mohrbacher 2014). Seventy-five percent of women in the United States begin breastfeeding their infants; yet by six months, only 43 percent of babies are breastfed, and only 13 percent are exclusively breastfed (American Academy of Pediatrics 2015; World Health Organization 2002).

Recognizing the challenge of combining full-time employment and breast-milk production, the Fair Labor Standards Act was amended in 2010 to include a mandate that organizations provide lactating employees with a non-lavatory place to express breast milk, allow break time to do so, and ensure a safe place to store the pumped breast milk. More than half of the states also had their own versions of a Lactation at Work Law at the time when the federal law was passed. This book draws on data from one state that had its own Lactation at Work Law in the 2000s (Indiana) and another state that never had a state-level Lactation at Work Law (Wisconsin). Both states applied the federal law once it was in force. The data are strikingly similar for both states.

The Lactation at Work Law requires that workers must be allowed "reasonable" break time to express milk and that workers who usually were required to take their breaks at their work stations would be allowed to use their breaks to pump milk elsewhere. It required a private room "shielded from view and free from intrusion" for lactating workers (Fair Labor Standards Act 2010). And, symbolically, it declared that breastfeeding was of sufficient societal importance that employers needed to accommodate their employees expressing milk at work in order to breastfeed at home.

This law – like many others – has some ambiguity. The law does not stipulate what "reasonable break time" means, what employers must do if employees' milk pumping requires more time than is provided by their break time, nor how convenient the private space must be for the employee. Extant research in the area of law and organizations has found that laws with "broad and ambiguous principles give organizations wide latitude to construct the meaning of compliance" (Edelman 1992: 1532). Even when the law's directives are unambiguous, organizations may intentionally misinterpret the law to their advantage (Kelly 2003). Structures and procedures, initially created to signal compliance with the law, often transform the legal imperatives into conventional managerial goals in a process that scholars call "managerialization." Occasionally, these structures and procedures produce real change, such as the placement of ramps in key locations that enable convenient access for wheelchair users. Often, however, the organizational changes created in response to new legislation result in mere symbolic structures that produce few substantive effects, such as new internal procedures purported to further employment equality that actually stifle discrimination rights claims and serve to smooth out employment relations (Edelman et al. 2011; Edelman, Erlanger, and Lande 1993; Krieger, Best, and Edelman 2015; Pedriana, and Stryker 2017; Stryker 2007). This is particularly true when a law is new and organizations are wrestling with how to understand and apply it.

In struggling with how to apply a law, managerial personnel sometimes transform the law's goals, such as access and fair treatment, into goals conventionally held by management, such as efficiency and morale. As a result, the policies or structures that appear to be complying with the law are symbolic, creating little real improvement for the covered employees (Edelman et al. 2011; Edelman, Erlanger, and Lande 1993; Krieger, Best, and Edelman 2015).

Although the Lactation at Work Law has some ambiguity, it mandates more specific accommodations than most other civil rights laws do. By specifying that employers provide private, non-lavatory space and adequate break time, the law stipulates exactly how employers should comply with the law, unlike other employment laws that include vague concepts such as "equal opportunity" (Pedriana and Stryker 2017; Stryker 2007). The law's substantive directives provide a context for discussing how to implement it and, by codifying the needs of lactating employees, the law legitimates those discussions. In this way, the Lactation at Work Law overcomes what is often the most difficult aspect of workplace civil rights laws: initiating change in organizations.

If Margie and Josie wished to express milk at work today, the Lactation at Work Law should have removed the difficulties they faced. Margie's employer would have been required to provide her access to a private place to pump that wasn't a bathroom stall. Josie would have been allowed to leave the reception desk to express her milk. The law would have mandated these provisions.

EFFECTIVE LEGISLATION AND ORGANIZATIONAL COMPLIANCE

Did the law create the organizational changes that would have helped Margie and Josie? New workplace legislation does not automatically manifest as expanded workers' rights and improved employment conditions. Various actors within organizations must translate these laws into polices and those policies into day-to-day realities. Human resource specialists craft new policies in reaction to civil rights laws, and their supervising managers apply those new policies to their employees' work lives.

Despite legal mandates, organizations enjoy substantial discretion regarding their actual policies and practices, with some organizations' compliance more successfully fulfilling the goals underlying new laws. This book addresses key questions to understanding organizational compliance and effectiveness of legislation, specifically asking: "How did organizations interpret and apply the Lactation at Work Law, and which of those interpretations and applications succeeded?" and "How did the organizational actors' reasons or motivations for complying with the law affect its success in ameliorating the workplace issue and expanding those employment rights?"

I studied the Lactation at Work Law at two times: immediately after it was passed and approximately five years later. By reinterviewing many key personnel over time, this study explores how sometimes formal policies produce substantive change in the organizations, while at other times the changes are purely symbolic (Albiston 2007; Edelman 1992; Edelman, Erlanger, and Lande 1993; Edelman and Suchman 1999; Edelman, Uggen, and Erlanger 1999; Meyer and Rowan 1977). These data indicate multiple frames for understandings of accommodation – frames that affected how well the needs of lactating employees were, in fact, accommodated.

This study finds that the effectiveness of the law in ameliorating barriers for lactating employees is substantially affected by how their organizations' human resource specialists and supervising managers understand and apply it. The law is not a monolithic force that asserts its edicts on civil society. Instead, its effects are mediated by the organizations and individuals responsible for interpreting and enacting it. These organizations and individuals can actively produce compliance with the law's original intention, they can skirt the original intention to meet organizational goals, or they can draw on morality frames external to the organization to broaden their understanding of compliance. Moreover, organizations do not act as single entities when it comes to their legal compliance. Rather, individual actors within the organization, particularly at the level of supervising managers, develop their own understandings of the law and its subsequent policies as they interact with the employees they supervise and by drawing on their own personal experiences. These understandings may shift over time.

This study found variation both between organizations and within organizations. Often, human resource specialists and supervising managers reinterpreted the law's dictates into conventional management goals. In doing so, some created policies that complied with the letter of the law, but did not ameliorate the struggles of lactating women employees, creating lactation accommodations that satisfied the law but were purely symbolic. In other cases when employers shifted from legal goals to management goals, human resource personnel and supervising managers created accommodations that were viable solutions for their lactating workers, accommodations that were substantive.

In some organizations, some human resource specialists and supervising managers were supporters of the new law and the subsequent organizational policies without first embracing managerial goals as a way to understand and apply the law. These early supporters tended to have personal or close secondhand experience with expressing breast milk and became allies for the lactating employees. Often, their proximity to the issue of lactation at work meant that they already both understood the practicalities of milk expression and supported the goal of combining breastfeeding and employment.

Over time, the focus of some supervising managers who did engage in managerialization changed even farther. Their understanding of the lactation accommodations shifted away from both the legal directive and the managerial objectives to health-related reasons for supporting the mandated policies. Rather than using legal or managerial goals, these supervising managers drew on a health-focused morality frame from outside the organization, thereby "moralizing the law."

In many ways, the Lactation at Work Law is a success – a much-needed law that helps a sympathetic group of women workers. However, while activists, scholars, and politicians have all praised the Lactation at Work Law for mandating necessary accommodation for lactating employees, some scholars and activists question whether the Lactation at Work Law truly helps lactating workers. Indeed, some might describe this law as not *family* friendly, but *work* friendly. The presence of this law encourages women to return to work as quickly as possible, while still maintaining the effort of caring for children. From a policy standpoint, this type of law allows employers to shift the discussion away from the lack of effective, paid maternity leave in the United States. Some speculate that if US mothers did have longer paid leave, they might not want or need to pump at work.

Thus, while lactating employees may appreciate the Lactation at Work Law and their organization's subsequent policies because they enable milk expression, pumping milk might not be their first choice. To be clear, these women may prefer workplace milk expression to the alternatives of working full time and not pumping, or of not receiving a paycheck. But combining employment and breastfeeding may not be their aspiration.

In capitalist societies, an important marker of competent adulthood is full-time employment, and women who exit full-time employment are penalized in various ways, from diminished career trajectories to denial of welfare assistance from the state. The Lactation at Work Law allows nursing mothers to remain in the workforce; yet, in doing so, it perpetuates inequalities of neoliberal capitalism by compelling greater social reproduction labor from workers while demanding the very resources they require (time, energy, mental health, physical health, money) to sustain that social reproduction.

While feminism and other progressive movements have worked to bring more women into the paid labor force in order to increase women's personal and financial empowerment, the pro-woman or pro-mother benefits of the Lactation at Work Law are only tangential to its capitalist goals. As an outgrowth of neoliberalism, some assert that its main goal is to keep more workers – including lactating employees – in the labor market. By enabling the further separation of family and work, the Lactation at Work Law reinforces a double responsibility for working mothers. In this way, the success of the Lactation at Work Law might be considered an immediate success for lactating employees in some ways; but in other, broader ways, it might actually be more problematic.

METHODOLOGY

When new laws to protect workers' rights are enacted, organizations respond by translating these new laws into new workplace policies and practices. But they have considerable latitude to determine what kinds of policies and practices they create, and some of these may be more effective than others at meeting the law's underlying goals. This study asks, "How did different organizational responses translate the Lactation at Work Law differently, and how did those different translations affect the lactation experiences of the workers whose rights the law was intended to protect?" To answer this question, I selected a law that would allow me to easily observe responsive policies and structures and permit focused discussions with key actors. Previous research in this area has largely focused on managerial responses to legal change (Dobbin and Kelly 2007; Edelman 1992; Edelman, Fuller, and Mara-Ditra 2001; Edelman and Suchman 1997; Fuller, Edelman, and Matusik 2000; Kelly 2003; Kelly et al. 2010). However, because various groups of actors within organizations have different perspectives on how the processes and policies worked, I needed to interview more than management. In particular, I wanted to include the voices of those lactating employees who were affected by the law and the subsequent organizational policies devised by management.

As a qualitative study based on in-depth interviews, this research draws on each group of actors' own words to understand the application of the Lactation at Work Law. While this study has a relatively large number of participants for a qualitative study – 361 total: 188 management + 173 employees – it does not apply to all workers or all management in all organizations. Yet, unlike studies that draw on a large number of statistics, I am able to look more deeply at the data and thereby draw on the thoughts and experiences of the people involved to understand the social processes going on in organizations (what Levi-Strauss calls "mechanical models" [Lévi-Strauss 1969: 254]). Thus, this book draws on rich data and personal narratives to build theory about the processes described across the organizations in this study.

Whose Voices Are Speaking in This Book?

To understand how management and employees actually think about and experience legal compliance, workplace policies, and worker accommodations as they evolve over time, I spoke with people from 113 businesses from 10 industries – construction, dining/hotel/tourism, education, finance, government, health/medical, manufacturing, media, retail, and transportation – as well as from professional firms. Thus, this study draws on viewpoints and experiences from varied, multi-sited fieldwork across a range of industries (Hind 2007; Lévi-Strauss 1969). I selected these industries because they provided a mix of businesses to include variation in the types of occupations and purposes of organizations and because characteristics of jobs and worksites could affect the ease with which organizations implemented lactation accommodations (variation in manufacturing and service sectors); in the proportion of female workers, as a higher density of women workers could affect the level of need for lactation accommodations (variation in gender composition); and how easily workers could enter various fields and occupations, because lactating workers might be reluctant to quit if they fear they would not be able to reenter the same or similar jobs (variation in entry costs).

I conducted interviews with supervising managers, human resource specialists, and lactating employees working in each of these industries. Human resource personnel were those working in human resource departments, or similar employee benefit departments, who oversaw their organizations' interpretation and application of new laws. Supervising managers were those who directly oversaw workers and engaged in activities such as performance evaluation, scheduling, and assignments. For example, in hospitals, these manager-supervisors were clinic or division managers; in school systems, these managers-supervisors were principals; in the tourism and finance industries, these were the general managers for a specific hotel or bank, respectively.

I used a two-wave approach to explore how organizational responses to the Lactation at Work Law evolved over time, since previous single-time research theorized that organizational response moved from having less legal focus to having more organizational focus in crafting interpretation and compliance. Beginning in 2009, I interviewed lactating employees, human resource personnel, and supervising managers in Indiana to learn how businesses were interpreting and applying the new state law. In 2011, I expanded the study to include lactating employees, human resource personnel, and supervising managers in Wisconsin. Approximately four to six years after the initial interviews, I reinterviewed many of those same human resource specialists and supervising managers to assess whether their interpretations, practices, or viewpoints had changed. These second-wave interviews produced crucial data about how certain supervising managers changed from focusing exclusively on how compliance could help the organization ("managerialization") to how compliance furthered moral goals of community wellness ("moralizing the law").

Initially, I conducted the Wisconsin interviews in order to explore how organizations responded differently to federal laws than to state-level laws addressing the same goals. Interestingly, I did not find any meaningful differences between the Indiana and Wisconsin interviews. This similarity is very important for this study; the similar reactions to federal and state lactation-at-work laws suggest that the findings are valid beyond the two states I studied.

Why Two Waves of Interviews?

These data were collected in real time, just as the human resource specialists and supervising managers were first encountering the law, and then again once those new organizational policies had been in place for several years. Thus, this study observes, first, how this law was freshly interpreted and then, later, how those understandings evolved over time. I believe this is the first time the interpretation of a new law has been studied longitudinally beginning with its introduction.

What Exactly Is This Law?

This study examines the Lactation at Work Law in two different manifestations: as state-level legislation and as a federal law in the United States. First, I studied this state law when it was passed in Indiana. In 2008, the Indiana legislature passed Ind. Code §5-10-6-2 and §22-2-14-2, which mandated that employers accommodate lactating employees. At that time, twenty-six other states had passed similar legislation.

In 2010, the state-level Lactation at Work laws were mirrored in an amendment to section 7 of the Fair Labor Standards Act ("FLSA") through the passage of the Patient Protection and Affordable Care Act. The state and federal laws are very similar except for three differences: First, the federal law specifies a cutoff time of one year after the birth of the child, while Indiana's has no time limit for its applicability (as is true for most the other state Lactation at Work laws). Second, the federal law applies to employers with at least fifty employees, while the Indiana law applies to workplaces with at least twenty-five employees. Third, the state-level law has no enforcement mechanism, although noncompliance sets up a business for a civil suit, enabling a lactating employee to sue. The federal law is enforceable under the Federal

Department of Labor. Despite these differences in their respective laws, I found no differences in practical application between the two states.

To study the federal Lactation at Work Law, I turned to a state that had not had a state-level lactation-at-work law. In Wisconsin, the federal Lactation at Work Law addressed a new workplace issue, just as the state-level law had been new for Indiana. I chose Wisconsin as the comparison state because, like Indiana, it is a central Midwestern state with some industry and much farming. Both states have similar demographics. Throughout this book, I refer to "the Lactation at Work Law" in the singular, not differentiating between state and federal level.

In many ways, this was an ideal law to study in order to examine various aspects of sociological and socio-legal theory about how organizations apply laws, how organizational understanding of laws shifts over time, and how compliance varies depending on the degree of ambiguity and the resulting variation and breadth of organizational interpretation. In particular, the Lactation at Work Law was ambiguous enough to require interpretation by organizational actors – human resource personnel and supervising managers. Interviewees discussed how they interpreted the law, how they made decisions about new workplace policies to respond to those laws, and how they experienced those new policies. Yet the Lactation at Work Law was not as ambiguous as many other employment civil rights laws because it mandates accommodations that are sufficiently specific so that compliance was more transparent – for example, a private room was accessible for milk expression or it was not. Because the mandated accommodations were more concrete than those of many other civil rights laws, assessing the adequacy of accommodations could facilitate discussion between supervising managers and lactating employees.

How Does This Study Analyze What People Said?

This project uses a longitudinal panel of qualitative, in-depth interviews. A key benefit of qualitative research is the high validity possible; that is, success of actually capturing what the research purports to address (Hind 2007; Lévi-Strauss 1969). The interviews ranged from twenty minutes to about two hours, with most lasting between thirty and ninety minutes. All interviews were recorded and transcribed. Thus, all quotations used in this book are direct quotes.

The transcribed interviews and field notes were coded, using the qualitative data software NVivo, for various themes. Sometimes these themes were responses to specific questions (e.g., "What sort of internal publications to do you use to communicate about this law?" "What would an employee do if she felt she needed more accommodations for pumping breast milk?" "How would she appeal if she didn't receive the accommodation she requested?"). However, many others were extracted from the responses of interviewees to broader questions (e.g., "How would you handle an employee who takes offense to a co-worker's decision to express milk at work?" "How would you explain the law to someone else in your industry?" "What would you change about this law if you could just snap your fingers and it would be different?"), or to follow-up questions to other responses. Thus, many codes were not the result of a direct question or set of questions intended to measure a particular phenomenon, but were produced by analysis of interviewees' responses.

FOUR WORKPLACE RESPONSES TO THE LACTATION AT WORK LAW

Often, human resource personnel and other supervising managers, such as Helen and Greg, discussed shortly, translated the law into classic management goals, soon after the law was passed. Some organizations made changes that resulted in ineffective symbolic structures, policies that abided by the requisites of the law, but did very little to ameliorate the difficulties experienced by lactating employees, such as Amber, also discussed shortly. In other places, the law resulted in real change: new policies that directly helped lactating employees successfully express milk at work, as was the case for Olivia (see next section). Sometimes this resulted from managerialization that occurred in organizations where workplace milk expression enjoyed sufficient legitimacy, adequate space, and enough time to result in successful lactation accommodations. Other times, change was driven by allies – those in management who understood and supported workplace lactation even before the law was passed. Others in management became advocates over time after educative conversations with their lactating employees.

Symbolic Compliance

Helen's approach to implementing the law and her work's lactation policy provides an example of legal compliance that created mere symbolic change, without providing sufficient accommodation. Helen was a supervising manager at a midsized department store who valued the law's managerial benefits but did not implement sufficient accommodations to enable her employees to succeed at workplace milk expression. In the first-wave interview, Helen said that the Lactation at Work Law is good for business because it furthers preexisting management goals: "It reduces absenteeism; it's good for morale. It's a good law." In response to the law, Helen's organization created a new lactation policy, stating that lactating employees could use their break times to express milk. While Helen's organization recognized the legitimacy of the law's mandate and obeyed the letter of the law, the organization changed little to facilitate their employees' lactation success. This approach appeared to meet the prescriptions of the law, but did little to meet the needs of lactating workers, the law's goal.

When Helen's employee, Amber, returned from maternity leave, Amber told both Helen and Bruce, the human relations specialist in charge of work-life issues, that she wanted to pump milk at work. Bruce told her the store had designated the basement sick room as its lactation room. The room satisfied all requirements under the Lactation at Work Law: It was private, but not a bathroom. However, Amber found the setup unworkable. Just her travel time to and from the lactation room, along with necessary sanitation and set-up time, consumed most of her fifteen-minute break – leaving no time to actually express milk. What's more, her milk-storage cooler was kept in the employee break room on the third floor, and she needed time needed to clean and de/construct her pumping apparatus each time she pumped. Sometimes she was able to pump in ten minutes and return to her area within twenty-five minutes; this exceeded her official fifteen-minute break time, but fell within the "grace period" that her manager would occasionally allow. When she was consistently unable to return within twenty-five minutes, Helen told her she'd have to clock out and clock back in for any time beyond a twenty-four-minute over-break. Not wanting to lose income with each pumping session, Amber began pumping in the women's restroom located on the third floor.

In this way, Helen's organization met the requirements of the law, but did not make sufficient accommodations to enable Amber to achieve the goal of the law: successfully expressing breast milk at work. The law conferred adequate legitimacy on employee lactation for the company to meet the specific legal requirements. Yet, Amber's need to pump at work lacked sufficient legitimacy to warrant her employer granting the additional organizational resource of a few more minutes of paid breaks time.

Although Helen stated the law was "good for business," she did not implement any changes beyond those minimum legally required.

The law did not stipulate longer break time or that the designated place to pump be particularly convenient. Yet, without additional break time or a more convenient place to pump, Amber had to choose between losing wages, not expressing milk, or pumping in a lavatory (even though the law explicitly states that the employees should not need to pump in a restroom).

Substantive Managerialization

Greg also saw compliance with the Lactation at Work Law primarily as being good for business, but this managerialization created successful accommodations, what I refer to as Substantive Managerialization. Greg directly supervised about thirty-five employees. When one of his employees, Olivia, returned from her maternity leave, she told him she would be making use of the company's lactation policy. Olivia contacted the human resource department, which told her locations of rooms available for milk expression, and informed Greg that Olivia would be using her breaks and lunchtime to express breast milk. This worked well for Olivia. She only had to walk down the hall to the nearby "lactation room," where she both stored her expressed milk and refrigerated parts of her pumping apparatus so she would not need to clean the attachments between each day's pumping sessions.

Greg voiced support for the Lactation at Work Law because it furthered management goals; it enabled employees to come back from maternity leave, rather than quit. He felt that it helped those employees feel better about returning to work and enabled them to be more productive at their jobs. He articulated the law's value as its contribution to furthering managerial goals, specifically reducing worker turnover and increasing morale.

While locating private space nearby was not difficult, sometimes Olivia's pumping sessions exceeded the fifteen minutes of her official break. However, this was never seen as a problem. In part, her breaks were not problematic because other workers would also push the time limits if they were running errands or going out for lunch, creating a culture of flexibility around break time. While workplace lactation might not have enjoyed sufficient legitimacy to allow for multiple lengthy breaks, it certainly was accorded the same legitimacy as other employee needs that warranted occasional longer breaks. Lactation at work received sufficient legitimacy at the organization because its preexisting culture of flexibility about break time and availability of unused rooms that could be used for lactation created successful accommodations.

Although Greg's organization's focus on legal compliance was on how the law would benefit management, and his organization did not make substantial changes in reaction to the law, this Substantive Managerialization resulted in successful accommodations for Olivia. Fortunately, the organization had preexisting lockable/private rooms that could be used for milk expression. It also had a cultural norm of flexible break time so that Olivia's longer breaks were not troublesome.

Allies Already

One group of management interviewees needed neither the law nor managerial advantages to convince them to support the Lactation at Work initiatives: I call these actors Allies Already. Because of the momentum for change created by these allies, their organizations were poised to act when the law came into force and to implement lactation accommodations swiftly and successfully.

This group of human resource personnel and supervising managers were aware of the benefits of breastfeeding and the barriers to expressing milk at work. Before the law was even passed, and often even before lactating employees approached them, these employees were already proponents of workplace milk expression. Because they had personal or secondary experience with expression of breast milk – through wives, sisters, daughters, mothers, or friends – they understood the physiology of expression and lactation. They also embraced many of the goals, values, and beliefs of their lactating employees. Even before the law was in force, they welcomed the new law and organizational policies.

Chad was a supervising manager of a large hotel. He had suggested that the hotel provide a lactating room several years before the Lactation at Work Law was passed, but the board refused. "Once [the law] was passed, I thought, 'Yes! *This* the board will understand.' They might not have understood the need to support nursing moms, but they can understand what the law says to do." With newly bestowed legitimacy of the Lactation at Work Law, Chad's suggestions for lactation accommodations were approved and implemented speedily – lactation rooms were created near the various work stations of employees who needed them.

Chad, like many other managers and human resource personnel, had social proximity to breastfeeding before the law was passed. These people served as allies to their lactating employees, and the law became their ally as they used its passage both instrumentally and symbolically to create desired changes in their organizations. These human resource personnel talked of using the law to create new policies to help lactating employees, policies that otherwise would not have been approved without the law. These supervising managers frequently described embracing the policies not only to make legally required changes but also to exceed the baseline that the law set. Once the law legitimized lactation accommodations and workplace lactation, these Allies Already were in a better position to convince others in their organizations to embrace pro-lactation changes.

Morality-Motivated Advocates

One group of supervising managers actually shifted in how they understood the lactation accommodations, and, over time, became Morality-Motivated Advocates. Here, the law created opportunities for employees to educate their supervising managers, expanding their view of compliance with lactation accommodations by sharing lactation information and health-focused morality.

When I began my interviews shortly after the Lactation at Work Law was in force, both human resource personnel and supervising managers often engaged in managerialization of the law. Both groups appreciated the law for its potential to further managerial goals and typically complied with the letter of the law only. While this could accomplish substantive change in some organizations, in other organizations it resulted in symbolic policies.

However, when I returned to these human resource personnel and supervising managers about five years later, approximately two-thirds of the supervising managers who had not been allies at the first interview had changed how they approached the law, as did their organizations' subsequent policies; however, none of the human resource personnel had changed their approach. Those supervising managers now viewed the issue in terms of the morality of health benefits – health benefits for those inside as well as outside their organizations. Their broadened focus was not just health benefits as a means to a managerial end, such as healthier babies resulting in fewer sick days and lower absenteeism, but health benefits for the employee, her children, and even members of the community not associated with the organization in any way. With this new appreciation, these Morality-Motivated Advocates were more willing to work beyond the minimum requirements of the law to create effective accommodations.

Although not all supervising managers shifted how they understood the benefit of the law, the people who did experience this shift were all supervising managers, not human resource personnel. That is because supervising managers were the ones having educational conversation with their lactating employees. As these workers used lactation accommodations or requested changes in accommodations, they discussed breastfeeding, pumping, and related issues with their supervising managers. These conversations taught the managers the practical reasons for expressing milk at work, but they also explored the employees' beliefs and norms. The human resource personnel had more contact with lawyers, human resource organizations, and higher management, but they had significantly less day-to-day contact with lactating employees. As a result, they maintained their classic managerialization of the law, seeing its benefits through the lens of profit to the organization.

For example, Brian, a sixty-something supervising manager of a manufacturing company, admitted that when his organization instituted its lactation policy, he didn't understand much about pumping and lactation and why a mother would want to breastfeed at all, much less express milk at work. Yet, over the last several years, he had supervised several employees who chose to pump milk. He said he would "just let them do whatever it was she had to do." Over time, these lactating employees would talk with him about their decision to pump at work. Sometimes, these educational conversations were brief; other times, they were extended discussions.

"I didn't understand," Brian said. "My wife never nursed; I never really knew about it. But breast milk is amazing. It really helps babies be healthy. But you have to keep making the milk all the time, or the milk dries up. And then the baby won't have it. And it's so important for babies to stay healthy . . . and grow well and have a good start. We talk about crime, and education, and tax dollars, but this is something that directly helps those kids grow up to a good life." By his second-wave interview, Brian, new Morality-Motivated Advocate, embraced the rhetoric of health to explain the lactation at work policy.

Table 1.1 summarizes the book's main findings. In doing so, it provides an overview of the interpretive frames of how the various organizations approached legal compliance and accommodations.

TABLE 1.1 Lactation at work and pathways to social change

Approach to the legal compliance	Motivation/ Frame	Primary/Specific use of law	Goal	Furthering effective compliance	Outcome
Noncompliance	Refuse to comply with the law, but often deny noncompliance	Noncompliance with law permitted if posing hardship to business; a rare exception	Deny responsibility of, or minimize change to, organization	–	Substantial hurdles to expressing milk
Symbolic managerialization	Minimal accommodation as possible	Compliance with law ceremonial only; accommodations only incidentally useful	Minimize change to organization	–	Hurdles to expressing milk remain
Substantive managerialization	Managerial and organizational goals	Law used to further organizational priorities	Further conventional organizational needs (efficiency, employee retention and morale)	Preexisting Resources Culturally, flexibility for employees' needs; Structurally, private places for employees' (own offices; wellness rooms), or spaces easily adaptable	Adequate milk-expression accommodations if needs align with preexisting resource

Table 1.1 *(cont.)*

Approach to the legal compliance	Motivation/ Frame	Primary/Specific use of law	Goal	Furthering effective compliance	Outcome
Allies Already	Personal or close secondhand experience with lactation	Used to lend workplace lactation legitimacy; bolster effectiveness of allies	Fully meet lactating women's needs	Allies in place before law's passage	At least adequate milk expression accommodations; swift, immediate change; some beyond compliance
Morality-Motivated Advocates	Educational conversations with lactating employees Moral commitment	Used to lend workplace lactation legitimacy and extend accommodations' importance to outside of organization	Promote public health within and beyond organization	Morally committed new advocates	At least adequate milk-expression accommodations; some beyond compliance; child & health focus obscures worker rights

COMPONENTS OF SUCCESS

Workplace accommodations for lactating workers were more successful when the organization could adapt the workplace culture and organizational structures already in place to the needs of the lactating employees. For example, workplaces that had wellness rooms could adapt them for lactating employees to pump breast milk. Similarly, workplace cultures that were flexible enough to allow employees to leave their work stations for running errands, medical appointments, or to shift start or end times were more able to harmoniously integrate the needs of lactating workers.

However, even in organizations with preexisting structural or cultural aspects, compliance is only symbolic if workplace lactation lacks legitimacy. Even if a workplace has flexible time for employees' outside needs, a lactating employee might not step away to pump if her supervising manager has communicated disapproval by scheduling meetings during established break times. If co-workers have expressed similar annoyance regarding the employee's need to pump, a lactating employee might feel she must sneak away to express milk or be concerned that someone might "tattle" on her for using lactation accommodations. Similarly, if milk expression only has enough legitimacy to allow it, but not enough to warrant using organizational resources, such as paid time off, a lactating worker might feel she must punch out if she takes enough time to pump, in order to not see herself as a "bad worker" wasting company time. Yet, by punching out, she diminishes her income.

Without understanding workplace milk expression as fully legitimate, available accommodations will not be successful and hurdles to their availability will become barriers, making potentially successful accommodations into merely symbolic compliance. Thus, the key to truly effective compliance with the Lactation at Work Law is the legitimacy it can command within organizations. With sufficient legitimacy, the law and the practice of workplace lactation command sufficient organizational resources, wresting control from management over workers' time and physical placement. Without legitimacy, lactating employees' experiences with milk expression will not be consistently successful, and legal compliance will remain more symbolic than effective.

For those in management who already saw workplace milk expression as legitimate, the law provided useful – often necessary – legitimation of workplace lactation. After legitimacy was established, they could effectively advocate for lactation accommodations within their organizations. The Lactation at Work Law's substantial symbolic power communicated that breastfeeding and milk expression were sufficiently important issues that the state and federal governments passed laws to protect and encourage them (Gusfield 1967; McAdams 2017). In legitimizing lactation accommodations, the law reframed them as important, rather than a lesser "women's issue."

STRUCTURAL AND CULTURAL CONSTRAINTS ON WORKERS' RIGHTS

Laws designed to protect workers' rights do not automatically result in workers actually being able to exert those rights. Organizational culture generally opposes anything that distracts workers from their work. Organizational structure often resists any change that diminishes management's control over their employees' time and bodies.

Scholars in a range of disciplines have studied employment law (see Albiston 2007) and many of these studies have documented employment discrimination against mother-employees, including active bias by those intending to treat these employees differently, and disparate impact resulting from ostensibly neutral policies and seemingly benign actions (see Agocs, Langan, and Sanders 2015; Albiston 2010; Gangl and Ziefle 2015; Glass 2004; Goldin 2006; Kelly 2005; Kelly and Dobbin 1999; Perlow and Kelly 2014; Waldfogel 2001; Whittington 2011; Williams 2000; Woodward 2015). Indeed, as noted employment law scholar Catherine Albiston observed, concern over workers' difficulties in meeting both work and family responsibilities, and the law's ability to address this concern, has changed the focus "from marginal concern to center stage" (Albiston 2007: 398).

Mother-employees' family obligations usually center around absences from work (see e.g., Budig, Misra, and Boeckmann 2016) or wanting fewer hours of work time (see e.g., Reynolds and May 2014). Parental leave, pregnancy bed rest, sick-child days, and leaving early or arriving late due to childcare complications all result in the employee being away from her place of work. Her nonconformity is demonstrated by her absence. Various workplace-focused laws have been passed to address these issues, such as the Family and Medical Leave Acts and the Pregnancy Discrimination Act.

In contrast, expressing breast milk takes place while a breastfeeding mom is at work. In order for women to maintain their milk supply and to alleviate the discomfort of accumulating breast milk, they must express milk throughout the day. While physiologically understandable, this physical need to regularly pump milk makes these workers substantially different from co-workers.

Lactating workers thus might fall short of the image of the "ideal worker," one dedicated exclusively to the employer, without the distractions of family, health issues, or other concerns. The need to regularly pump breast milk might physically separate lactating employees from their co-workers and make them appear less committed to their jobs, more distracted, and less willing to focus on their job duties. The extant research documents that employers often discount and even punish employees whom they see as falling short of their image of the ideal worker (Beauregard 2014; Pedulla and Thebaud 2015; Perlow and Kelly 2014; Roth 2004). In this way, it can be quite difficult for workers to deviate from standard expectations of how the organization usually functions. These institutionalized expectations hinder provision of lactation accommodations by making necessary alterations seem indulgent, inappropriate, or impossible according to the organizational culture (Berger and Luckmann 1966). As Albiston noted, "many of the characteristics of work that seem natural, normal, and inevitable involve practices regarding time and employer control" (2010: 1104). Yet, this law addresses the *employee*'s control over her time and place in order to have the necessary private space and minutes to pump milk.

Thus, the Lactation at Work Law faced various obstacles to reaching its goal of creating successful accommodations for lactating women. Cultural and structural organizational bias against allowing employees to control their own time created resistance to any substantial changes the law might enact. To achieve true success, measures taken to implement the law must overcome discrimination against lactating workers as well as overcoming reticence by those lactating employees to use the accommodations, lest they not be seen as "ideal workers."

SUMMARY OF CHAPTER FINDINGS AND ARGUMENTS

To understand organizational actors' perspectives on the Lactation at Work Law, the project needed to include a sense of the general cultural history and understanding of breastfeeding that the interviewees might have as background knowledge. Both the law and health care entities have helped frame the public's understanding of lactation and expressing milk at work. Chapter 2, "Lactation Law as Public Policy," provides background for subsequent chapters by explaining the cultural context of breastfeeding both in the United States, where this study occurred, and internationally. This chapter explains the new law and the rationales for lactation-at-work policies. While the right to pump breast milk at work is now a federal right in the United States, this legal protection varies worldwide.

As with all laws, the official law is filtered by various institutions and their actors into working people's everyday lives. Chapters 3, 4, 5, and 6 explain how organizational actors applied the Lactation at Work Law, interpreted the law into policies, and applied those policies to workers' specific situations. Interviews with lactating employees, human resource personnel, and supervising managers explain how organizational policies and workplace rhetoric sometimes evolved the longer the law was in force.

Organizations' formal policies addressed the mandates of the law – provision of a private space that is not a lavatory, a place for storing pumped milk, and break time to pump. However, the law does not stipulate how convenient a private space needs to be, how secure the storage place for milk must be, or to what extent the employer must accommodate if the employee needs additional break time. Within these under-clarified areas human resource specialists and supervising managers displayed a range of attitudes in how they approached and executed their organizations' lactation policies.

Moreover, the seemingly straightforward provisions could be difficult to implement. Secure milk storage was the easiest. However, organizations often struggled to locate a private space that was sufficiently easy to access. For example, some women had to leave their floor, or even their building, to go to a designated lactation room. Others had to ask a supervisor or a receptionist for the key to the designated room, causing not only additional time and hassle, but also some level of embarrassment.

The allotted time itself also could be a hurdle in many organizations. This was especially true if the employee had to leave her work area, adding travel time to the minutes she used for her break; the typical fifteen-minute break was often insufficient. Even if no travel time was necessary, it often took more time than a standard break to assemble the pumping apparatus, express milk, disassemble and wash the pump.

For the Lactation at Work Law to create more than merely symbolic policies, the existing organizational structures, workplace culture, or management initiative needed to make the legally mandated accommodations into effective changes. For example, this could be an organization where private offices or at least easily accessible private rooms were easily available to all employees. Or it could be an organization with a strong norm of flexible time for fluid breaks, with little direct accountability for exact work time so long as the workers complete their tasks. Or it could be an organization with neither structural nor cultural factors contributing to lactation accommodations' success, but whose lactating workers have human resource specialists or supervising managers who viewed lactation at work as a legitimate endeavor that led them to embrace a level of accommodation beyond the minimum requirements of the law. As a result of these variations, some organizations' accommodations were only symbolic and resulted in no substantive change for employees. Other organizations, even if they were focused on managerial goals, considered workers' ability to express milk at work to be legitimate enough that they were willing to utilize organizational culture and available physical structures to create effective accommodations. A third set of organizations had human resource personnel or supervising managers who embraced the legitimacy of workplace lactation to champion swift, substantive compliance soon after the law was in place. And finally, some organizational responses changed over time as supervising managers began to draw on health-focused morality to motivate their extensive compliance. Chapters 3–6 address each of these variations in turn.

Chapter 3, "Expressed Frustration: Noncompliant, Insufficient, and Inconsistent Accommodations," shows that sometimes organizations interpreted the Lactation at Work Law in ways that created only symbolically compliant structures; these policies appeared to abide by the law, but were insufficient accommodations – when organizations complied with the law at all. Here, managerialization of the law resulted in mere gestures of compliance that did little to assist the employees who needed lactation accommodation. The Lactation at Work Law had sufficient legitimacy that organizations created some policies, but workplace lactation lacked enough legitimacy to compel these organizations to implement successful changes. Where managerial goals clashed with the goals of the law, "managerial norms and needs" (Albiston 2005: 38) trumped the lactation needs of employees. Even when a pumping space was provided and the break time was allowed for milk expression, some lactating employees faced many obstacles to pumping milk. For these women, the policies, although often legally compliant, were ineffective and mostly symbolic.

In these situations, lactating employees met with substantial resistance, resentment, and unhelpful stances regarding pumping accommodations. The onus often would be placed on the employee to devise a way to pump successfully. These employees could not successfully pump without devising their own creative initiatives. For example, sometimes women in these organizations would have to clock out and clock in, reducing their paychecks. Other women, perhaps not having this option, simply snuck away for longer than was allowed and hoped that their absence wasn't noticed – or, if it were, that co-workers would cover for them. And, of course, a substantial proportion of those lactating workers simply gave up pumping milk at work.

However, other times managerialization of the law created policies that led to substantive change and supported lactating employees' pumping needs. Chapter 4, "Milk and Management: Substantive Compliance through Managerialization," shows examples where the Lactation at Work Law moved beyond symbolic compliance to creating substantive, sufficient lactation accommodations. This is in stark contrast to the findings of most other studies of managerialized law, where managerialization of laws – often laws that are more vague and with less concrete mandates – create symbolic compliance that appears to satisfy the letter of the law but fails to improve workplace civil rights.

In the cases explored in Chapter 4, organizational response to the law created lactation policies that resulted in easily accessible, convenient pumping places and enough time to do everything necessary, with the Lactation at Work Law viewed as furthering management goals (e.g., morale, turnover, absenteeism). Although management in the Chapter 4 organizations also focused on how the law could benefit business, the changes the organizations in Chapter 4 made resulted in effective accommodations. Success was often aided by preexisting structures of the organization, such as a workplace with many private offices, and established culture, such as scheduling flexibility. These organizational cultures viewed workplace milk expression as a legitimate issue. Human resource personnel and supervising managers implemented lactation accommodations by drawing on rationales focused on the legal mandate or on how the lactation accommodations benefited the organization.

The "Allies Already" of Chapter 5 present a stark contrast to the resistant managers of Chapter 3 and the organizations of Chapter 4. These eager supporters were the human resource personnel and supervising managers who had wives, mothers, daughters, other close friends or relatives who pumped milk at work, or who did so themselves. Their proximity to the practice of expressing milk at work familiarized these interviewees not only with the pragmatics of pumping and safely storing milk at work, but also with the health philosophies and child-rearing ideologies that accompanied pumping milk.

The law provided legitimacy to workplace lactation accommodations and gave these Allies Already leverage to swiftly make the pro-lactation changes – often changes they had unsuccessfully attempted earlier – as soon as the law was passed. They embraced the Lactation at Work Law and organizational policies from the beginning, often making accommodations that extended far beyond the legal mandate. While they utilized the Lactation at Work Law to compel their organizations to initiate effective lactation accommodations, their own motivation emanated from the empathy and solidarity they had with their lactating employees.

Chapter 6, "Moralization of the Law: Listening in the Shadow of the Law and the Transformation of Supervising Managers," shows how the law creates opportunities for relational work that can generate another group of enthusiastic supporters of lactation accommodations, Morality-Motivated Advocates. By the second-wave interviews, some supervising managers had begun to "moralize" the law, drawing on morality-based arguments regarding children's health and wellness to support their compliance. As a result, they often embraced accommodations beyond the basics specified by the law. This group of supervising managers (about two-thirds of those managers who were not allies at Time One) had learned about lactation physiology and breastfeeding values through educational conversations with their lactating employees.

These Morality-Motivated Advocates *initially* took the legal mandates and created arguments for legal obedience based on management goals – like the managers in the organizations in Chapters 3 and 4. Over time, though, some of them began to draw on health-focused morality perspectives to expand past traditional management goals, often creating accommodations beyond basic compliance. This approach to legal compliance was not simply reconfiguring management goals. For example, this approach does not include a supervising manager who finds that breastfed babies have fewer earaches and supports her organization's lactation policy because her nursing employees miss less work due to sick children. That example would still be categorized as managerialization of the law because it embraces the policy for its furthering of the management goal of absenteeism. Instead, these supervising managers embraced a health-focused morality around breastfeeding and lactation for the sake of the wellness of their employees, their families, and even the larger community, regardless of the direct impact on managerial goals.

Human resource personnel, without day-to-day employee contact, were not privy to these educational conversations. Without the impact of the educational conversations, human resource personnel continued to understand legal compliance solely through managerialization. This illustrates how organizational actors' responses to the law can be strongly affected by their location within the organization, challenging the theory of a single institutional culture permeating each organization, (see Gray and Silbey 2014 for somewhat similar findings regarding regulation of safety practices).

The concrete specifics of the law created the opportunities for lactating employees to have these critical conversations with their supervising managers, while the law's mere presence legitimized the issue of workplace milk expression, thereby enabling those conversations to occur. This evolution in compliance rationales – from legal mandate, to managerial concerns, and finally to overall health goals – presents a significant contrast to what other scholars have found, where managerialization results in only symbolic compliance (Dobbin and Kelly 2007; Edelman 1992; Edelman, Fuller, and Mara-Ditra 2001; Edelman and Suchman 1997; Fuller, Edelman, and Matusik 2000; Kelly 2003; Kelly et al. 2010). My data show the possibility that, in some circumstances and with certain laws, managerialization could result in effective, substantive compliance. This is a very hopeful message.

This book examines the Lactation at Work Law and the policies it inspired as ways to better understand possible pathways to social change. It discusses how organizational actors understood and applied the law and how these understandings and applications might vary across an organization and change over time. This research identifies four key ways that organizational actors interpret and comply with new workers' rights legislation; the four sets of organizational policies and practices organizations enacted in response to these interpretations created very different experiences for the targeted workers and their civil rights at work.

This work speaks to how society might create greater change in the workplace and how the law and other institutions might intersect, reinforce each other, or hinder social change. While this book focuses on a particular law, its findings have implications for many other laws, such as the Americans with Disabilities Act (ADA). Compliance with the ADA might be heightened by preexisting structures that accommodate disabilities; organizational cultures that appreciate the legitimacy of a range of accommodation needs; and advocates who push for compliance with the law as well as organizational changes that surpass the legal minimum. These findings also have implications for other civil rights issues, such as transgender accommodation. Transgender, nonbinary, and queer-plus workers may be able to identify advocates already in place to further their civil rights or create new advocates through educative conversations with supervising managers about their experiences and needs.

Nevertheless, the nature of the research also suggests various observations specific to the Lactation at Work Law and its policies. In Chapter 7, I offer suggestions regarding the law and organizations, generally, and the Lactation at Work Law, specifically. For example, in addressing how some changes initiated by new laws might take hold and continue over time, I suggest that normative shifts within the organizational culture actually might result in the laws becoming institutionalized in more substantial ways. In the case of the Lactation at Work Law, reification of lactation accommodations and greater acceptance of workplace milk expression were more likely when the law and its subsequent organizational policies created normative shift in organizational culture, more than when compliance was focused on the managerial benefits or the force of the law itself. In the case of the Lactation at Work Law, however, such cultural shifts were characterized by a focus on health, rather than workers' rights. Ironically, then, this particular moralization of the law could eventually result in regressive, rather than progressive, social policy when the morality of health concerns trumps workplace rights.

CHAPTER TWO

LACTATION LAW AS PUBLIC POLICY

For millennia and in every country around the globe, women have breastfed their babies. More recently, however, the increase of women in the paid labor force and the heightened awareness of the health benefits of breastfeeding have focused attention on the question of how mothers can combine breastfeeding and full-time employment. The Lactation at Work Law addresses this timely issue: the need for some female employees to express breast milk at work in order to continue breastfeeding. Today, in the United States, not only are more middle-class women in the workforce, but more women are choosing to breastfeed than in past decades. These two trends make accommodations for workplace milk expression a key issue in the modern workplace.

The cultural shift toward valuing milk expression was fueled by changes in science and health care, greater maternal labor force participation, and developments in the technology that allows for the convergence of the two. The growing presence of breast pumps, especially among middle-class postpartum women, represents the conundrum nursing mothers face: How do they breastfeed if their children are not with them during the day – for example, if the mothers are at work. This chapter briefly discusses this context, although it is beyond its scope to provide a history of lactation, a full analysis of the culture around breastfeeding, or a greater exploration of many of these issues.

Supporters praised the Lactation at Work Law as addressing many concerns, including child health and employment discrimination. Even more than from modern lactation technology, lactating workers benefited from many organizations embracing, rather than resisting, this new law. My research demonstrates that the law can be used as a tool for social change. However, despite its success in improving lactation accommodations, the Lactation at Work Law might actually do little to advance workers' rights.

BREASTFEEDING WOMEN'S LABOR FORCE PARTICIPATION IN SOCIAL AND HISTORICAL PERSPECTIVE

Distinctiveness of Breastfeeding

The Lactation at Work Law emerged from an understanding that breastfeeding issues are distinct from other health issues and other family-related concerns (e.g., Dinour and Bai 2016; Elliott and Bowen 2018; Jantzer, Anderson and Kuehl 2018; Kozhimannil et al. 2016). The World Health Organization (WHO), along with other health organizations across the globe, recommends that babies be exclusively breastfed for the first six months and then given breast milk in addition to food until they are at least two years old (World Health Organization 2002). The WHO cites various breastfeeding benefits. For example, compared with babies who are not breastfed, breastfed babies experience lower rates of asthma, allergies, ear infections, and postneonatal death. Breastfed babies also show strengthened immune systems, better cognitive development, and heightened performance on intelligence measures (Adams 2017; American Academy of Pediatrics 2005; Kim, Shin, and Donovan 2019; Welmer 1999). The WHO's recommendations are also informed by breastfeeding's benefits to mothers, including less postpartum bleeding; lower rates of breast, ovarian, and uterine cancer; and less likelihood of osteoporosis and type 2 diabetes compared with mothers who do not breastfeed. Moreover, breastfeeding offers social benefits, including furthering mother–child bonding and positive feelings about mothering (Adams 2017; American Academy of Pediatrics 2005; Kim, Shin, and Donovan 2019; Lindberg 1996; Mun and Brinton 2015; Welmer 1999).

Despite these social and physical benefits of breastfeeding, nursing mothers face significant hurdles when combining lactation and employment. Once mothers return to work – and 66 percent of mothers in the United States return to work within six months of delivery (Kim, Shin, and Donovan 2019) – their likelihood of continuing to breastfeed drops significantly. Hours of employment negatively impact breastfeeding incidence, so that only 11 percent of employed mothers who started breastfeeding their infants were nursing after one year (May 2017). Breastfeeding advocates hoped that the Lactation at Work Law might ameliorate this situation (Adams 2017; Boone 2018a; Hoffmann 2019; Jantzer, Anderson, and Kuehl 2018; Kim, Shin, and Donovan 2019; Kobayashi and Usui 2017a; Shortall 2015).

Some scholars argue that breastfeeding needs to be framed as a health concern, a social issue, or a family-friendly policy, because otherwise it risks being framed as a "mother issue" – and "mother issues" historically have received inadequate public support (Boswell-Penc and Boyer 2007; Elliott and Bowen 2018; Jantzer, Anderson, and Kuehl 2018; Kozhimannil et al. 2016). However, lactation at work is different from maternity leave and similar accommodations that enable the working parent to be away from work. Workplace lactation accommodations, by definition, facilitate the employee's body being at the work site. But milk expression at work poses unique work challenges, and the need to express milk regularly complicates the conventional control of management over employees' work spaces and times in ways that are unlike most other health issues (Kozhimannil et al. 2016).

Workplace breastfeeding is also complicated by being a gendered activity. While both men and women can parent, only mothers can breastfeed. Especially in the United States, breasts are highly sexualized parts of women's bodies. Discussion of breasts, including their functions, is often considered inappropriate for the public space – particularly the workplace. Additionally, because breast milk is not essential for infant survival, breastfeeding often is viewed as a choice (Stevens, Patrick, and Pickler 2009).

Although it is a natural process, breastfeeding and expressing breast milk involve a learning curve and some focused effort; lactating workers may need to focus their attention on milk expression in order for lactation at work to be successful. Nevertheless, once lactating, breastfeeding mothers *must* breastfeed or express milk every few hours. When lactating mothers do not nurse or express milk for substantial periods of time, their breasts become uncomfortable and painful. They risk milk duct infections (i.e., mastitis), and eventually lose their ability to lactate. These physical needs mean that lactating employees must conduct a nonwork activity (either breastfeeding or expressing milk) while at work.

Race and Class

Socioeconomic status and race significantly affect breastfeeding practices (Stevens, Patrick, and Pickler 2009). At the turn of the twentieth century and prior, working-class women in the United States were more likely to be working outside the home and therefore less likely to be breastfeeding for an extended duration, especially if they lived or worked in urban areas (Papastavrou et al. 2015). Today, children in low-income families are far less likely to be breastfed for extended durations than children in middle- and high-income families (Jones et al. 2015).

Jones and co-authors note that "[m]others with lower rates of breastfeeding tend to be young, low-income, African American, unmarried, less educated, participants in the Supplemental Nutrition Program for Women, Infants, and Children (WIC)" (2015: 186). In particular, African American mothers are least likely to intend to, initiate, and continue breastfeeding when compared to similar white mothers, as well as other racial and ethnic groups. Of African American mothers, 61 percent initiate breastfeeding, and of those women, their mean duration of nursing is 6.4 weeks, compared to 78 percent and 16.5 weeks, respectively, for white mothers (McKinney et al. 2016). African American moms also are more likely to live in poverty and less likely to have a college degree, both of which correlate with lower rates of breastfeeding (Bentley, Dee, and Jensen 2003; McKinney et al. 2016).

Additionally, poor women and African American women are more likely to work in jobs without lactation accommodations, and they are less likely to be able to take advantage of such accommodations when they are offered. African American and poor women are more likely to work in smaller organizations, and the federal law explicitly excludes businesses that employ fewer than fifty employees if compliance would impose an undue hardship (although state-level laws apply to smaller businesses). Poor women and African American women are also more likely to work multiple jobs for fewer hours with each employer; yet the law does not apply if, due to short durations of work time, the woman would not qualify for breaks. Even if the woman has a job that provides breaks and is covered by the law, those breaks are not required to be paid, and poor and African American women are less likely to be able to afford the luxury of unpaid break time (Bentley, Dee, and Jensen 2003; Federal-Lactation-at-Work-Law 2010; Jones et al. 2015; McKinney et al. 2016; Welmer 1999).

Often relying on only their own paycheck to care for their families, poor women often are too vulnerable to demand breastfeeding-friendly childcare and too desperate to hold out for family-friendly employment. As a result, mothers of families at or below the poverty line are 19 percent less likely to initiate breastfeeding, in contrast to those 350 percent above line (Welmer 1999). Similarly, 59 percent of teenage mothers are below 200 percent of the poverty line, and only 43 percent of teenage mothers are like to breastfeed, in contrast to 65 percent of those 20–29 years old or 75 percent of mothers over 30 years old (McDowell, Wang, and Kennedy-Stephenson 2008). Thus, the lower a woman's household income, the less likely she is to initiate breastfeeding, the fewer weeks she will exclusively breastfeed, and the less time she will continue breastfeeding at all for her child's first year (Bentley, Dee, and Jensen 2003; Jones et al. 2015; McKinney et al. 2016; Welmer 1999).

Structural, institutional, and overt racism contribute to this difference in breastfeeding. A commercial formula milk substitute is more likely to be offered to mothers in predominantly African American communities, with 32 percent of African American mothers feeding their children formula by their second day post birth (Jones et al. 2015; McKinney et al. 2016). African American women also receive less encouragement and education regarding breastfeeding from health-care providers, even though breastfeeding might help African American women in particular because they are disproportionately affected by some of the health issues that are ameliorated by lactation (e.g., diabetes and cardiovascular disease) (Jones et al. 2015). Jones and coauthors found that African American women are more likely to receive formula instead of breastfeeding counseling from Women, Infants, and Children (WIC) counselors (Jones et al. 2015).

The negative correlation between breastfeeding and being working class or African American is poignantly ironic in that breastfeeding requires little financial outlay, while formula costs money and requires bottles and other supplies. But breastfeeding has hidden costs: time and flexibility. A working mother who wants to exclusively breastfeed for at least the first six months of her child's life requires generous maternity leave, milk-expression breaks in a private room, or easy access to her nursling, such as through on-site childcare. In the United States, where this study took place, such benefits are rarely available to African American and working-class women. The Lactation at Work Law promised to address this inequality by applying to jobs held by many working-class and women of color.

The Separation of Infant Feeding from Nursing and Lactation

The issue of accommodation for expressing breast milk at work emerges from the history of the separation of feeding babies from actual breastfeeding and lactation. Social forces and technological innovations as well as greater social acceptability contributed to separating infant feeding from nursing and lactation. While wet nurses had fed babies of wealthy, sick, or deceased mothers for centuries, artificial milk substitute – that is, "formula" – was first introduced in the late nineteenth century, with Nestle first to sell a complete artificial formula in the 1870s. Despite this availability, proprietary formulas were still considered too expensive in comparison to cow's milk, as a breastmilk supplement (Jung 2015; Stevens, Patrick, and Pickler 2009).

When World War II required more labor in the war industries, nearly 6 million women joined the workforce in the United States alone. Internationally, during the war almost one-third of married women were employed outside the home. Corporate polices, federal laws, and social mores shifted to enable this influx of women workers; for example, in 1941, the United States expanded the Lanham Act to provide more day care for the children of women who were employed in war industries. The availability and acceptance of infant formula grew significantly as well (Jung 2015).

Internationally, by the mid-twentieth century, import controls were loosened or lifted, which allowed companies to expand their markets for infant food (Cohen and Otomo 2019). Women's equality movements perceived bottle-feeding as emancipating and breastfeeding as old-fashioned (Thulier 2009). An uncritiqued relationship between infant food companies and the medical establishment grew that normalized bottle-feeding so that "practice became institutionalized in the hospital's maternity and postnatal procedures" (Martucci 2015: 113). The trend away from breastfeeding was also driven by what Martucci calls the "century's dominant ideology of scientific motherhood" in which women's experiences and control over their maternal processes were subjugated to the objectivity of "science" (Martucci 2015: 111). Women who eschewed formula for breastfeeding were viewed as "backwards and unsophisticated" (Joyce 2015).

After World War II, women's employment rates plummeted to prewar levels in the United States and Great Britain, but by the 1950s their workforce participation again increased, with a coinciding growing market for baby formula in North America, parts of Asia, and Europe (Cohen and

Otomo 2019). In Japan, for example, formula availability began in 1917, but it only became commonly used in the 1950s when female labor participation rate reached 50 percent (Inoue et al., 2012). At one-third of prewar costs, formula became accessible to more than just wealthy families in many countries (Rose 2018).

Milk-expression technology also has separated nursing from infant feeding. Breast pumps enable the lactating woman to produce breast milk without the suckle of her child by pulling the nipple through the opening of the pump's flange and then releasing the nipple at regular intervals to simulate the stimulation from the child's mouth and trigger the release of milk through the nipples' ducts (Palmer 2009; Wolf 2001). While the usefulness of a milk-expression apparatus is not disputed, criticisms have been leveled at the industry that produces the devices. And some studies indicate that breast milk produced without child-to-mother physical contact lacks the feedback loop from the baby's mouth to cause the breast to create specific antibodies. Pumps also eliminate the skin-to-skin contact that facilitates parent–child bonding, and they may extract a higher proportion of the thinner "fore milk" versus the richer "hind milk" than actual nursed milk (Galtry 2000; Palmer 2009; Wolf 2001). Additionally, the growing milk-expression industry often deemphasizes the physicality of breastfeeding as physical contact, promoting nursed and pumped milk as equivalent. With entire product lines of milk-expression contraptions, innovations, and accoutrements, such as designer bags to carry pumping equipment, "breastfeeding, which was once seen as a challenge against big business, [now is] big business itself" (Jung 2015: 128). The US market for breast pumps will reach $1 billion in 2020 (Jung 2015).

The tight association between women's employment and use of formula and/or milk-expression apparatus and supplies raises the possibility that these industries have financial interests in preventing US states and organizations from adopting longer maternity leaves. Additionally, the formula industry, in particular, is situated in opposition to policies that accommodate breastfeeding/lactating mothers at work. This concern applies to legislation such as the Lactation at Work Law (Allers 2017: 50).

INTERNATIONAL CONTEXT

The International Formula Industry

In the late 1970s, increasing numbers of first-world countries enacted more stringent formula advertising regulations in a successful effort to encourage breastfeeding and discourage women from using formula. To recoup the resulting losses, manufacturers turned to markets in developing and low-income countries. This aggressive formula marketing in lower-income countries contributed to a decline in breastfeeding in those countries. For example, in Mexico 100 percent of children were breastfed until they were six months old in 1960; by the mid-1960s, less than half of six-month-olds were breastfed. In Chile in 1960, more than 90 percent of thirteen-month-old babies were breastfed; in 1968, only 5 percent. In 1951 in Singapore more than 80 percent of three-month-olds were breastfed, but only 5 percent by 1971 (Halabi 2018: 82). Lower-income and nonwhite markets continue to be particularly lucrative, with the global infant formula industry seeing $11 billion in annual sales and representing the largest segment of the baby food market (Jung 2015; Martucci 2015).

Nestle soon accounted for 50 percent of the global market share, spending millions on marketing and advertising in Latin America and Africa. In Brazil, for example, formula became the third most advertised product after cigarettes and soap (Jung 2015: 39). Perhaps consequentially, in the 1970s, Brazil saw a precipitous drop in breastfeeding rates compared to the previous decade (Oliveira et al. 2017). Nestle disguised formula representatives as health-care experts whose visits were to "educate" new mothers in hospitals; their true agenda was to push formula – the infamous "Nestle nurses." Free formula samples not only psychologically discouraged new mothers from breastfeeding; they created a physical need for infant formula. When women did not nurse their babies during the free-formula weeks, their breasts stopped producing milk. They stopped producing breast milk, compelling them to purchase more formula (Jung 2015).

Formula containers were often not even printed in the countries' common/native language, making instructions unclear for both literate and illiterate mothers. Particularly in the poorest countries, because of the cost of the now-necessary formula, women often diluted the formula to stretch their supply, inadvertently malnourishing their infants. Formula-fed babies were more prone to diarrhea-complication death, both because formula lacked the immune benefits of breast milk and because their families lacked access to clean water with which to mix formula (Cohen and Otomo 2019; Jung 2015).

An international boycott was officially launched in 1977 by the US nonprofit Infant Formula Action Coalition (INFACT), gaining many supporters in France, Finland, Canada, Australia, and many other countries. The World Health Organization, UNICEF, and IBFAN convened international meetings soon after; the WHO introduced the International Code of Marketing of Breast-Milk Substitutes in 1981, a nonbinding code designed to restrict formula promotion. The United States was the only one out of 119 countries to vote against it, expressing concern that it restricted communication between consumers and manufacturers, perhaps foreshadowing a similar US vote in 2018 against a new WHO statement encouraging mothers to breastfeed in crisis situations (Jacobs 2018; Solomon 1981).

The boycott marked an international shift in how countries understood breastfeeding. Formula and breastfeeding were no longer viewed as interchangeable, equivalent choices. International activism around the Nestle boycott "elevated the status of breastfeeding among international health organizations . . . almost overnight, breastfeeding advocacy became an institutional priority" (Jung 2015: 46).

La Leche League International

Encouraged by scientific research documenting the benefits of breastfeeding in the 1970s, women resisted feeding with formula, and breastfeeding rates increased among predominantly white, middle-class women, often contradicting advice from medical professionals. Second-wave feminist movements of the 1970s felt that using formula liberated women from the physicality of lactation but also alienated them from a quintessentially female activity (Thulier 2009). La Leche League, a breastfeeding advocacy group formed in the mid-1950s, rose in prominence at this time, asserting that "mother-to-mother help was better than doctor-to-mother help in regards to breastfeeding" (Thulier 2009: 90). Beginning with small meetings in the wealthy Franklin Park, Illinois, community, La Leche League eventually gained the support of a network of medical professionals. By the 1960s, chapters had been established across the United States (Martucci 2015; Thulier 2009).

Internationally, La Leche League spread across North America and beyond, renaming itself La Leche League International (LLLI) in 1964. Currently, most LLLI chapters are in Europe and North America, although the organization has a growing presence in South America. However, La Leche League's presence in Africa was limited to seven countries, and the bulk of its network remains in Europe and the United States. With LLLI, a mother-to-mother approach to encouraging and empowering breastfeeding women spread internationally, including multi-language publications (Hicks 2005; Wiessinger, West, and Pitman 2010).

WORKPLACE LACTATION INTERNATIONALLY

The question of workplace lactation is especially complicated in countries that lack maternity leave policies and offer little assistance for lactating workers. Countries vary greatly when it comes to policies concerning breastfeeding, milk-expression breaks, and maternity leave policies. According to the World Policy Analysis Center and MACHEquity (Maternal and Child Health Equity Project), North and South America and the East Asian and Pacific regions have the greatest proportion of countries that do not guarantee breastfeeding breaks (approximately 45 percent), in contrast to Europe and Central Asia which have the lowest (13 percent) (Assi et al. 2014: 4). Indeed, of the 182 nations that Earle, Heymann, and Raub examined, 25 percent have no policy on breastfeeding breaks at work. A total of 71 percent of these countries guarantee paid breastfeeding breaks, and 4 percent guarantee unpaid breaks (2013: 400).

While US businesses often provide only the required six weeks (eight weeks for Caesarean-section births) of maternity leave, many other countries guarantee far more time. Longer maternity leaves can affect the level of need for workplace lactation accommodation – but not necessarily so. In countries with long maternity leaves, fewer women might return to work needing lactation accommodations, because by the time they return, they may not need to express milk more often than over their lunch hour; may not need to do so at all; or might no longer be breastfeeding. However, some women will elect to return to work sooner than required, because their commitment to their organizations compels them to remain involved or because maternity leave remuneration is at a lower rate than the usual salary and they need the additional money. Others may return to the workplace for strategic career reasons, such as fearing that extended time away from the workforce will limit their advancement or overall earning potential (see Olivetti and Petrongolo 2017 for a discussion of the "tipping point" when maternity leave length becomes detrimental). These women, despite their countries' maternity leave policy, might need additional time to express milk at work. Additionally, unlike most women in the United States, these women might have support that could enable in-person breastfeeding during the day, such as on-site childcare or nearby relatives to transport the children for nursing during the mother's break times.

Nevertheless, breastfeeding rates continue to be an important international health issue. Despite pro-breastfeeding proclamations by the WHO and other organizations, no country currently meets the WHO's recommendations to exclusively breastfeed babies for their first six months and continue breastfeeding with supplementary feeding until the age of two.

The Convention on the Rights of the Child, adopted by the United Nations in 1989 and ratified in 190 countries as of 2012, includes access to knowledge about breastfeeding benefits as a key part of child health and nutrition (United Nations 1989: 11). In 2016, the UN released a statement on breastfeeding, calling it a human rights issue that should be "protected and promoted for the benefit of both" mothers and children (United Nations 2016). The UN has issued specific guidance to promote, support, and protect breastfeeding mothers, including paid maternity leave, workplace spaces for nursing or expressing and storing milk, and greater acceptance and awareness of breastfeeding. The International Labour Organisation (ILO), a UN agency, established the Maternity Protection Convention in 2000 (No. 183), setting international standards for protecting and supporting breastfeeding among working mothers across industries and job types, establishing that lactating workers should have one or more milk expression paid breaks daily. As of 2016, thirty-four countries had ratified its recommendations (Calero, Giroud-Castiella, and Sici 2016).

Researchers agree that formal policies implementing maternity leave and breastfeeding breaks at work are associated with increased breastfeeding rates and lower infant and child mortality rates (Assi et al. 2014). A study conducted using 2012 data from 182 nations concluded that substantially higher rates of exclusive breastfeeding could be achieved from government policies providing paid milk-expression breaks for at least six months post-birth (Heymann, Raub, and Earle 2013). Another study analyzed the relationship between the implementation of the WHO/UNICEF Global Strategy for Infant and Young Child Feeding and trends in EBF over the twenty years prior to 2013 and found that countries that enacted the Global Strategy saw significant increases in exclusive breastfeeding rates (Lutterman, Kand, and Morrow 2013: 216).

The WHO/UNICEF Global Strategy includes a directive for countries to "enact imaginative legislation to protect the breastfeeding rights of working women" (Lutterman, Kand, and Morrow 2013: 214). The directive noted that the relationship between formal policies that facilitate breastfeeding at work, increased rates of breastfeeding, and childhood health, then, is clear. However, it's important to note that these studies, like others, only looked at formal industries/workplaces. Many of the world's poorest women work in informal industries, so the data may not speak to their experiences (Heymann, Raub, and Earle 2013; Lutterman, Kand, and Morrow 2013, 1989).

While lactating workers internationally might encounter various levels of structural and cultural support for combining lactation with employment, the issue of workplace lactation accommodation often remains a factor for working mothers around the world. In the next section, I review the various levels of structural and culture support internationally by region.

Europe

The European Union enacted breastfeeding protections for working women in 1992 with COM (1990) 406, "Protection at work of pregnant women or women who have recently given birth." States had two years to put the legislation in place after it went into effect on November 24, 1992, but the legislation is essentially a directive. EU states were free to meet the goals of the directive in any way, so long as they met the overall standards. The directive guaranteed maternity leave for fourteen weeks and guaranteed that leaves for other reasons (e.g., if work would expose someone to dangerous chemicals), must be paid. It also guaranteed that pregnant workers may have prenatal medical exams during work hours without loss of pay and protected them from being fired for pregnancy or maternity. However, the directive did not guarantee that maternity leave must be paid, and states have approached that issue in different ways. A report in 1999 indicated that some states paid full wages throughout maternity leave, while others paid only a percentage for part of the leave (2019).

A proposed update in 2009 would have set the minimum time for maternity leave within the EU to twenty paid weeks. It would have also added two weeks of paid paternity leave. It seems that the EU Parliament supported the legislation; however, a group of states including the United Kingdom and Germany opposed the directive. As a result, when the EU Commission sent it to the Council of the EU for approval, it was tabled for four years and ultimately withdrawn.

The nations that opposed its passage were worried about financial consequences and inflexibility regarding individual nations' needs (2019).

European countries are some of the highest income countries in the world, yet Europe also has some of the lowest breastfeeding rates (just 25 percent of infants in the WHO European Region were exclusively breastfed for the first six months). Denmark, Norway, and Sweden provide for up to fifty-two weeks of paid leave. Furthermore, Norway and Finland have provisions for partially paid childcare leave up to three years after birth. In general, the Nordic countries and Finland provide generous paid leave policies that often allow mothers to avoid the need to breastfeed or express milk at work altogether (2019). Breastfeeding rates in Norway are the highest in Europe, and *The New York Times* cited Norway's "homogenous" income equality as a main contributor, attributing Norway's high rates of breastfeeding to a grassroots–led PSA campaign in the 1970s, which eventually turned into government-backed advocacy that continues strong to this day (Alvarez 2003; Phelan 2015). Finland is famous worldwide for its Finnish Baby Boxes, which are government-provided maternity-resource packages available to all Finnish mothers, pregnant or adoptive (this can also be taken in the form of a tax-free, lump-sum grant). Finland also has the lowest breastfeeding rates among the Nordic countries (Assi et al. 2014).

Continuing through Europe, one may expect some uniformity in policies across EU member states, but this does not appear to be the case. France, Latvia, the Netherlands, Austria, Portugal, Germany, and Poland are among those that offer less than eighteen weeks of maternity leave. Malta is the sole EU country that does not pay for maternity leave with public funds (WABA Women & Work Task Force 2011). Meanwhile, the United Kingdom, Denmark, Malta, and Finland are the only EU countries that do not have nationally mandated breastfeeding breaks (Iceland, although not in the UE also lacks mandated breastfeeding breaks) (Assi et al. 2014; Heymann, Raub, and Earle 2013; Menon and Mulford 2007).

While EU law forbids discrimination against breastfeeding mothers (European Parliamentary Research Blog 2018), both in public and the workplace, some countries have instituted specific legislation to enumerate further protections. For example, in Italy, maternity leave is compulsory for female workers, and the law guarantees that. Belgium, additionally, does not allow pregnant employees and women who are breastfeeding to work overtime (Valk et al. 2014).

Asia

The government laws and policies on lactation at work or maternity leave varies substantially across Asia. Mongolia is an outlier, providing more than a year of paid maternity leave. Exclusive breastfeeding rates in Mongolia are 57 percent for children under the age of six months, with mothers breastfeeding for an average of twenty-one months (2019, Centre 2013). In contrast, Singapore, one of the consistently richest countries in the world, grants only eight paid weeks of maternity leave, and has no laws regarding lactation breaks or milk-expression places. In Singapore, as of 2011, 42 percent of six-month-old babies were breastfed at all, and only 1 percent were exclusively breastfed (Centre 2013). One of the very few studies of Singaporean working mothers found that the median breastfeeding duration for stay-at-home mothers was nine weeks and working mothers was eight weeks (Choo et al. 2005). Yet, the most oft-cited reason of mothers in the study who stopped breastfeeding during this time was "work-related factors." (Assi et al. 2014; Valk et al. 2014).

In general, breastfeeding in China is not widely accepted, and formula, particularly foreign-made formula, is often used (Pak 2018). Yet, a survey of more than 2,000 participants found that "almost 95 percent believed that public places should have lactation rooms . . . and 65 percent of respondents agreed that it was acceptable for mothers to breastfeed in public . . . More than 90 percent of respondents approved of policies supporting breastfeeding in public" (Redding, Ouyang, and Zhao 2017: 316). The Chinese government also launched a pro-breastfeeding campaign in 2013–2016, creating an app to help women locate lactation rooms, with more than 1,600 verified during the period of the campaign (2019, Centre 2013).

In the workplace, China has mandated paid sixty-minute breaks for lactating workers. However, one study found that that this accommodation disproportionately benefited wealthier lactating workers, and advocated "expanding coverage of paid maternity leave in the informal/private sectors should thus be a policy priority. Universal paid leave entitlements would not only reduce income disparities among women in different socioeconomic groups but also minimize intergenerational inequality" (Jia, Dong, and Song 2018: 53).

Lactating workers in Japan also experience work–family struggles. In 2017, a Japanese city counselor wrote for *The Guardian* about the hostility she experienced in the workplace when she attempted to bring her infant son to work; not surprisingly then, her previous proposals to breastfeed him in the chamber or gain access to day care in the building had been rebuffed (Ogata, 2017). Indeed, "support for breastfeeding in the Japanese workplace has been quite limited" (Kobayashi and Usui 2017b: 580). Additionally, while Japan has a policy of sixty-minute paid lactation breaks for twelve months after birth, "over the past 20 years [in 2017], approximately 60 percent of working women quit their jobs because of pregnancy or childbirth" with approximately a fourth of nursing mothers fully employed by the time their children are a year old (Kobayashi and Usui 2017b).

The lactation policies of India, which has an infant mortality rate of 34 per 1,000 live births with nearly 35 percent of children under five suffering from some form of malnutrition, have been of interest to scholars (Ministry of Health and Family Welfare 2017). India's average exclusive breastfeeding rate is 54.9 percent, on the higher side in Asia, despite the absence of a law protecting breastfeeding in public. India's Maternity Benefits Act requires employers to provide nursing breaks for fifteen months after birth to lactating workers, but does not prescribe the length of such breaks. India is also one of at least twenty-nine countries that prohibit the firing of a woman during maternity leave for any reason (Pareek 2019). However, a survey by Medela India, a breast pump manufacturer, showed that 33 percent of women found the lack of nursing facilities at work the biggest challenge to continued breastfeeding, and 31 percent cited a lack of adequate time to pump at work (Medela India 2018: 13). Only 2.4 percent of women in this survey reported that they felt supported at work in their breastfeeding needs and choices (Medela India 2018: 19).

Workplace protections are almost nonexistent in Pakistan and Indonesia, where maternity leave is just twelve weeks in both countries and nursing breaks are not mandated in Pakistan. While Indonesia does mandate breaks, they are unpaid and their length unspecified by law (Menon and Mulford 2007). A survey of 297 workplaces in Karachi, Pakistan found that just "45 percent of the sites were offering task adjustment to mothers during [the] lactation period. Only 15 percent of the sites were offering breastfeeding breaks to working mothers. Physical facilities that include a breastfeeding corner, refrigerator for storing breast milk, breast milk pump and nursery for childcare were provided in less than 7 percent of the sites" (Soomro et al. 2016: 24). Over half (52 percent) of employers in the survey claimed that they were not aware of national guidelines or policy regarding their responsibilities to lactating workers, and 46 percent of employers asserted that the lactating workers were at fault for not approaching their employers for assistance (Soomro et al. 2016: 28).

Africa

Three of Africa's five most populous countries provide paid breaks for breastfeeding mothers at work. Egypt mandates three-month maternity leave and one-hour paid lactation breaks at work. However, many women report that the break is insufficient time for women to travel home, nurse their children, and return to work; moreover, the breaks are often denied to lactating workers. Women working in informal/unorganized and agriculture sectors are also not entitled to this same right (Menon and Mulford 2007).

The Democratic Republic of the Congo mandates paid breastfeeding breaks for working women nationally, but the states do not specify the daily length or duration after birth that a mother can take them (WABA Women & Work Task Force 2011). Leaving such decisions solely up to employers places the onus on working women to secure these lactation accommodations. In a country where women are generally economically and socially disadvantaged yet provide the majority of the agricultural labor, choosing between working and breastfeeding essentially means choosing between not eating or not nursing one's baby (US Aid 2019).

Likewise, sharp inequalities exist between women and men in the Congo that have an impact on breastfeeding mothers' access to workplace accommodations. South Africa, like Nigeria, does not mandate paid milk-expression breaks nor does it mandate paid maternity leave for mothers. South Africa's Code of Good Practice on the Protection of Employees during Pregnancy and After the Birth of a Child secured guaranteed breastfeeding breaks of thirty minutes twice per day for breastfeeding or milk expression for the first six months of the child's life (Department of Labor South Africa 1998). Many mothers must choose to return to work sooner than they prefer. Additionally, no law specifies which accommodations employers must provide during those two thirty-minute breaks, nor are there "discernible public financing of systems to support" the Code of Good Practice (Martin-Wiesner 2018: 54).

Latin America

Most Latin American countries do not meet the UNICEF–recommended fourteen weeks of maternity leave. Cuba is the greatest outlier with fifty-eight-week publicly funded leaves, followed by Chile at thirty weeks and Venezuela at twenty-six (Carreño 2019). These three countries also mandate paid breastfeeding breaks at work (WABA Women & Work Taskforce 2011). Costa Rica, in addition to providing four months' paid leave, also is unusual for its workplace accommodation efforts. Not only are breaks mandated and paid, but as of April 2018, companies with at least thirty female employees are obligated by law to have an adequate lactation space, which must include a refrigerator that is used exclusively for breast milk; an armrest and back support; a trash can; curtains; proper air circulation; and many more requirements (Rico 2018).

Lactating women in Peru also have explicit legal protections on breastfeeding at work and in public. Peru has one of the highest rates of exclusive breastfeeding in Latin America, at 70.6 percent, despite a rising poverty rate (World Health Organization 2013). Peru's government committed to increasing the exclusive breastfeeding rate by 2 percent per year by 2021 through a Multisectoral Strategic Plan for the Promotion and Protection of Breastfeeding 2013–2021, which includes a directive for workplaces to have lactation rooms. Already existent are breastfeeding laws No. 27240 and No. 28731 and Act No. 29896, which required creating lactation spaces for public and private organizations (World Health Organization 2013). Illustrating Peru's innovative pro-breastfeeding activities, the Ministry of Health holds a competition every year for breastfeeding babies to see which baby could drink the most milk in a single sitting, called "Baby with Best Suck" (Phelan 2015).

Mexico, like the majority of South and Central America countries, offers twelve weeks of paid maternity leave. Women are legally entitled to sixty-minute paid breaks, but the experience of Mexican Senator Martha Cecilia Márquez raises questions about the ways women experience lactation laws in their daily lives. In January 2019, Senator Márquez was harassed by her colleagues for bringing her baby to a Congressional session, with one news outlet even stating that she "exceeded the limits of tolerance in Congress this week"(Mexico News Daily 2019: 1). Given that the Senate building itself lacked designated breastfeeding areas and changing stations, protections for women working in informal industries may be particularly lacking (Mexico News Daily 2019).

UNICEF also decried both the lack of information about breastfeeding and availability of lactation rooms as key factors to Mexico's low exclusive breastfeeding rate of 14 percent in 2015, one of the lowest in Latin America – and one that actually decreased in the 2000s (Slim 2015; Unar-Munguía et al. 2019). In fact, between 2012 and 2014, Mexico saw a substantial increase (37 percent) in the promotion and sales of infant formula, to which one study attributed the drastic drop in breastfeeding rates. In possible response in 2015, the Mexican government banned hospitals from giving away free baby formula in an attempt to increase breastfeeding rates. Mexico City even adopted a PSA campaign in 2014 to encourage breastfeeding, but this backfired spectacularly as women interpreted the call to not "turn their backs on their babies" as insulting and implying that they were not good mothers if they did not breastfeed (Slim 2015; Unar-Munguía et al. 2019).

Conversely, Colombia saw a dramatic increase in exclusive breastfeeding between 1986 and 2010, from 15.4 percent to 46.8 percent, attributed to a variety of protections from the government. For example, Colombia mandates a sixty-minute break each day for six months from birth for breastfeeding, though maternity leave is only twelve weeks (Lutter and Morrow 2013).

Brazil has been lauded as an international standard for breastfeeding promotion and support after the country showed a substantial increase in exclusive breastfeeding rates from 2.5 percent to 38.6 percent between 1986 and 2006. While it doesn't have the highest breastfeeding rate in Latin America, Brazil demonstrates strong protection for mothers with many policies and programs, which have been frequently amended and strengthened since their inception. Furthermore, Brazil bans advertisement and promotion of infant formula, and Sao Paulo, for example, fines businesses that discriminate against breastfeeding mothers (Lutter and Morrow 2013).

Middle East

The Middle East is a region that has seen "the largest number of conflicts in any major region worldwide since World War II," which scholars speculate has affected breastfeeding rates and lactation rights (Diwakar, Malcolm, and Naufal 2017: 2). Indeed, it is "the only region in the world where breastfeeding rates actually fell in the decade leading up to 2006" (Diwakar, Malcolm, and Naufal 2017: 5). While Iraq mandates sixty-two days of maternity leave and one-hour paid breaks for breastfeeding, it is unclear how well mothers are able to take advantage of these rights, particularly in conflict zones (WABA

Women & Work Task Force 2011). The government launched a national nutrition strategy in 2012, which included the promotion of breastfeeding, but the Geneva Infant Feeding Association was unable to conclude if it had been implemented or what impact it had (Geneva Infant Feeding Association 2015).

Iran has mandated paid breastfeeding breaks at thirty minutes, every three hours, for twenty-four months after birth (WABA Women and Work Taskforce 2011). But research suggests that these protections did not translate into support in the workplace. "The [study's] participants stated that their children and husbands expected them to do their roles with the best of their capabilities, without any complaint. Similar expectations were presented by their employers and colleagues without granting any especial work privilege in the workplace" (Valizadeh et al. 2015: 488).

Saudi Arabia, one of the richest countries in the world, offers no legal protections to breastfeeding mothers and offers maternity leave shorter than twelve weeks (WORLD Policy Analysis Center 2019). It is difficult to find consistent statistics on breastfeeding rates, though generally rates are much lower than recommended and "the most common feeding practice among Saudi mothers is mixed feeding, where they initiate formula at age three months" (Alhabas 2016: 11). Rates of working women have been increasing, and in 2014, "Saudi women working outside their home made up around 30 percent of the country's employment rates" (Nabbout 2019: 15). These include private bathrooms, prayer spaces, and gender-separate work areas as well as curfews in certain industries and bans against women and men working together. However, it is unclear if these measures provide any protections for lactating workers (Nabbout 2019).

Israel's public health ministry's explanation of breastfeeding rights exemplifies the substantial level of legal protection for breastfeeding women in Israel. Public breastfeeding is allowed, and the Ministry goes so far as to call breastfeeding "not the mother's exclusive responsibly. It is society's responsibility" (Ministry of Health 2019: 1). Maternity leave is granted by seniority, with twenty-six weeks after being at a workplace for over one year, and fifteen if less than a year. During the four months following return to work, mothers receive a "nursing hour," sixty minutes of paid time to express milk, breastfeed, or address other family issues (Kol-Zchut 2019).

Workplace lactation is indeed a global issue, one that different countries are addressing in more and less successful ways. Key factors in success include specific procedures for workplace milk expression, longer maternity leaves, pro-labor environments, and cultural support for breastfeeding and shared family duties. When supportive policies are in place, we see greater success for women combining work and breastfeeding, but the experiences of some countries suggest that (specific) additional structural and cultural factors mediate how successful these policies are.

LACTATION AT WORK IN THE UNITED STATES: FEDERAL AND STATE LEGISLATION

This study actually examines two lactation-at-work laws, the federal Fair Labor Standards Act, as amended by the Affordable Care Act, and also the Indiana lactation-at-work law, which was passed four years earlier.

US Federal Law

Until the Fair Labor Standards Act was amended in 2009, no federal legislation addressed the needs of lactating employees. The Family Medical Leave Act (FMLA) secured the right to twelve weeks of unpaid leave, which facilitates infant breastfeeding; yet this legislation does not apply to workers in small businesses or in part-time jobs. Of those who do have this right, many workers cannot afford to take weeks of unpaid leave; they need that income to support themselves and their families. The Americans with Disabilities Act (ADA) does not consider lactation to be a disability, despite the physical demands of breastfeeding on the lactating worker (Lepore 2009).

On September 17, 2009, Senator Tom Harkin (D-Iowa) introduced to the Senate S. 1679, the *Affordable Health Choices Act*. The act included the following language:

Section 7 of the Fair Labor Standards Act of 1938 (29 U.S. USC. 207) is amended by adding at the end the following:

(r)(1) An employer shall provide—

A a reasonable break time for an employee to express breast milk for her nursing child for 1 year after the child's birth each time such employee has need to express the milk; and

B a place, other than a bathroom, that is shielded from view and free from intrusion from coworkers and the public, which may be used by an employee to express breast milk.

(2) An employer shall not be required to compensate an employee receiving reasonable break time under paragraph (1) for any work time spent for such purpose.
(3) An employer that employs less than 50 employees shall not be subject to the requirements of this subsection, if such requirements would impose an undue hardship by causing the employer significant difficulty or expense when considered in relation to the size, financial resources, nature, or structure of the employer's business.
(4) Nothing in this subsection shall preempt a State law that provides greater protections to employees than the protections provided for under this subsection (Federal Lactation at Work Law 2010).

This amendment to the FLSA was passed as part of the Patient Protection and Affordable Care Act (ACA). The ACA was amended on November 19, 2009 to include this breastfeeding portion of the law. The amendment was proposed by Senate Majority Leader Harry Reid (D-NV), along with thousands of other sections of the law, without discussion of motivations or rationales for the particular lactation-at-work addition. In fact, some scholars characterize this provision as an obscure clause that was "slipped into the massive 2,074-page Health Care Reform Bill" (Orozco 2010: 1293).

Prior to the amendment, however, in June 2009, Representative Carolyn B. Malone (D-NY) and Senator Jeff Merkley (D-OR) introduced bills ("Breastfeeding Promotion Act of 2009") in each of their houses to amend the Civil Rights Act of 1964 to include breastfeeding. That law also would have provided tax breaks for companies that provided lactation equipment. Crucially, it would have amended the FLSA to require employers of fifty or more people to provide time and private space for lactating mothers to express breast milk. However, both bills died in committee (Senate–Finance; House–The Education and Labor Committee). Nevertheless, much of the ACA's text came from these bills, which contributed to the relevant discourse.

In introducing the Breastfeeding Promotion Act, Representative Malone noted that mothers of infants under one year of age are increasingly participating in the labor force, and yet experts recommend that children are breastfed for at least their first year, with the first six months being exclusively breastfed. She also observed that research indicated that breastfeeding reduces the likelihood of various illnesses (e.g., ear infections), health conditions (e.g., asthma), and infant mortality. She also mentioned breastfeeding benefits to mothers, such as reduced risk of some cancers. She did not mention benefits to businesses, such as decreased absenteeism (Maloney June 11, 2009).

Similarly, Senator Merkley opened by commenting, "The science is undisputable – babies who are breastfed the first six months of life have a greatly reduced risk for acute and chronic disease – yet only ten percent of all infants receive this nourishment that they need to remain healthy. One of the primary reasons for this is that working moms face real and serious challenges to expressing milk when they return to work." He went on to note that 72 percent of mothers work full time, often due to economic necessity, and characterized protections to enable them to continue to breastfeed as "simply an act of human decency." Drawing on experiences from his home state of Oregon, which already had similar legislation, he cited examples not only from employees, but also from employers, to demonstrate how lactation laws benefited organizations, without significant disruption to businesses. Finally, he cited a finding by a Mutual of Omaha study showing that health care costs were three times lower for breastfed infants, as well as a USDA study that estimated a savings of $3.6 billion in health care costs if half of US babies were exclusively breastfed for six months (Merkley June 11, 2009).

Previously, Representative Maloney had introduced amendments to the 1964 Civil Rights Act to promote breastfeeding since 2001. She introduced breastfeeding promotion acts in 2001, 2003, 2007, and 2009. In 2011, she further pushed breastfeeding legislation.

The Lactation at Work law does not mandate that the milk–expression break time must be paid, although if the employer provides paid breaks, lactating employees must be allowed to use those paid breaks before taking any unpaid break time. The law also would not apply if, due to short durations of work time, the employee would not qualify for breaks. In addition, the law explicitly excludes businesses that employ fewer than fifty employees if compliance would impose an undue hardship (although state-level laws may apply to smaller businesses). Also, the law is limited to nonexempt workers – basically hourly wage workers categorized as eligible for overtime pay; not salaried workers (Federal Lactation at Work Law 2010).

The federal law includes enforcement by the Department of Labor Wage and Hour Division (WHD). Employees contact the WHD to file a complaint. The WHD keeps complaints confidential, and, if it investigates, the department usually conducts a more general investigation to avoid singling out the lactation accommodation issue (Cardarelli 2016).

US-Indiana: State Level

Twenty-nine states, the District of Columbia, and Puerto Rico have laws related to breastfeeding accommodations in the workplace (Maternal and Child Health Bureau April 30, 2019). Some scholars assert that, on average, states with Republican-controlled legislatures and those overtly supporting traditional gender roles passed breastfeeding laws earlier than more progressive, Democratic-controlled state legislatures (Boone 2018a).

Moreover, some legal experts note that many lactation-at-work laws, which may have been initially suggested by feminist and women activists, are delineated to reinforce gender norms and conventional views of motherhood. For example, most state lactation-at-work laws stipulate that the woman may express milk for her child (or, in the case of the FLSA, until the child is one year old). The laws specify that the accommodation is for the benefit of the child, not the mother. A salient example is that some women whose infants had died were denied accommodations to express milk (Boone 2018a; Orozco 2010).

Thus, although it is the employee who has the legal right to the accommodation, the right is intended to also benefit someone else – the child for whom she is lactating. This makes this right unlike most other civil rights. Although the infant does not possess legal rights, it is a powerful fiction and a significantly unique discursive connotation. This law has a strong cultural resonance around the issues of maternity, infant health, and care that makes it easy to frame a discussion around the formal legal right.

The Indiana law states:

> IC 22-2-14-1
> As used in this chapter, "employer" means a person or entity that employs twenty-five (25) or more employees.
> IC 5-10-6-2
>
> Sec. 2. (a) The state and political subdivisions of the state shall provide reasonable paid break time each day to an employee who needs to express breast milk for the employee's infant child. The break time must, if possible, run concurrently with any break time already provided to the employee. The state and political subdivisions are

not required to provide break time under this section if providing break time would unduly disrupt the operations of the state or political subdivisions.

(b) The state and political subdivisions of the state shall make reasonable efforts to provide a room or other location other than a toilet stall, in close proximity to the work area, where an employee described in subsection (a) can express the employee's breast milk in privacy. The state and political subdivisions shall make reasonable efforts to provide a refrigerator or other cold storage space for keeping milk that has been expressed. The state or a political subdivision is not liable if the state or political subdivision makes a reasonable effort to comply with this subsection.

IC 22-2-14-2

Employer provide private location where employees can express milk; employer provide cold storage for expressed milk; employer not liable.

Sec. 2. (a) To the extent reasonably possible, an employer shall provide a private location, other than a toilet stall, where an employee can express the employee's breast milk in privacy during any period away from the employee's assigned duties.

(b) To the extent reasonably possible, an employer shall:

(1) provide a refrigerator or other cold storage space for keeping milk that has been expressed; or

(2) allow the employee to provide the employee's own portable cold storage device for keeping milk that has been expressed until the end of the employee's work day.

(c) Except in cases of willful misconduct, gross negligence, or bad faith, an employer is not liable for any harm caused by or arising from either of the following that occur on the employer's premises:

(1) The expressing of an employee's breast milk.

(2) The storage of expressed milk.

The Indiana legislature offered no floor debate on this bill. The bill's author, Senator Vi Simpson, offered one amendment from the floor: It added "to the extent reasonably possible" to the requirements regarding provision of private space and the refrigerated storage of the expressed milk. In contrast to the federal legislation, the Indiana lactation-at-work law stipulates no penalties for employers that fail to comply with mandated provisions, so that enforcement falls to individual employees to bring civil suits (Rudavsky May 15, 2008). Some states have more stringent regulations such as Oregon, where a business that does not comply could face a $1,000 fine. The stronger wording originally included in Indiana's proposal was removed after the proposal failed to garner sufficient support, partly due to complaints from business representatives (Rudavsky May 15, 2008).

Legal Consciousness

The law as it is formally written, "law on the books," is seldom identical to how it is experienced in civil society, "law in action," as many socio-legal scholars have documented (e.g., Bumiller 1988; Galanter 1974; Lovell 2012; Macaulay 1963; Nielsen 2000; Pound 1910; Young and Billings 2020). The Lactation at Work Law is no exception. The law as it was written needs to be filtered through various frames and understandings. As various actors interpret it, it changes its focus, its strength, and even its substance.

Understanding how laws and rights work within organizations requires discerning organizational actors' relationship with the law – that is, their legal consciousness (Ewick and Silbey 1998, 2003; Hull 2016; Marshall and Barclay 2003; Merry 1990; Nielsen 2004; Young 2014). Although legal consciousness is collectively constructed, it is constrained by individuals' interpretation of meaning and setting (Ewick and Silbey 1998). Their legal consciousness shapes what is seen as possible and, even, what is legitimate (Calavita and Jenness 2013; Edelman 1967, 2016; Gelber and McNamara 2015; Hoffmann 2004, 2005; Pedriana and Stryker 1997; Stryker and Wald 2009; Suchman 2003; Young 2014).

Relationships with the law vary among different organizational actors. For example, legal texts are human resource specialists' touchstones; they work more closely with lawyers and focus on the specific mandates of legal compliance (see Edelman, Fuller, and Mara-Ditra 2001; Marshall 2005; Stryker 2000, 2007; Suchman and Edelman 1996). In contrast, supervising managers are further removed from the letter of the law, often being less cooperative when it comes to legal compliance than human resource specialists would be. Indeed, extant research shows that, while human resource specialists often are the actors who bring the law into the organization, the supervising managers are the ones who might block full compliance with the law in quest for efficiency, control, and managerial or organizational goals (e.g., Gwartney-Gibbs and Lach 1992; Hallden 2015; Hodson and Roscigno 2004; Kelly et al. 2014; Marshall 2003).

Organizational "practices implementing the policies can alter the very definition" of those laws within the organization (Marshall 2005: 87). As the organizations respond to, interpret, and apply the law, that law becomes institutionalized and transformed by the very organizations that the laws are intended to control (Dobbin and Kelly 2007; Edelman 2005; Fuller, Edelman, and Matusik 2000; Kelly, Moen, and Tranby 2011; Marshall 2005; Stryker 2007). "As organizations become increasingly legalized, the law becomes managerialized," and the focus shifts from legal concepts to managerial goals, creating policies that might only serve to symbolize compliance, yet engender no true changes (Edelman 2005: 340). This minimal compliance with the letter of the law is a way to circumvent the law's goals and allow management to maintain control over their employees' time and space, while formally, if ineffectively, adhering to the law. Thus, the organizations' compliance superficially might satisfy legal requirements while these symbolic structures advance the actual goals of the law very little, if at all.

For example, research on violations of the Family and Medical Leave Act (FMLA) showed that, rather than fully complying with FMLA law, employers prioritized managerial control over workers' bodies, time, and placement, thereby deflecting the impact of the law and maintaining workplace power (Albiston 2005: 40). Employers "did not completely ignore the law," but partially complied so they could maintain "managerial norms about work schedules and staffing" so as to "subtly transform leave rights in the workplace to be consistent with managerial needs" (Albiston 2005: 39)

The translation of law on the books into the law in action often results in rights becoming diluted and much-heralded laws being ineffective. In addition to the FMLA violations discussed (Albiston 2005), various scholars have found amble violations of the Americans with Disabilities Act (Barnes and Burke 2012; Engel and Munger 2003), sexual harassment laws (Marshall 2003), FMLA (Albiston 2005), equal employment law (Edelman 2016), housing and voting rights (Pedriana and Stryker 2017), and other workplace antidiscrimination laws (Berrey, Nelson, and Nielsen 2018). Given the plethora of unsuccessful civil rights laws, examination of the Lactation at Work Law, provides an important – and in some ways hopeful – contrast to many of these studies.

WORKING MOTHERS, LAW, AND ORGANIZATIONAL CHANGE

Just as different countries respond to lactating workers' needs with myriad policies and programs of varying success, so too do different organizations respond in a continuum of ways to regulatory laws, complicating observation and analysis of organizational compliance. Organizational responses to any law can range from minimally compliant to enthusiastic overcompliance, going well beyond what is necessary for compliance. Because interpretation of the law can be decentralized, legal consciousness – nonlegal actors' understanding of the law and new legislation – changes over time (Dobbin 2009) (Barnes and Burke 2012; Kagan, Gunningham, and Thornton 2012). Moreover, changes to employment law do not automatically translate into improved working conditions (Dobbin and Kelly 2007; Edelman 1992; Edelman, Erlanger, and Lande 1993, Edelman, Fuller, and Mara-Ditra 2001; Edelman and Suchman 1997; Edelman, Uggen, and Erlanger 1999; Fuller, Edelman, and Matusik 2000; Kelly 2003; Kelly et al. 2010; Pedriana and Stryker 1997; Stryker 2000, 2007).

Discrimination

Workplace lactation accommodations are one component of a collection of employment laws focused on increasing access and protection of underrepresented groups, such as women. Employment law has been studied from a range of disciplines (see Albiston 2007), and employment discrimination against mother-employees has been well documented (see Agocs, Langan, and Sanders 2015; Albiston 2010; Gangl and Ziefle 2015; Glass 2004; Goldin 2006; Kelly 2005; Kelly and Dobbin 1999; Perlow and Kelly 2014; Waldfogel 2001; Whittington 2011; Williams 2000; Woodward 2015). Indeed, concern over workers' difficulties in meeting both work and family responsibilities, and the law's ability to address this concern, has shifted "from marginal concern to center stage" (Albiston 2007: 398). However, usually mother-employees' family obligations – and motivations for discrimination – center around absences from work (see e.g., Budig, Misra, and Boeckmann 2016) or desiring fewer hours of work time (see e.g., Reynolds and May 2014). Parental leave, pregnancy bed rest, sick-child days, and leaving early or arriving late due to childcare complications all result in the employee being away from her place of work, and laws such as the Family and Medical Leave Acts and the Pregnancy Discrimination Act address these absences. Indeed, the maternity leave employee's nonconformity is demonstrated by her absence.

Expressing breast milk at work involves an employee's activities *while* at work. Lactating bodies must regularly express breast milk, and doing so comfortably means that management has to deviate from the way organizations usually operate. Laws would have little effect if human resource personnel and supervising managers insisted on maintaining the status quo and refused to deviate in order to make necessary accommodations. However, deviation can be very difficult because many aspects of a workplace appear to be unchangeable – institutionalized within the organizational culture (Berger and Luckmann 1966). As Albiston has noted, "many of the characteristics of work that seem natural, normal, and inevitable involve practices regarding time and employer control" (2010: 1104). Yet, the *employee*'s control over her time and place in order to have the necessary private space and minutes to pump milk is exactly what this law addresses.

The "Ideal Worker" Norm

The need to express breast milk at work also distances lactating workers from the "ideal worker" norm. The narrow "good employee" definition can thwart the success of ideal accommodations – even when an employee's "good status" is because she is "doing good work" in another context – such as caring for her child. This tension between struggling to fulfill family obligations and needing to reach out beyond the family for assistance has been documented (see Kelly et al. 2010). For example, Levitsky's study of people providing long-term care to their family members demonstrates how they resisted requesting government assistance. The ideology that they must care for their own or risk losing their status as good people frequently prevented caregivers from reconceptualizing the government's role as a possible source of assistance – often until they were quite desperate or had spent many years providing long-term care without relief (Levitsky 2008, 2014).

Hochschild's research in a large organization discovered that very few employees were utilizing the company's generous pro-family policies, such as flextime. They did not want to be seen as less committed employees, were unaware of the policies, or feared using these accommodations would be read as harming the "Total Quality" of the organization (Hochschild 1997). Other researchers have documented that, even when the law provides clear rights, people do not always assert those rights in their daily lives (see Berrey, Hoffman, and Nielsen 2012; Bumiller 1988; Gallagher and Yang 2017; Hull 2016; Kirkland 2008; Levitsky 2008, 2014; Marshall 2003). For example, Marshall's research on sexual harassment found that women only considered legal remedies when objectionable behavior reached a certain threshold (Marshall 2003). Similarly, Albiston's research on Family and Medical Leave Act (FMLA) violations shows that workers are hesitant to pursue FMLA accommodations, fearing they would be perceived as bad employees (Albiston 2005). Rather than fully complying with FMLA law, these employers prioritized managerial control over workers' bodies and time, thereby deflecting the impact of the law and reverting the balance of power to how the workplace traditionally had always been (Albiston 2005: 40).

When workplace norms and expectations prevent lactating workers – or any employee – from taking the time necessary to have their needs met, accommodations will fail. Fear of "making a fuss" (a pejorative that can be highly gendered) prevents employees from requesting the accommodations their employer is obligated to provide. Women employees, in particular, may struggle to ask for accommodations (see Albiston and O'Connor 2016). In this way, management-lead approaches to workplace issues – for example, management adopting a new policy – might not be successful if an employee culture exists that prevents affected employees from using the policy.

Employees' concerns about deviating from the ideal worker norm are not unfounded. Extant scholarship documents that employees who depart from the ideal worker norm often incur many penalties at work (Beauregard 2014; Pedulla and Thebaud 2015; Perlow and Kelly 2014; Roth 2004). Workplaces, therefore, might need to adjust how they usually operate in ways that will remove or reconceptualize the label of "ideal worker."

The lactating employee may need to overcome both her own internalized ideas about being an ideal worker as well as those of her co-workers and management. If the ideal worker is one who is focused solely on the job, then a worker who breaks to pump milk or leaves her post do so, could not be an ideal worker. No lactation accommodation, however ideal, will be successful if pressures to be an ideal worker are paramount.

Managerialization and the Lactation at Work Law

The Lactation at Work law mandates accommodation of lactating workers' needs, yet it doesn't stipulate exactly what employers must provide terms of space or time. Laws with "broad and ambiguous principles give organizations wide latitude to construct the meaning of compliance" (Edelman 1992: 1532). However, even if the law has minimal ambiguity, organizations applying the law might reinterpret the text in ways substantially different from the original intent of the law, often in a way that is more advantageous for the organization (Kelly 2003; Stryker 2001).

When facing legal mandates to alter the workplace, organizations might "offer creative, self-interested interpretations of law, even when the law is explicit and seems to point unambiguously to particular interpretations" (Kelly 2003: 615). Their official response to the law diverges from how the organization actually approaches the issue; that is, "decoupling" the formal procedure from the day-to-day organizational action (DiMaggio and Powell 1983; Harrison, Lopez, and Martin 2015; Meyer and Rowan 1977). As the law addresses more specific aspects of organizations, often only providing organizations with vague concepts of what constitutes compliance, the law becomes "managerialized"; that is, the focus shifts from legal concepts, like equality and access, to managerial goals, like turnover and morale, with the resulting policies only serving to symbolize compliance, engendering few true changes (Edelman 2005: 340, 2016).

Advocates for the Lactation at Work Law capitalized on the potential overlap of managerial and legal goals by highlighting exactly those benefits when promoting legal compliance to businesses. The new law capitalized on such possible synergy to get public support, but in doing so risked undermining the original legal goals of equality and access. The Business Case for Breastfeeding website says:

> The payoff is significant: more satisfied, loyal employees and cost savings to the business. These savings are seen in such areas as:
>
> - Retention of experienced employees;
> - Reduction in sick time taken by both moms and dads for children's illnesses; and
> - Lower health care and insurance costs. (Office on Women's Health last updated: October 26, 2018)

Likewise, the fliers from the Department of Health and Human Services have two main headings: "Lactation Support Requires Few Resources" and "The Return on Investment." This second portion has three main bullets: (1) "Breastfeeding employees miss work less often," (2) "Breastfeeding lowers health care costs," and (3) "Investing in a worksite lactation support program can yield substantial dividends to the company" (Health Resources & Services Administration 2015: 1).

In transforming legal ideals into organizational goals, human resource personnel resolve any ambiguity about the law with specific organizational structures through which the law enters the workplace. Sometimes these structures are merely symbolic, "rules that are unenforced, procedures that are biased, programs that are ineffective, and ideologies that legitimate extant racial and gender inequality" (Edelman 2016: 116). Rarely have researchers found these structures producing substantive change that concretely improves employees' lives (Albiston 2010; Berrey, Nelson, and Nielsen 2018; Edelman 2016; Edelman and Suchman 1997; Stepan-Norris and Kerriessey 2016).

This scholarship would predict that the Lactation at Work Law would follow in a similar vein. Its ambiguity would allow for managerial leeway, resulting in managerialization. As in previous studies of other laws, managerialization, here, too, would create the appearance of compliance, while offering few effective organizational changes.

This is what the literature would predict, but this is the first study to investigate these questions empirically: Have organizations managerialized the Lactation at Work Law? If so, what have the consequences been for lactating workers? If not, what organizational factors have saved this law from being managerialized? I find a range of organizational responses that complicate the question of managerialization and its effects on the success of worker protection laws.

Organizational Actors and Compliance

For a law to create effective compliance and useful accommodations, well-positioned allies and advocates are key. Contrary to some earlier scholarship, organizations are not monolithic bodies driven solely by short-term, narrowly defined business goals. Rather, organizations are driven by many actors reflecting legal, economic, and societal contexts (Albiston 2005; Asta and Vacha-Haase 2013; Gunningham, Kagan, and Thornton 2003; Hoffmann 2003, Hoffmann, 2012; Kagan, Gunningham, and Thornton 2012; McCann 1994; Trautner, Hatton, and Smith 2013). For example, in their study of compliance with the ADA, Barnes and Burke found that compliance, and possible over-compliance, hinged on "finding the 'right' person inside the organization, meaning someone who will internalize the social model perspective and serve as an advocate within the organization" (Barnes and Burke 2006: 508). Similarly, in their study of environmental law,

Kagan et al. documented differences in compliance between "committed compliers" who followed exactly what the law dictated, and the "true believers" who saw environmental law compliance as important to their corporate identity (2012).

Organizational change advocates frame or reframe their desired organizational change in ways that encourage other groups not personally committed to the particular value to support the change and also "mobilize constituencies to infuse new beliefs, norms, and values into social structures" so that the change becomes established in the organization (Rao, Morrill, and Zald 2000: 240). Successful advocates often involve the innovation being incorporated in structures and processes of the organization (Wijen and Ansa 2016: 1079). Thus, compliance with a new law or regulation increases when its advocates are positioned to affect the daily workings of the organization (Barnes and Burke 2012). Organizational actors, even if they are not in key positions of power, can be effective, so long as they are situated within the organization and have contact with important decision makers (Bockhaven, Matthyssens, and Vandenbempt 2015).

However, organizational actors may be unable to champion innovation and create change within an organization if they are constrained by the norms and structure of their organizations – what scholars label "the paradox of embedded human agency" (Battilana 2006: 654; Scott and Davis 2007). DiMaggio argues that actors can overcome this paradox and advocate for organizational change – becoming what he called "institutional entrepreneurs" – when they have sufficient resources and recognize an "opportunity to realize interests that they value highly" (DiMaggio 1988: 14). Institutional entrepreneurs comply with the structure of their organizations yet challenge specific practices to advocate for alternative practices (DiMaggio 1988).

Additionally, powerful decision makers can be swayed even through explanations of values-neutral information. For example, in Weinberg and Nielsen's study of judicial empathy, parties could sensitize judges who were not originally empathetic by educating them on matters with which they may have had little personal experience (Weinberg and Nielsen 2012). In this way, the judges' understanding expanded past the legal focus of the case to also consider realities within civil society.

Unfortunately, lower-status, disempowered people often bear the task of providing the additional information and educating powerful actors to the realities they face. Much research has documented that members of underrepresented groups often find themselves asked to explain their situations and experiences to underinformed members of the majority (see Herring 2009; Royster 2003). These tutorials of the powerful by the less powerful are often critical in creating "moral allies" who will support their cause (Becker 1963).

Successful transformation of powerful actors into moral allies can be critical in developing "policy entrepreneurs" for this law within organizations (Raymond et al. 2013). This occurs when less powerful actors are able to "use the strategy of normative reframing to invoke alternative norms for a given issue, thereby creating new opportunities for institutional reform" (Raymond et al. 2013: 207). Placed in supervisory or policy-development positions within the organization, these policy entrepreneurs are able to broaden the organizational attention beyond its immediate managerial foci – such as efficiency and production – to include various normative issues. An example would be organization concern for employees' well-being for its own sake, beyond the "economic rationale for wellness" (Kirkland 2014: 958).

Scholars have demonstrated that sufficient access to those in power is often only available to people with adequate power themselves (e.g., Abel 1982; Crenshaw 1988; Delgado et al. 1985; Edelman, Erlanger, and Lande 1993; Galanter 1974; Grillo 1991; Hoffmann 2001, 2005; Lazerson 1982; McEwen, Mather, and Maiman 1994; Sarat 1990; Silbey and Sarat 1989). Homosocial socializing, however, can keep traditionally underrepresented groups outside of the circles of power. For example, within most organizations, men hold more management positions and within workplace social circles, male employees generally socialize with men co-workers and women with women co-workers, leaving women employees outside of the social networks that include the actors with greater power (Haveman and Beresford 2012; Hoffmann 2005).

Additionally, initiating discussions with powerful actors in attempt to educate them to become organizational allies involves some level of risk. By providing new information to the powerful actors, these underrepresented employees risk annoying or angering the people they hope will become their allies. New information, especially when it belies previously held beliefs, is not always welcome and can be a source of aggravation (Boyle and Corle 2010; Plumm and Terrance 2009).

Critically, and in contrast to much past work in this area, this study demonstrates how the law can enable such supporters and create opportunities to educate management. By providing a tool for demanding organizational compliance, the law facilitated Chapter 5's Allies Already to come forward and forcefully advocate for lactation accommodations. The law also generated a space for discussing lactation, motivations for these efforts, and the accommodations they require, creating Morality-Motivated Advocates as a result of educational conversations between supervising managers and lactating employees in Chapter 6.

ORGANIZATIONAL CHANGE AND THE LAW

Existing literature establishes that legitimacy is a priority for organizations (Battilana 2006; Deephouse et al. 2017; DiMaggio and Powell 1983; Harrison, Lopez, and Martin 2015; Powell and DiMaggio 1991; Stryker 1994; Suchman and Edelman 1996; Weber 1946). Suchman's classic definition of legitimacy – "a generalized perception or assumption that the actions of an entity are desirable, proper, appropriate" – asserts that the legitimacy of the organization rests on "some socially constructed system of norms, values, beliefs, and definitions" – asserts that the legitimacy of the organization rests on "some socially constructed system of norms, values, beliefs, and definitions" (Suchman 1995: 574). An organization could be concerned about its own legitimacy as well as the legitimacy of "an act, a rule, a procedure, a routine, a distribution, a position, a group or team, a group's status structure, teamwork, a system of positions, an authority structure, an organization, organizational symbols, an organization's form, practices, services, programs, a regime, a system of power, and a system of inequality" (Johnson 2004: 11).

Scholars have identified various organizational strategies utilized to maintain legitimacy among peer organizations. Coercive isomorphism reflects formal and informal pressure from other organizations, legal mandates, and societal expectations. Alternatively, when organizations experience uncertainty about how to interpret and apply a new law, like the Lactation at Work Law, they often copy what they perceive other organizations to be doing in order to maintain legitimacy, that is, mimetic isomorphism. Organizations might also change if they perceive their legitimacy will be enhanced if they reflect emerging norms, as communicated by the organizations' professionals, such as human resource personnel. This innovation reflects the education and socialization they receive from their professional organizations, that is, normative isomorphism (DiMaggio and Powell 1983; Powell and DiMaggio 1991).

The new institutionalism theorists, in discussing an organization's legitimacy, emphasized the importance of congruence with norms and perceptions of morality. Most discussion of legitimacy within the organizations literature focuses only on the organizational level. For example, although the definition of "subjects of legitimation" by Deephouse et al. includes numerous "entities, structures, actions, and ideas" whose assessment by internal or external actors contributes to the legitimacy of the organization is quite broad, the recipient (or not) of the legitimacy remains the organization (2017: 54). Nevertheless, while legitimacy has generally been addressed by Suchman and others as being the legitimacy of the organization itself, those discussions can also inform this book's discussion of legitimacy of employee endeavors – such as workplace milk expression – *within* the organization (Deephouse et al. 2017; Deephouse and Suchman 2008; Meyer and Rowan 1977; Suchman 1995, 1997; Zucker 1977).

How might organizations' pursuit of legitimacy interact with employees' quest for legitimacy when it comes to their own needs? My research finds that the legitimacy of the lactating employees' needs was necessary for employees' success with workplace milk expression. The Lactation at Work Law helped establish this legitimacy from several different types of organizational actors in order for lactating workers to receive fully effective accommodations.

LAW, NORMS, AND ORGANIZATIONAL CHANGE

Although the Lactation at Work Law does involve the formal threat of sanctions, the coercive power of a law is only a small part of its ability to effect change. Indeed, laws often affect what people believe to be morally correct even when organizations lack instrumental power to enforce compliance. Laws have substantial symbolic power to communicate the values and norms – sometimes shifting norms – within a society (Gusfield 1967; McAdams 2017). In this way, people who initially disagreed with the purpose of a law may change their beliefs to internalize new norms because the law "redefin[es] the normative value of old practices or by creating the cognitive building blocks for new ones" (Suchman and Edelman 1996: 929). These "expressive powers independent of the legal sanctions threatened on violators" can create changed behavior even when enforcement is unlikely, sporadic, or not possible (McAdams 2017: 6). Also, new rights articulated by the law may have empowered those affected to act differently and engage in confrontations or "rights talk" they might not otherwise have engaged in (McCann 1994). The presence of the rights-conferring law allows those affected to question and confront the status quo (Kostiner 2003).

Simply learning that the law now permits something otherwise forbidden, or forbids something previously allowed, will begin an internalization of this new norm with corresponding law-abiding behavior, demonstrating the law's "expressive powers independent of the legal sanctions threatened on violators" (McAdams 2017: 6). The law not only creates new official rules, but proclaims loudly what is deemed acceptable, laudable, and constructive – and what no longer should be tolerated (Bernstein, Marshall, and Barclay 2009). Legislation, especially recently passed laws such as the Lactation at Work law, can communicate that public opinion has shifted, what McAdams calls "attitudinal signaling" (McAdams 2017: 145). Thus, the law can effect change by "redefining the normative value of old practices or by creating the cognitive building blocks for new ones" (Suchman and Edelman 1996: 929).

Past scholarship demonstrates the impact of normative arguments within organizations (e.g., Harrison, Lopez, and Martin 2015; Nielsen and Parker 2012; Skitka and Morgan 2014). For example, Desai and Kouchaki found that employees could influence greater ethical behavior by their supervisors by invoking and displaying moral symbols, such as religious icons or images of Gandhi (2017). By displaying moral symbols, these workers were able "to guide their leader's behavior and reduce the occurrence of unethical acts in the workplace" (Desai and Kouchaki 2017: 7).

Similarly, regulatory requirements add weight to the normative pressures around laws, heightening compliance (Kagan, Gunningham, and Thornton 2012). Deterrent effects and organizations' fear of violating regulations interact with feelings of duty to be a "good corporate citizen" and normative commitments. This desire can produce a more willing compliance than mere fear of the law could elicit. In fact, some organizations' actors will "over-comply," embracing accommodations that are well beyond those required by law (Kagan, Gunningham, and Thornton 2012).

The literature indicates that laws can act as a symbolic resource for legitimacy. Is that the case with the Lactation at Work Law? Do workers and managers invoke the law in this way? To what extent does the mere passage of the law create legitimacy for employees to engage in workplace milk expression, and what other factors are important? How do actors use the law's symbolic power to influence the legitimacy of milk expression at their specific organization? I find that in some organizations, the existence of the law itself was enough for sufficient legitimacy to create adequate accommodations. In other organizations, workers used the law to more actively pursue and gain legitimacy. Sometimes, the law legitimized workplace milk expression enough for employees to have educational conversations with their supervising managers, discussing values and physiology (McCann 1994).

Breastfeeding is internationally acknowledged as important for public health. Nevertheless, modern workplaces have not been designed to accommodate breastfeeding. This has particularly been true for women who are already societally disadvantaged by class or race. In recent decades, countries around the world have enacted policies designed to facilitate breastfeeding by working mothers, with varying degrees of success. The United States has been part of this movement, first at the state level and then, in 2009, the federal level. The laws stipulate a private, non-bathroom place to express milk and break time do so, but they leave accessibility of the place and the adequacy of the breaks up to interpretation by individuals and workplaces. The literature suggests that the Lactation at Work Law's success may be influenced by various factors, including organizational structure, managerial norms, well-positioned advocates, and the power of the law to legitimize workplace milk expression. This book pays particular attention to these factors.

In some ways, things played out exactly as the literature might have predicted. For example, the passage of the Lactation at Work Law had substantial symbolic power (Gusfield 1967; McAdams 2017) and communicated that breastfeeding and milk expression were sufficiently important issues that the state and federal governments passed laws to protect and encourage them. The law often was able to legitimize workplace lactation, which empowered lactating employees and their advocates to demand support for lactation accommodations.

In other ways, however, my findings revealed some surprises. Values that support lactating workers' breastfeeding efforts, along with a greater understanding of the physiology and health benefits of lactation, shifted the understandings of some of the supervising managers, evolving them into strong advocates. Conversations between managers and workers reflected societal norms and morals from outside the organization to engender cultural shifts that allowed some organizations to embrace accommodations even beyond the law's requirement.

CHAPTER THREE

EXPRESSED FRUSTRATION

Noncompliant, Insufficient, and Inconsistent Accommodations

> *If the employee's job is very busy, [taking a break to express breast milk] can be almost impossible sometimes. Then there's not much we can do about that. [107]*
>
> —supervising manager at a government agency

> *For factory line workers ... they now have a law supporting their needs, but it's very difficult for them to find the time and do what they need to do within the very short breaks that are allotted for factory line workers. And then from their supervisors' point of view, if they allow someone to go to pump breast milk, you know, they have the quandary of 'Do I allow them to do it? Do I not allow them to do it? Do I shut the line down? Do I let everyone have 20 minutes off instead of 15?' [061]*
>
> —human resource specialist at a large engine-producing factory

In organizations where official compliance with the Lactation at Work Law resulted in only symbolic changes that produced few substantial improvements, lactating workers struggled to continue to express milk at work. Workers who were granted insufficient break time took time away from their families, or received less compensation, in order to pump. Some of these employees came in earlier or stayed later to satisfy their employers. Others clocked out for at least one of their lactation breaks in order to have sufficiently long breaks. Lactating workers who struggled with adequate space resorted to pumping in lavatories or in their cars. Some faced painful medical issues when they could not express milk when their bodies needed to. Of course, others simply stopped trying to pump at work.

When lactating employees' pumping needs interfered with management norms – such as control over workers' time and physical location – the needs of management overrode the pumping needs of the employees. Even when employers were following the letter of the law, the resulting work situations still left many employees with insufficient accommodation. In these situations, formal compliance with the law was decoupled from accommodation that would actually enable the lactating employee to successfully express milk.

In these situations, little real change happened; the mere gestures of compliance did not sufficiently assist the employees who needed lactation accommodations. Where managerial goals clashed with the goals of the Lactation at Work Law, "managerial norms and needs" (Albiston 2005: 38) trumped the lactation needs of employees, creating only symbolic compliance. Even when a pumping space was provided and break time was allowed for milk expression, lactating employees faced obstacles to successfully pumping milk. For the women in this chapter, the policies, although usually legally compliant, often were ineffective.

Although I encountered little active resistance when conducting this study, many employees in this chapter experienced frustration with their organizations' application of the law and the inadequate accommodations they received. In other words, while only a few organizations were fully noncompliant, a substantial minority of the organizations complied with the letter of the law yet failed to provide sufficient accommodations.

In these cases, legal compliance was so insufficient that the lactating employees felt that the accommodation almost did not "count." The organizations could list specific ways they were meeting the law's demands, but the goals of the law were forgotten. As a result, the organizations failed to enable many of their lactating employees to successfully express milk at work and continue to breastfeed their children. This demonstrates that simply passing a law that requires employers to provide lactation accommodations does not automatically guarantee that lactating employees will receive adequate accommodations.

This chapter examines the gaps between the law as it was intended and the frustrated lived experiences of the lactating employees whose organizations fail to consistently provide adequate lactation accommodations. In some cases, lactating workers experienced intransigence or resistance from management. But, in other cases, organizations seemed willing to comply, but were more passive, resulting in accommodations that are symbolic without actually being sufficient or effective.

Sometimes human resource departments and supervising managers were passive in assessing whether the accommodations were adequate – waiting for the employee herself to demand improved accommodations. Management appeared to be unaware of the gap between a letter-of-the law compliance that may seem adequate and the struggles of lactating employees.

In these circumstances, lactation at work was not deemed sufficiently legitimate to warrant the level of accommodation that was needed for lactating employees to successfully express milk. For example, management might see milk expression as having sufficient legitimacy to allow an employee to use the single wellness suite to pump milk, but lacking sufficient legitimacy to warrant providing additional locations that would be more convenient to her work area. Or pumping milk might have achieved sufficient legitimacy for the company to allow lactating employees to leave their work area to go to a private place provided for pumping, but it would not provide sufficient paid time off in the form of extended breaks for the employee to travel to the designated area, set up her equipment, and still have time to express milk. Often when accommodations that appeared to meet the letter of the law were, in fact, unsuccessful, either the time permitted was too brief or the available space provided was insufficiently accessible. It appears in these cases that the act of milk expression lacked sufficient legitimacy for the organization to alter their usual ways of working and accept partial responsibility for narrowing the gap between those resources of time and space, instead leaving the burden to the employee.

CONTINUUM OF ACCOMMODATION FAILURE

Organizational reactions to the law that fail to deliver consistently adequate lactation accommodations fall along a continuum. On the far end, are organizations that boldly refuse to accommodate. These cases represent a very small portion of the data in this study.

The next three categories of organizational reaction along the continuum fall under the category of symbolic compliance, indicating that the organization formally complies with legal mandate, but the accommodations are insufficient to actually assist lactating workers. The first symbolic compliance point on the continuum is when the failure to accommodate is so consistent that the lactating employee must choose between continuing in her job without repercussions or ceasing regular milk expression. These organizations observe the letter of the law without realizing its goal.

Farther down the continuum of symbolic compliance are the companies where some accommodations are sufficient for some employees, but insufficient for others. Sometimes, this involved the specifics of the accommodation – such as a lactation room being near some employees' cubicles but not others'. Other times, an organization provided adequate and accessible space and time, but, without sufficient legitimacy, workplace milk expression could not be prioritized above other workplace demands.

Finally, some organizations achieved success in providing accommodations for lactating workers, but the success was inconsistent. For example, they might have permitted pumping at certain times or days, but not others, not allowing for biological needs. Sometimes the physical space provided for milk expression was adequate, but access was intermittent.

Noncompliance: Failure to Accommodate

The changes an organization needed to make to provide sufficient lactation accommodations often required deviating from the ways the organization usually functioned. The aspects of the organization to be altered – such as control over workers' time and physical location – could be perceived as unchangeable or as inappropriate to change (Albiston 2010). However, any law that mandates employee accommodations takes a small step in shifting some power away from the employer. The following human resource specialist for a midsized school district expressed a sentiment shared by those in management in other organizations as well.

> The employer should not be penalized in terms of the expectations of work production and so forth and so on. It's real important that . . . the employers' point of view is maintained because if it's going to be so intrusive that we're not able to get the work done, then I think the person should remain on leave 'til they can come at a time when it would not be harmful to the child and/or to them emotionally or physically, you know, to be able to pump the milk themselves, or to store it or whatever, but, I don't think we should be penalized for it. [021]

In interviews, noncompliant managers consistently emphasized employer priorities.

Other lactating workers were less fortunate in accessing accommodations, even though no supervising manager or human resource specialist in the study stated that their organization wished to evade the law entirely, or that they refused to implement any workplace accommodation. In fact, interviews with human resource personnel and supervising managers always produced statements reflecting compliance with the law. Nevertheless, subsequent discussion later in the interviews and employee interviews provided contrary perspectives.

Sometimes, organizations' efforts fell short of the legal requirements. The Lactation at Work Law clearly stipulates that employees should be given access to a private place to express milk that is not a bathroom and be allowed sufficient break time to do so, using paid break time if they have paid breaks. However, sometimes non-bathroom space was not provided or break times were not allowed. For example, the office worker, mentioned shortly, explains that two lactation spaces had been set up in her building, but they both were parts of women's restrooms that had been sectioned off with curtains.

> In [my] building they did not have a private room set aside for that sole purpose. They had put up a shower curtain in the corner of the bathroom, so you had to sit there and you had to listen to the gossip and the chatter and the noise. And the smells and all of that. And you really felt exposed because you were behind a curtain. It was the only thing separating you from everyone else.
>
> Additionally, for that entire building, they only had [those two spaces]. I actually had to coordinate with other people. If I found an opportunity to leave my desk and I got upstairs and someone else was using it, then I couldn't use it. I actually went to the building manager and asked them if there was another place that I could use.
>
> A couple of times I used a conference room that didn't have a meeting posted on the door, and so, I was able to lock that door. But, of course I always had a fear that someone would unlock it if they decided they needed that room because there were plenty of people in the building that had keys. So, I used the conference room, and of course you were always on edge, ready to cover up at any minute if you needed to.
>
> I talked to the building manager to say, "Is there a room or something available?"
>
> [W030]

Not only were the designated lactation areas unacceptable and noncompliant, they were not always available when she needed to use them.

Her supervising manager was much more positive when describing the accommodations. She focused on the flexibility of the work schedule and believed the physical spaces provided were adequate:

> We're really lucky that our workplace lets employees pretty much do what they need to do. So long as you're not scheduled for a conference or for something else – and that you're getting your work done, obviously – you take a longer break, go talk to your child's teacher, run to the store. It's a great place to work. [Interviewer complements the flexibility and asks about physical accommodations] We're not a big place. That's why we can be so flexible. But that also means that we don't have a lot of extra rooms, not always a lot of space. So we have to be creative. Sometimes, it's not ideal, but not everything is perfect.
>
> [063]

Eventually, the building manager offered a utility closet, which met the letter of the law, but this space was unappealing to the worker because it served as storage for cleaning supplies and was quite dirty.

> They said, "Oh well, there's a utility closet that we can clear out." But, it was literally a utility closet off the hallway before that maze of cubicles and it had cinder block walls and a utility thing ... There were dirty brooms and mops and things in there. I was like: I don't want to close myself up in the utility closet; that doesn't seem sanitary either! So I told them, "Thank you, but no thank you." I used the bathroom and the conference room a few times, but that was difficult also because there aren't that many conference rooms in that building, so those are always being used as well. A few times – I have tinted windows in my car – so a few times I just went out to my car and used the battery power from the pump. It was not a good set up.
>
> [W030]

As discussed further in subsequent chapters, while lactating workers often need concrete accommodations in terms of both a private place and sufficient break time, the third key component for successful milk expression is a less tangible need for legitimacy of the activity. Workplace milk expression needs to be understood as legitimate for workers to successfully overcome hurdles.

Organizations that focus on children, health, or children's health are types of organizations where one might anticipate substantive and enthusiastic accommodations for employees' lactation needs. Yet managers' need to control their workers' time and placement sometimes overrides the possible synergistic effects between an organizations' mission and that of the Lactation at Work Law. For example, the human resource director of a large childcare facility indicated that milk expression was not compatible with her employees' jobs.

> We encourage, as a quality child care employer, and a place of employment, we encourage not only our clients to breastfeed, but also our employees ... [But] it makes it a little difficult to actually get things done while [an employee is] pumping [laughs] ... Their job is to care for the children, and when they're pumping; they're not caring for the children, obviously. So that makes it a little difficult.
>
> [007]

In fact, the worker interviewed at that childcare facility stopped trying to pump at work shortly after returning from maternity leave.

> I could use my lunch break, but I needed more break time, but there just wasn't the break time. Someone was always out [so we were short-handed] and I often missed breaks [therefore]. I tried to talk with [#007] about this and she said she'd try to get [a floating teacher] in to help me take breaks, but it never happened. We are always [short-staffed.] I just couldn't step out [of the classroom] whenever [I needed to pump].
>
> [W168]

Although the law formally shifted the balance of power in the workplace slightly away from management by bestowing more workplace rights to the employees, informally, management still controlled employees' bodies and their schedules.

This supervisor at a manufacturing supply company explained that, because his employees were often on the phone or traveling to meet with clients, time and space for expressing milk would always be a challenge – a challenge that he felt remained with the employee herself:

> We're a small company [although over sixty workers]. We're all always working with clients, meeting with them at their factories, or helping them on the phone ... Our job is being there for them. If they don't [use our products] then we don't have [our jobs]. [I told W171] I'd do whatever I could for her, but she'd have to figure it out.
>
> [110]

This employee confirmed that both time and space were problematic. However, the issue of legitimacy was also present; her characterization of taking time to express milk as "sneaking" and worrying that a client might "tattle" illustrates how her organization did not view lactation and the associated accommodation it required as legitimate.

> If I had a day when I was just at the office, I could always go find a storage room [where I could express milk] . . . But if I had to travel – and that's a lot of my job – then I'd be like, "How can I sneak in a little extra time somewhere so I can pump?" I'd try to arrive early and park far enough away that I could sit in the back [of my car] and pump . . . If I couldn't park [in a discrete place] I'd try to sneak in [to the client building] and pump in their bathroom. It worked, but I was always worried someone would say something. Tattle on me! [laughs]
>
> [W171]

Elsewhere in the interview, this lactating worker explained that she had approached the human resources manager to see if she could change her job to providing phone support. She was told those specific job duties fell under the control of the supervising manager. That human resource specialist confirmed that it was not possible for the employee to alter her job duties.

> We had one woman who wanted us to just completely change how we did things in order to [accommodate her milk expression]. We can't just change everything. If we had changed what [job duties] she had to do, then that would mean that someone else's [job duties] would have to change to do what she had been doing before. We can't make everyone change just to accommodate one person.
>
> [111]

After about two months, when accommodations did not improve, the employee stopped trying to express milk at work and discontinued breastfeeding her child about a month later.

Women, Infants, and Children (WIC) offices are places where one might expect some synergy between the Lactation at Work Law's goals and the organizational goals; yet, here, too, workers struggled to receive adequate accommodations when their own lactation needs lacked sufficient legitimacy to warrant adequate organizational support. Structurally, WIC offices would seem to be ideal because many had lactation rooms in place for their clients to use. Yet the following somewhat lengthy portions of a lactating worker interview, especially when compared to the interview with her most senior supervising manager, exemplifies employees and management divergence in understanding their shared workplaces (see Hirsh and Kornrich 2008).

This lactating worker had regularly pumped breast milk at her desk while covering her body and the pump.

> I worked at the Head Start home-base program working with children, [birth] to two years old or up until they enter preschool. I [had] been working there about a year before I became pregnant. I had expressed my desire to nurse to everyone, and after the baby was born and I went back to work. I share an office with two other ladies, and they both said that they didn't mind if I pumped. I had a shawl that I put over me and stuff, so it was nothing that anyone would see.
>
> [W141]

Several weeks later, while waiting for a meeting to start, she used her pump to express milk, as she usually did, but a new, young co-worker complained about this to the supervising manager.

> [At one point] we were [in the "family room," which is where we hold our meetings, and I was] waiting for a meeting and so I pumped while I was waiting and I had everything covered. You couldn't see anything. All you could do was hear the pump. One of the new girls that was there – she was fresh out of high school – she said that she thought it was gross that I was pumping. And, so, my supervisor came to me and told me that I could not pump anymore at work. And I said, "You can't tell me that." I said, "If you want to give me a [different] place to pump, then I can do that." But I thought that my office and the family room, that's set aside for those things. [I thought those rooms] were safe places to do that.
>
> [W141]

Even though the law explicitly states that a restroom is not an acceptable place for the employee to express milk, this social worker's supervising manager told her to move her pumping to the restroom.

> And I asked her where I could pump and she said, "You can pump in the bathroom." And I told her that I was not going to pump in the bathroom, that she would have to figure something else out, 'cause I already had permission from the other people in the office to, that it was okay for me to pump because I didn't have anywhere [else] to pump. And she told me basically, "You have to pump in the bathroom." And I said, "That's disgusting. You don't eat lunch in the bathroom. So I'm not going to pump in the bathroom."
>
> [W141]

This lactating worker contacted other supervising managers at her location, as well as their supervisors, to try to appeal the decision.

> I sent out several emails about the issue to [other supervisors and management] and had nothing returned. Nobody would answer any of my emails, any of my phone calls. They wanted me to drop it. And, I was already struggling to keep my milk supply up. And, there was no way that I could be at work all day long and not have my milk dry up, or at least, decrease. My [milk] supply went down at least half, just going back to work, let alone not being allowed to pump, too. It was even worse. I could only pump enough at work to get her one bottle for the day. And, then to be told that I have to pump in the bathroom?!
>
> So I tried to go the right way and talk to the right people and got nowhere. I actually saved my emails to show them that I had tried ... [I had talked to my supervisors about the law before I left for maternity leave] so they already knew it was illegal to ask someone to pump in the restroom or to not provide facilities and they just totally didn't even listen to it or give any validation to it at all.
>
> [W141]

Unable to remedy the situation on her own, she reached out to her state's breastfeeding coordinator, an informational government position to address questions about the lactation laws.

> [The state's breastfeeding coordinator] actually called the people at Head Start, and they were very taken back that she had called them ... They finally talked to her and told her that they had no clue that this was going on and I hadn't said anything and blah blah blah. [But they were lying.] I had the emails showing that I had talked to people and it was just a bad situation.
>
> [W141]

When the state's breastfeeding coordinator confronted the managers, they denied knowing about her workplace difficulties.

> They pretty much just wanted me to not say anything. And I wasn't going to do that because this is my job. I had been there two years and, over two years. I didn't want this to be the reason why I wasn't working there anymore ... [When the breastfeeding coordinator and] I went in to meet with them, they kind of said, "Well maybe you're just emotional. Maybe you were taking things differently. You just had a baby. Maybe you're just missing your daughter or something." I said, "No." I said, "Yes, of course, I'm missing my daughter. It's not easy to go back to work after having a baby. This is my job, I love my job. Don't make me having an issue with nursing in the bathroom my fault!"
>
> [W141]

This worker felt betrayed that an organization that encourages women to breastfeed could not see the legitimacy in her own milk expression needs. When she felt that management was pressuring her to leave, she quit.

> They were upset that I had gone to [the state breastfeeding coordinator] about it. And so, I just lost all that; I just felt like they wanted me to leave. And so, I left . . . They tell you to be a whistle blower but as soon as you blow the whistle then you're like the black sheep.
>
> [W141]

The toxicity of her workplace was confirmed when co-workers, hearing of her imminent exit, asked her to raise grievances on their behalf; they were too scared to do so themselves, and felt that by leaving, she had nothing left to lose.

> Even the last meeting [illustrates how contentious this workplace was]: My last day of work we had a team meeting where everybody could come and talk. [And I had received] 13 emails, 14 emails, [that had] come in from different staff wanting me to bring up issues at this meeting that they were too scared to bring up because they [had] seen what happened to me. It was just a really bad situation; the last meeting was terrible.
>
> [W141]

The supervising manager, during her interview, said that her employees often preferred to nurse their babies at home, for their own personal reasons, and she would not want to pressure them to breastfeed or pump at work if they did not want to. She did not indicate any awareness of any problems lactating workers had experienced.

The human resource manager at this Head Start office initially expressed no knowledge of this employee (W141), but discussed, in general terms, that employee's situation, reframing the story and sanitizing any actual dispute out of the narrative. She began by saying that mother-employees often elect to not return to work, and some of those who do return simply elect to pump milk in restrooms.

> We've had a lot of moms that haven't returned to work lately . . . That happens when you get home. You fall in love with that baby and you decide, "You know what? I'm not coming back to work" . . . We wanted to make sure that we were in line with that bill or that law that was passed . . . We would already make those accommodations for them [before the law was passed]. Some moms were choosing to pump in the restroom. So, we were just making sure . . . we let them know that

> that wasn't, if that was their choice, they could do that, but this new law came out and, by the law, we weren't promoting that they pump in the restroom. We would provide them a separate space to do that.
>
> [042]

When asked if she had a sense of why they would choose to pump in the restroom, she responded:

> I think some folks were feeling that we have a lot of space that's shared office space, so I guess they felt that [the restroom] was the most private, intimate space that they could have. 'Cause all our restrooms, most of the restrooms are private restrooms. They're not public restrooms that have several stalls in them . . . [They are individual little rooms, each with its own sink.] . . . I don't ask mothers when they're returning, "Are you going to breastfeed?" I don't ask that question. If they choose to share that I provide them with the information and the lactation support in the workplace information.
>
> [042]

I asked directly about how she managed supervising managers who might resist some aspects of lactation accommodations. She succinctly answered, "I haven't had any issues, honestly." She then qualified that statement to be referring to the past year, and began to talk specifically about the lactating worker I had interviewed (W141).

> We did have one [situation] before this, so, I had to educate that manager that we want to make sure that we're working with this employee and providing her the time that she needs and if that means that she's flexing that time, takes that break in the day and takes that 15 minutes at the end or works that out on Friday, or however. We just make sure that we're working with that employee. So we have satisfied employees that can do the job that we need them to do. [Interviewer asks her to elaborate.]
>
> So, about a year and a half ago, maybe, we had one manager that, you know, [portraying the manager's voice:] "I need her here and I don't know if I can allow her to pump." I said, "No, we need to work with this mom, we need to allow her to do those things, to accommodate her for her choices that she's making." Especially because it's in the business that we do. We serve individuals, families, and children in our community and we're supporting moms in these same services outside of our work. So we need to make sure we're providing the same internal environment as we're promoting externally.
>
> [042]

When asked how the supervising manager responded, she portrayed the difficulty as a simple lack of knowledge about breastfeeding, which would be surprising since the organization officially supports and teaches its clients about breastfeeding.

> Just working with that manager to make sure that they were educated on providing for breastfeeding, what breastfeeding was about, and the nutritional value of that for that child. Just working with them to find out a place to talk with the employee and address what issues she may have had and to find her that intimate space for that 15 or 20 minutes that she needed … I guess, [that supervising manager] didn't quite understand the committed choice that she was making by providing, by feeding her child through breastfeeding … So we just educated that manager on that value of breastfeeding and that bond between mother and child.
>
> [042]

The human resource specialist then broadened her discussion to indicate that the problem was not just with the supervising manager, but also with the lactating worker's co-workers and with the employee's immodesty:

> Let me also address … the employee had some concerns. She was pumping in an office with several other people. So other employees had concerns about that as well. So, it was a larger, a much larger issue. It was educating the manager and the employee about that need for a private space to do that … She just needed to do that in a private setting, or with other folks that were comfortable being in the room during that time. So … the employee was very open. [Laughs.] [Interviewer: Oh? What do you mean?] By pumping in front of other co-workers … We worked with the employee and the manager, both, to educate them about the need for a private space and she very much understood and didn't mean to offend anybody. But … in the business that we're in, she thought that was a pretty natural thing to do, that others wouldn't take offense. So … we just provided a designated space for her to do that privately.
>
> [042]

The "designated space" she referred to, according to the employee, was a one-seater bathroom. I asked the human resources specialist if these steps had adequately addressed the situation, and she said they had. But the employee decided to resign shortly after that.

> So we just worked with her and she, then, very shortly made the choice to leave our organization to go home and stay with her baby. So we weren't 100 percent successful, I guess, but that's a personal choice. [042]

Her admission that the attempted accommodations "weren't 100 percent successful" is a mild way of acknowledging that the accommodations were insufficient.

These stories illustrate that sometimes the actions of human resource officers and supervising managers can display significant intransigence to complying with the law. Even some organizations with official pro-breastfeeding policies for clients or patients resisted sufficient accommodations for their own employees. In these instances, the worth of breastfeeding may have been seen as legitimate generally, but its workplace legitimacy was insufficient to override the needs of the employers to control their employees' bodily space and use of time.

Symbolic Compliance

Sometimes organizations provided a space for employees to conduct milk expression and allowed time to pump; yet the spaces were not accessible or the amount of allotted time was too short or inconsistently available. In these situations, the employees experienced formal compliance but still faced substantial hurdles, such that they often had to choose between breastfeeding and continuing in their jobs. These stories illustrate how organizations that provided symbolic compliance – obeying the letter of the law – may appear to be creating decent accommodation while failing to make substantive changes to the workplace.

Consistent Failure to Accommodate

Some organizations provided fully compliant, more amenable spaces – clean rooms that were private and not bathrooms with locks, and an electrical outlet for the pump. Yet the number of locations and their distribution across the organizations' areas were insufficient for many lactating employees to reach easily. For example, a research assistant at a university explained that the lactation space her university provided was in another building, necessitating too much travel time.

> I knew I wanted to breastfeed so I asked where [the lactation rooms] were and it turns out there's none in [my building.] The closest one is [the next building over]. So, if I want to use that space, I have to get my [milk pumping] stuff, walk down [stairs], go over there, to [the other

> building], and walk up[stairs] to that room. And if it's cold out, then I'm running between buildings without a coat and stuff. I mean, the room is fine; it's nice; it's okay. But I use up, like, half an hour, going there and coming back.
>
> [W131]

A human resource specialist at that same organization confirmed the lack of lactation rooms:

> I have had calls from people that wanted closer rooms [to where they work]. Either they call me or their supervisors call me . . . I think the big thing is the location; we don't have them in every building. I wish we did so some people don't have to walk to a different building, and I wish they didn't have to do that.
>
> [035]

The research assistant's supervising manager asked the employee to let him know when she left the building to express milk since she'd be gone so long. Yet, despite acknowledging how the poor placement of the lactation room took more time for her to reach, he never provided an alternative site closer to her work station. The research assistant soon found that she needed at least an hour for each pumping session, which was too disruptive to her work, so she soon stopped pumping altogether.

The need for lactation rooms to be sufficiently convenient was a key area where legally compliant accommodations became symbolic structures. The room itself might be an adequate accommodation, but providing it was an insufficient change if it was poorly accessible, often occupied, or unusable in other ways.

Issues of space and time were particularly intertwined when lactating employees needed to travel to their lactation rooms when they had limited break time. For example, a lactating health department employee explained that any lactation break that included travel time was going to exceed the usual fifteen-minute breaks.

> I think people thought [the lactating workers were] just goofing off but if you're on a 15 minute break it's probably gonna take more than 15 minutes to leave your setting, get the key, unlock the door, lock the door, pump, clean your pieces up, bring the key back, and then get back to your work site. Some managers, I think, are just more flexible and understood the importance of it and [that] it's gonna probably take more than 15 minutes – not that you can be gone for more than an hour on a 15 minute break, but it may be 20 minutes, it may be 22 minutes.
>
> [W109]

Sometimes management was unaware of the difficulty caused by providing a limited number of lactation rooms and how that affected travel time. One woman's supervising manager explained that, while he had supervised a few employees who pumped milk, they seemed to accomplish it without problems. His minimal understanding of the worker's situation was underscored when he indicated that he couldn't really say how many weeks or months any lactating employee he supervised had expressed milk at work, or at what times of day she would have left the area to do so.

Other times management was quite aware of the difficulties, as this human resource specialist at a small private college explained during her Time One interview:

> We have a women's center . . . that's been a designated place for the past year . . . and we're hoping to identify additional places across campus because if you work in this office, to walk to the women's center, it's not far. It's probably a five-minute walk, but that adds on ten minutes. So for hourly employees, the time issue is really important.
>
> [031]

Although this college intended to open more lactation rooms across its campus – as a number of organizations with large physical footprints did over the course of this study – only one additional lactation room had been created by the time of the second wave of interviews.

A data management worker at a large professional firm explained that her workplace had a wellness room, but it was very inconvenient from where she worked.

> People could use [the wellness room] if they needed to take insulin, or they needed a private place to pray, or needed to – I don't know – take care of some personal business or something. So I was told I could use that wellness room during my breaks and lunch hour. But it's on the second floor and I'm on the fifth floor, on the other side of the building. And, by the time I got my pump and then went to the wellness room, that was ten minutes right there. And then another ten to come back, that's twenty minutes. And it would often take me a while before [my milk would start to flow freely], so it would often take me about forty minutes.
>
> [W090]

Although her supervising manager allowed her to extend the length of her break times somewhat, this employee's needs lacked sufficient legitimacy in the eyes of her manager.

> [My manager] would be upset because I had been gone for so long. So, after a few weeks, I just couldn't make it work. I thought of asking if I could stay late to make up the time, but then that's time that I'm away from my kid. And the department pretty much shuts down [at 5 p.m.] so I'd have been the only one there. So, I stopped after a few weeks. I stopped pumping. I still nursed in the evenings for another month or so.
>
> [W090]

Although she was frustrated with her situation and worried about her manager, this worker did not bring her concern to the person in the human resources department, who, in his own interview, described this arrangement as being sufficient.

The following lactating worker, a salesperson at a large department store, also could not successfully express breast milk within the time her supervising managers considered a "reasonable break time," so she chose to punch out for her afternoon pumping break.

> I'm a [sales clerk at a large department store]. The employee locker room is in the basement. The lactation room is on the second floor. I work on the third floor, so [for my lactation breaks] I'd have to go down to my locker in the basement then up to the second floor, then walk the whole way (across) the second floor to the [lactation] room. Then I assemble my [pump and attachments], then I try to relax enough that I actually got any milk, then take everything apart, wipe [the pieces clean], get it back in my locker, and get back to the [sales] floor.
>
> It just took me a lot of time. I could just do it over my lunch break, but for my afternoon [milk expression break], no way. I get why my managers didn't like it. I didn't like that it took so long. I wasn't just wasting time; it took that long [to travel and do everything necessary]. I get why they felt it wasn't working. So then I would clock out when I went down to get my pump and clock back in when I put it back. That was better, but then it's like I'm working a couple hours less each week, and that money adds up.
>
> [W124]

While expressing milk was sufficiently important to her that she would sacrifice income, it was not a legitimate enough activity for her workplace's culture to provide the accommodations she needed within her usual work day.

The human resource specialist for the department store was enthusiastic about the store's support for its workers, extending that ethic to lactating workers as well. However, he believed the difficulties the employee had were her own problem.

> We really care about our employees ... They have a break room. They have lockers. And, yes, we provide a lactation room. That's both for our customers and for our employees. Employees use the lactation room, too. We support that ... If they need more time or can't manage without more time, then they have to work that out [on their own]. But it's always worked out fine.
>
> [063]

While this human resource specialist perceived the lactation accommodations as "work[ing] out fine," the employee's solution resulted in significantly less pay for her family because she had to punch out when she needed to express milk. If she spent about thirty-five minutes clocked out each day for milk expression, that totaled almost three unpaid hours each week.

Unlike the supervising managers and human resource specialists in the previous section who resisted legal compliance, the organizations in this category made sure to execute the letter of the law. Unfortunately, such accommodations were legally compliant on the surface yet were symbolic in practice. For substantive changes to occur, lactation at work would need to have greater legitimacy within these organizations. Greater legitimacy would command sufficient organizational resources and wrest from management enough control over workers' time and physical placement so that their lactating employees could have a successful accommodation for expressing milk.

Intermittent or Inconsistent Success

Some organizations provided accommodations for lactating workers that were inconsistently effective. In these workplaces, scheduling problems arose due to fluctuations in the rhythm of the workplaces or appropriate spaces were only intermittently available. The intersection of time and place created problems, such as when provided spaces were occupied when the lactating worker needed to pump.

This low-level manager at a restaurant explained that sometimes she would miss her breaks to express milk because her schedule placed substantial time constraints on her.

> [Day shift was easier], but night shift, as soon as you get there three hours from my four o'clock shift was during dinner rush, so it's not like I could just be like "Hey, pardon me for 20 minutes; I'm going to go pump some

> milk." (laughs). So you just kind of fit it in wherever you could, 'cause being a manager on the floor – everybody [always] needs a manager.
> [020]

Because servers needed a manager to be present on the floor, she felt that if she stopped to express milk during busy meal times, her servers would be disadvantaged. Her workplace culture prioritized the nonstop rhythm of certain shifts, like the dinner rush and certain holidays or festivals, and her need to pump lacked sufficient legitimacy to counterweigh those demands.

> [Some times were really hard], like the weekend of the car show. [Last year], I worked Friday morning, Friday night, Saturday mid[night], Sunday morning, [and] by Sunday afternoon I had mastitis because I wasn't able to pump enough. So by Sunday night when I came in for inventory I couldn't even raise my arms up. The lump that I had this time it went the whole circumference of my boob, and it was like three inches thick. And it hurts really, really bad. I couldn't even pick up my arms that night so I called my boss and I was like "I'm done counting for tonight. I'll count the rest in the morning." And she was like "Why?" I'm like "I'm in too much pain I can't pick anything up" . . . So she said "Ok well just get me the numbers in the morning."
> [020]

Although she had a place to express milk, she skipped many pumping breaks, which eventually resulted in painful mastitis from unexpressed milk. When her discomfort rose to the level of substantial pain, her need to leave became legitimate enough for her to insist to her boss, despite the fact that more work remained. The human resource specialist for restaurants in her region said that he trusted his managers to work with the employees to figure out solutions, recognizing that the restaurant industry posed special challenges. He was not aware of any problems.

Issues of adequate space and sufficient time sometimes converged when the lactation space was shared among a number of employees. The organization referenced in the following set of quotations [#W058, #105, #107] left coordination of the lactation room to the women themselves; they informally communicated with each other about when they would need the space. While often this resulted in successful sharing, sometimes women's lactation times overlapped, leaving one woman without access to the lactation room. Other organizations avoided this situation by having lactating workers use calendar apps or hard-copy schedules to reserve the lactation rooms. Nevertheless, even in those organizations, if one woman was running late or needed a few more minutes to express milk, she could delay the pumping schedules of all the workers scheduled after her.

This lactating worker at a government agency discussed her frustration in mobilizing herself to get to the lactation room only to discover that it was already in use; this difficulty was invisible to her supervising manager.

> They created this little room for women to go to pump milk. We could keep our [milk expression] equipment and such in there, too. It wasn't big – just enough room for a table and chair and lamp and a little cot. But it had an outlet, no sink or anything, though. But it could only be for one person at a time. If some other [lactating employee] had gotten there before you, too bad. And sometimes you can't get away again for several hours . . . you just missed that time when [your body was] ready to make milk. But usually it worked out. Usually we knew about when [the other women] would be using the room. It was just frustrating when it didn't work out.
>
> [W059]

Sometimes this organization's accommodations resulted in successful compliance, while other times the available accommodations were ineffective and merely symbolic. Yet, in his interview, her human resource specialist characterized the accommodations positively, focusing on the physical facility:

> We have three [lactating workers]. They have a room where they go. It all works well. It hasn't affected how [well the agency's office] works. It's not a problem at all
>
> [105]

He focused on whether the law and these accommodations changed the workplace at all, so from his perspective it is "not a problem" – not because the organization successfully addressed the law's priorities or the employee's needs, but because it found a way to avoid making any changes to how the organization functions in meeting management's priorities.

The employee's supervising manager was somewhat in touch with this ongoing struggle, but dismissed it as a problem for workers to figure out on their own:

> It works fine . . . Sometimes there are [problems]. Like, sometimes they don't coordinate it right and two people get there at the same time.

> I don't know. But they work it out there . . . That's not my thing to try to figure out . . . I don't know about exactly how [coordinating the accommodations] works . . . Of course, if the employee's job is very busy, [taking a break to express breast milk] can be almost impossible sometimes. Then there's not much we can do about that.
>
> [107]

He was aware of some accessibility problems, but, because the lactation at work lacked sufficient legitimacy for the organization to feel some responsibility for its success, he could dismiss the issues, shifting the onus to the lactating workers, exclusively.

Simply locating space was difficult for some lactating employees. In the next case discussed, the logistics of locating space became stressful; yet, because the organization offered legally compliant space somewhere, people in management assumed they had provided an adequate accommodation.

> Not too many people here have offices. We have a large area with cubicles, and so that's where that [lactating] individual works . . . We're a small company, and didn't have the ability to designate a room just for that, or just for her. However, we do have rooms that are not occupied most of the time, such as a conference room, or a library, or an individual that does have an office that isn't in that day, so she was told that any one of those locations, probably more than one of those, would be available at any particular time. And she could utilize those. They all have doors that lock and blinds you can draw, etc. So, that arrangement seemed to work okay.
>
> [043]

While the requisite spaces were provided – private, non-bathroom areas – the constantly shifting locations were stressful for this employee:

> They tried; they did. And I appreciate it. But from day to day it would change, and I wouldn't always know. I'd go to one room that was free before and now people are having a conference meeting in it. Then someone says, "Oh [co-worker] is gone today." So I use his office, but he's gone, so I never got his permission to use it, you know? Then he's back in a few days, and I'm somewhere else. It was fine, but it seemed like a lot of the time I had to spend time finding out where I could be pumping, rather than only taking time to *be* pumping.
>
> [W136]

Fortunately, her break time was not tightly constrained, so if she needed to spend some time searching for a private location to pump, she was not directly penalized.

Organizations often addressed the need for a private space for milk expression by using rooms already provided for other employee health issues. For example, this human resource specialist in an insurance company explained that the company had a wellness room for any employee to use for a variety of reasons, including expressing breast milk.

> Basically, what we have is, within our building we have what we call an employee health services area . . . We have a nurse over there and a staff person, and we have rooms that are cot rooms. It's for people if they get sick they can go lie down, but it's also for women that can come in for that purpose and they can go and use those rooms for that.
>
> [058]

However, at least one lactating worker who used this room found these accommodations unsatisfactory, not only because the small number of rooms meant that one might not be available when she needed it, but also because it might not be sufficiently hygienic.

> There are little, like, sick-person rooms, that [lactating workers] can use. They're fine; they're great. Except, like, sometimes they aren't. I mean, nothing big, but I've found a used Band-Aid and the wrapper for an alcohol wipe, and I just know that the person who was there before me was there for a health reason, not to pump . . . they had to take insulin or had some health problem or something. And then a few times I went there, I'd bring all my [milk pumping apparatus and supplies] and all the rooms were in use. Then I have to go find somewhere else. I get it. You can't always know when someone's going to be sick [and need to use those rooms]. But that's the point: I don't even like being where someone might have been sick.
>
> [W138]

This quote illustrates the thin line that exists between legally and medically approved spaces and spaces that meet employees' comfort expectations. The issue of the rooms being occupied when the worker needed to pump presented an unambiguous difficulty, but the dissatisfaction she felt because other unhealthy co-workers may have used the space is a separate issue. Some organizations acknowledged this distinction between providing "sick rooms" – where anyone with any health need can go – versus providing rooms for health maintenance activities like checking blood pressure, administering eye drops, or expressing milk.

Workers who had control over their schedules and had their own locking offices usually fared the best, but sometimes they still struggled if milk expression lacked legitimacy in their organization. For example, a data manager worked in an old, grand building with very high, ornate ceilings. To divide the large, open space into offices, portable but stable walls had been installed to create many smaller offices, each with a locking door and walls extending about eleven feet, providing ample visual privacy – no one could peek over the walls, as one could with cubicles. However, the offices had no ceilings, but simply opened up toward the original ceiling, approximately fifteen feet higher. The lack of aural privacy that this presented was problematic because of her supervisor's attitude toward pumping:

> I have my own space. It's completely private: my door locks, I have a little refrigerator. In many ways, it's perfect, except that people can hear the motor of my breast pump . . . [In particular], my immediate boss – her office is right next to mine – she can hear it and has commented about it. She doesn't approve of my pumping milk, she doesn't understand it . . . Fortunately, she has to travel a lot, so she's often not there. But when she is, I [pump elsewhere] so she doesn't hear me.
>
> [W019]

With her supervising manager denying the legitimacy of expressing milk at work altogether, the seemingly minor issue of aural privacy was exacerbated sufficiently that she left her locked office to pump elsewhere.

MEDIATING THE SUCCESS OF SYMBOLIC COMPLIANCE

Two factors mediated the relationship between management responses to the law and the experiences of the lactating employees: the attitudes of co-workers and lactating workers' socioeconomic status. When pumping lacked sufficient legitimacy in the workplace culture, co-workers compounded difficulties for lactating co-workers. In other cases where workplace milk expression had ample support from co-workers, they could help bridge the gap between the organization's symbolic compliance and successful accommodations.

Lactating employees with higher socioeconomic status were able to maintain successful workplace milk expression more easily, even if their organizations were unwilling to shift time constraints, create convenient private places for pumping, and demonstrated little support for employees expressing milk. These higher-status employees commanded their own time and space resources and were less affected by organizational unwillingness to accommodate adequately. Additionally, their status within their organizations allowed them to request or negotiate for better accommodations and their higher socio-economic status afforded them the possibility of exiting altogether if accommodations proved inadequate.

Co-workers

An older female co-worker exacerbated her lactating co-worker's struggles to pump milk at work when she objected to her expressing milk in their shared office even though the nearest lactation room was on the far side of the another building.

> The first week I was back [from maternity leave] it was all great. I didn't realize it was because [my office mate] wasn't there. [laughs] . . . Then she comes back [from her vacation] and is all, "You can't do that here." And I was covered up and everything. You know, I was very careful. I was discrete. She said the noise [of the breast pump] bothered her. What?! So then I'd have to go [to the other building] where the lactation room was. I told her I had a right to pump. She told me that I had no right to use "her" office. I told my [supervising] manager about her, and she basically said the same thing. But she wouldn't find me a better place to pump. Or couldn't. I don't know.
>
> [W020]

Her manager confirmed the tension between the two women, and in an ironic twist, used the language of inclusivity to assert that the lactating employee should leave her office to pump.

> Some people are more comfortable with that stuff than others. [This employee] was comfortable lifting up her shirt and pumping right there, but [her co-worker] wasn't. That's not okay. Everyone has to be welcome at their workplace. You can't make someone feel unwelcome in their own office. [Interviewer: So how was that resolved?]. [The lactating employee] would leave her office to [pump milk]. That's why that room is there [for women to express milk]. And I was very understanding of this, because it sometimes took her a long time to go there and do it. But we all try to help each other here.
>
> [117]

But this was not a good solution for the lactating employee who, in order to keep up with her workload, often stayed late or took work home, to compensate for the work time she lost with each pumping session.

> [Supervising manager] was okay. She'd say things like, "Now, don't worry if it's taking you longer. I'm not watching your clock" or whatever. So, fine, she's not counting the minutes I'm taking to go to [the lactation room] . . . Yeah, but she is watching whether I'm getting my work done, and I wasn't. So then I tried to stay late some evenings, but that's not fair to my family. Or I take work home, and just work when everyone's asleep.
>
> [W020]

Her experience echoes the experiences of #W141, the WIC employee discussed earlier. Although her supervising manager was much more sympathetic than the manager at WIC, she, too, did not locate a sufficiently convenient space for her lactating employee. Because of the substantial travel time involved in using space provided, the demand by her co-worker that she travel to the designated lactation room cost the lactating employee time that diminished her workday productivity.

In other situations, instead of exacerbating already difficult situations, co-workers, were able to substantially ameliorate relatively inhospitable provisions or poor employer accommodations. For example, this lactating worker explained how a co-worker, who had a private office down the hall from her, provided support.

> She had several kids and breastfed all of them, I think. We talked about that stuff, like breast pumps and breast shields. Whenever she'd see me walking to [the designated lactation room] she'd, like, smile at me or give me thumbs-up or something. It really made me happy. She went on vacation one week while I was still pumping and she even let me use her office then . . . That was great because it was a lot closer. When [another co-worker] saw that I was [using her office in her absence], I explained and it was really a good feeling.
>
> [W024]

This fellow breastfeeding mother regularly confirmed the legitimacy of her co-worker's efforts to breastfeed by conducting these positive signals. By publicly sharing the resource of her own office, that co-worker communicated her support to others in the organization.

Sometimes, co-workers who were not initially allies ended up providing crucial support. For example, this office worker's co-worker initially had little knowledge or compassion for women in that situation. However, after the lactating worker educated him and shared her frustration, he became quite supportive. She described the poor lactation accommodations provided for her after she returned from maternity leave:

> I was just so upset . . . I had every problem, it seemed . . . HR found me rooms that turned [out] to be already used [for an ongoing purpose]. My manager didn't get around to finding me a place. Then when I found a place, it was far, and so it took me longer to go pump and I was worried he'd get mad. None of it was working out . . . I told [my co-worker] that, even though I knew I had these rights [to a non-bathroom place], I ended up pumping in the bathroom sometimes. [My Co-worker] had no idea about any of this. He's married, but doesn't have any kids, I don't think. But I just opened my heart to him. I would just talk to him about everything. It reminded me why I was doing this . . . [Breastfeeding] was so important to me, but I was getting so frustrated . . . He knew someone higher up who had their own office who had just left, so I was able to use that office for a few weeks, until stuff got figured out. And then they found me even better space, but [sighs] that first week was really bad.
>
> [W079]

This lactating worker would not have had these conversations with her co-worker if the Lactation at Work Law had not been in place. The existence of the law served as a catalyst for lactating workers to have important conversations with co-workers.

Socioeconomic Status

There is an important association between lactating employees' socioeconomic status and the implementation of lactation accommodations. Workers' socioeconomic status – their level of education, their job type, their class identity – affects not only what sorts of accommodations they may need, but also their ability to negotiate for improved accommodations (see e.g., Gerstel and Clawson 2014). Working-class employees are more likely to have jobs with less flexibility in scheduling, posing challenges to finding sufficient time to express milk. Also, workers with lower socioeconomic status often have less control over their physical space, which presents hurdles to locating accessible, private places for pumping.

Retail store workers, for example, do not have any private space in the workplace. They hold jobs that require them to be publicly accessible, and are not able to successfully pump at work without their employer providing space and adequate time to use it. Despite having substantial need for lactation accommodations, these workers might not be able to challenge insufficient accommodations, even if the accommodations do not meet the legal minimal standard. In contrast, college professors are middle-class professionals who usually have their own locking offices and substantial flexibility and control over their schedules. They do not need their supervisors to provide them with a place to express milk or to approve certain break times.

Not only do workers with higher socioeconomic status face these difficulties less often; their interactions with management may be more effective. Lactating professionals often enjoy social status similar to their supervising managers and to their human resource personnel. In fact, they might even be members of management.

These differences in status affects people's ability to informally confront supervising managers, formally petition human resources offices, and both formally and informally invoke the law (Hoffmann 2012). Not only does socioeconomic class result in different outcomes from workplace disputes, but it also affects the sorts of previous experiences employees bring into the workplace that inform their ability to request accommodations (Trautner, Hatton, and Smith 2013). Class status also produces differences in workers' options; for example, is financial survival possible after quitting? If not, exiting might not be an option (Hirschman 1970; Hoffmann 2006).

However, the relationship between class and allocation of lactation resources is not determinative. Different types of jobs are associated with varying levels of socioeconomic status, but the association between class and lactation accommodation implementation is not absolute. For example, assembly line workers do not have private offices, but neither do bank branch managers. Some professionals might hold positions that structurally or culturally constrain their space or time, such as by sharing an office with an uncooperative co-worker or by needing to be immediately available to respond other employees, even those she "outranks," so that she cannot, in good conscience, take pumping breaks as needed. Conversely, a factory worker, while constrained by space and time structurally, might be part of a strong pro-union shop. Line workers are often privy to ongoing labor–management negotiations and disputes. Those experiences may empower a line worker who works in a union shop to confront management on myriad issues, including lactation accommodation.

EMPLOYEES, MANAGEMENT, AND POWER

The workplace exerts power over the worker's body, controlling it and constraining it. Institutions like the workplace affect how individuals experience their own bodies (Foucault 1980). Employers' control over employees' bodies – when they come to work, where they work, and what they do – all seem "natural and normal" within capitalist societies (Albiston 2005; Fraser and Jaeggi 2018). Workplaces have established norms about how workers present their bodies, how the placement of their bodies demonstrates job commitment, and how control of their bodies is seen as proof of being a good worker (Williams 2000). These all involve the worker submitting to the employer's control over time and physical placement. Yet, the Lactation at Work Law challenges these norms by reassigning to the employee some degree of control over her time and physical placement. By requiring employers to accommodate workplace expression of breast milk, the law shifts some small amount of power to the employee.

Human resource personnel's decisions can significantly affect how well laws, like the Lactation at Work Law, are translated into organizational policy. For example, a lack of understanding of the time and place-proximity needs of lactation workers can result in accommodations that are purely symbolic. In many situations, the supervising managers are the ones who are positioned to ensure effectiveness of the organization's accommodations – or to undercut potentially useful lactation provisions. Supervising managers enforce rules about where an employee must be physically located to do her job, and they are the ones who monitor the length of breaks. They can adhere to organizational norms in ways that render pro-lactation policies ineffective. Conversely, supervising managers are able to allow an employee to stretch her break if sufficient time is a hurdle to pumping; they can locate or even commandeer unused or underused spaces where the employee might pump, even in situations where ineffective organizational policies exist.

In contrast to the data discussed in the following chapters, where the data show more substantive and effective accommodations, the organizations discussed in this chapter often failed to meet employee needs. In a few organizations, management actively resisted compliance. More often, organizational changes were legally compliant but were merely symbolic, creating little change in employees' lived experiences. These cases demonstrate that mere legal compliance with a workers' rights law may not actually enhance workers' rights. While the law might on its face seem to further specific goals, these employees' lived experiences differed from the improved workplaces envisioned by the law's creators.

A MORE NEGATIVE PICTURE

This chapter reflects some of the most frustrating and negative experiences with workplace lactation among the women I interviewed, and it is the least optimistic. Yet, the picture it offers might actually be more positive than the reality for women attempting to breastfeed and pump while holding jobs. Some women's stories were not included in this book, despite my significant efforts to recruit them: women who never attempted to breastfeed because they doubted they would be able to sufficiently express milk at work; women who breastfed, but never tried to pump milk at work; women who never returned to work, because they thought combining nursing and employment would be too difficult or for another reason. Also absent are the voices of women who became so frustrated in their under-supported efforts to express milk at work that they declined invitations to be interviewed, whether invited by flier, word-of-mouth, or personal appeal. Women like #W141, who attempted to express milk at work and then left their jobs, are included in this study, but their number is very small – likely much smaller than actually occurs.

This means that the workplaces that were the most resistant to making accommodations and those that might even flaunt disobedience of the Lactation at Work Law are not captured by this study. For working women who continue breastfeeding, the frustrations explored in this chapter might only present a sliver of the struggles such lactating workers face. Yet, in contrast to these women's frustrations, the subsequent chapters examine full, adequate compliance with the Lactation at Work Law.

CHAPTER FOUR

MILK AND MANAGEMENT

Substantive Compliance through Managerialization

It doesn't just help the moms; it helps the organization. The women come back to work. We aren't hiring a new person, training a new person, each time. It's a win-win.
—Brian, human resource specialist from a large factory

The accommodations that organizations made for lactating employees generally followed the specific requirements of the law: They provide a place that is not a restroom and allow the employee to use break time to express milk. In some instances, the new policies and structures were mostly symbolic, producing little real change, as discussed in the preceding chapter. In other organizations, new organizational policies created substantive changes that directly improved the situations for the lactating employees; this chapter and the next discuss these cases. At still other organizations, the application of these policies evolved, with accommodations improving over time as the supervising managers' connection to the issue evolved, as I will discuss in Chapter 6.

The situations examined in Chapter 3 involve what many law and society scholars might expect to find – a gap between the law as its writers intended and the reality of how individuals experience those legally mandated changes. Many past studies have found that organizations tend to shift the law from its original objectives, such as equality, to serve managerial goals, such as improving morale. When it comes to accommodating the needs of breastfeeding women, managers filter the Lactation at Work Law through contrary organizational needs and norms and translate it into day-to-day practices. As a result, their success in implementing the law's accommodations is only partially successful.

This workplace reality reflects a challenge faced by human resource personnel, who must convince both upper-level management and supervising managers that complying with the new law is in their organization's interest, despite various costs and inconveniences. As Chapter 3 demonstrates, human resource personnel are often unable to achieve compliance simply by invoking the law; their efforts to comply run up against the assumptions that the organization's existing practices are impossible to change and cannot be compromised. Human resource personnel address this challenge by translating legal compliance into a managerial frame.

This process of managerialization is a common finding in research on civil rights and accommodations in the workplace. My findings differ from others when it comes to the consequences of this process. Most studies find that the translation of legal imperatives into conventional managerial goals generates only symbolic compliance.

By contrast, I found real improvement in targeted employees' workplace experiences. This chapter describes how managerialism created successful accommodations in those businesses where the Lactation at Work Law gained sufficient legitimacy throughout the organization – from upper-level management, human resource personnel, supervising managers, and lactating employees. In addition to benefiting from legitimacy, businesses that made effective changes tended to have preexisting culture and structure that were conducive to change, such as a culture of flexibility in scheduling or a physical structure of individual offices.

For managerialization to result in actual, substantive accommodations, the lactating employee needed the benefit of three organizational components: sufficiently flexible time, adequately accessible private space, and legitimacy of the act of expressing milk at work. In some organizations, all three necessary parts were present initially. In other organizations, however, organizational actors had to convince others of the legitimacy of workplace milk expression, create accessible places, and adjust time expectations during the workday.

Much of the work of establishing the legitimacy of workplace milk expression was accomplished by human resource specialists – somewhat through coercion, but primarily through their managerialization of the law. By reframing lactation accommodations as being in line with other managerial goals, supporting lactating workers became understood as a legitimate concern for the organization.

In contrast, adjusting the preexisting organizational culture and structure to adequately accommodate lactating employees' needs was accomplished by a wider array of organizational actors, but most often by the lactating employees themselves. With sufficient time, space, and legitimacy – even though legal compliance was managerialized, stripped of the law's original goals and transformed into a managerial agenda – they were still able to secure adequate lactation accommodations.

Thus, at least in certain circumstances and with specific laws, the transformation of legal goals into managerial concerns resulted in the creation of effective accommodations. This provides hope that managerialization need not be exclusively viewed cynically; sometimes it can result in effective substantive compliance.

SUPPORTIVE PREEXISTING CULTURE AND STRUCTURE: TIME, SPACE, AND LEGITIMACY

Managerialization most consistently resulted in more substantive, and less symbolic, compliance when the lactation accommodations complemented the culture or structure of that particular organization. When lactating employees had accessible private places and scheduling flexibility that allowed them time to pump, and the workplace culture valued the activity enough to enable them to use these resources of time and space, the lactation accommodations were successful. In those instances when employees had control over their own space and time – such as private offices and keeping their own schedule – legitimacy was less critical. A human resource officer for a government agency explained that most employees had their own offices with locking doors, so creating lactation rooms was rarely necessary:

> Most of us have offices, our own [private] offices, because of the work we do. If a woman is breastfeeding and she needs to pump, she just closes her door and does it. Other places might need to make separate rooms for their employees, but that's [not an issue] here because we have our own – albeit tiny! – offices.
>
> [095]

A similar situation was described in the interview, below, with a human relations specialist at a private university – the same university as the lactating professor (W153) quoted later in this chapter.

> Our faculty all have their own offices. It's not a problem for them. And our graduate students often have a [private] office or they share with

> only one or two others who might not be [on campus] that often. So, really, [in terms of employees (not students)] it's only an issue for our clerical workers and our office workers.
>
> [120]

Because human resource personnel saw most workers as enjoying significant autonomy and privacy, they were less concerned with widespread need for lactation accommodations.

Similarly, in some organizations, or departments within organizations, work time was quite fluid. Employees of any rank or seniority could excuse themselves to care for whatever personal needs they might have. A supervising manager in a manufacturing research-and-development department described this type of situation.

> Okay, we don't have a designated break time. People can take breaks whenever they feel they need to, so . . . people just let each other know [when they'll be gone and how long] . . . [Securing accommodations] is not so hard here. [It's] not such a big deal.
>
> [043]

Another research-and-development organization's human resource specialist, this one working in the pharmaceutical industry, characterized her organization as particularly helpful.

> We have a very flexible environment, so anything employees work [out] with their management, then they don't have to get approval. They really probably just schedule the room, and then go use the room, and then come back to their work . . . I don't think there is a philosophy behind the practice. We [simply] have a very flexible environment, work environment. And, whether you're a nursing mom, or you need to go work out, or take care of other business, you just manage your job, when and how it makes sense, given our flexible work environment and so you and your manager, I mean you're really accountable for the work that you do, and around here, you just communicate where you'll be, how you can be contacted, and when you're available, and where you are . . . It's very flexible. It's a very flexible environment.
>
> [017]

These cultures of time flexibility enabled lactating workers to leave their work spaces, express milk, and return without expending substantial effort to persuade supervising managers that allowing this flexibility was acceptable. Indeed, the human resource specialist just quoted (#017), had, elsewhere in the interview, characterized her workplace as "an ideal situation" for a lactating worker. Yet, as discussed by a lactating employee at this pharmaceutical factory, W291, elsewhere in this chapter, in practice, the situation was not without stress and hurdles for the worker.

Of course, employees with substantial control over their work space and schedules had little need for employer-provided accommodations. The lactating employee quoted next was a low-level manager.

> I have my own office with a door that closes. Although I have to be out [on the floor] a lot, I can come in and pump when I need to. [The supervising manager] knows what I'm doing and he's fine, I guess. I mean, I guess he knows. And I guess he's fine with it. And if he hadn't been fine, or if I couldn't have pumped milk at work for whatever reason, I probably wouldn't have come back. But everything worked out great.
>
> [078]

Her response demonstrates the importance of her having her own office: Not only was she not concerned with enlisting her manager's support for her milk pumping, but his support was so unnecessary that she wasn't even certain whether or not he knew she was pumping. Her statement about how she would have strongly considered leaving if she couldn't have been able to successfully pump milk at work, reinforces the human resource specialist's statement about the benefit of the law for the organizational goal of retaining workers and limiting turnover.

However, even in the most rigid organizations, in which nearly no one has private space or scheduling flexibility, those workers with more power were more likely to have private offices and control over their time. One interviewee was a senior architect at a medium-sized firm where most employees work in a large open space and even higher-ranking architects have open-and-accessible offices that give them little privacy.

> I have my own office. The door shuts and locks. Unlike some offices, my door doesn't have a window going into the hallway, so no one can see in. I have a little refrigerator that I brought in to store the milk – in fact, I store the whole thing [pump with apparatus attached] in there so I don't have to clean [the pump] in between pumpings. It would be different if I didn't have my own office, but I do.
>
> [W072]

This case highlights the impact of socioeconomic status on the need for lactation accommodations. Although a few high-ranking employees might require lactation accommodations – such as bank managers who lack a private office – most employees who are highly placed within their organizations' and society's hierarchies are unlikely to need lactation accommodations. The importance of class is much more about status than it is about salary – higher status workers often not only earn more money; they also enjoy an elevated status that makes negotiating accommodations and mobilizing legal rights easier.

CHANGING THE PREEXISTING CULTURE AND STRUCTURE: CREATING TIME, SPACE, AND LEGITIMACY

In some organizations, the preexisting organizational culture and structure was not sufficient for successful workplace milk expression. In those cases, organizational actors had to do additional relational work in order to establish the necessary facilities or time blocks, or to shift the existing cultural understanding or improve inadequate facilities. While human resource personnel and supervising managers were part of this process, much of this work was done by the lactating employees themselves.

Occasionally, human resource managers would compare expressing milk to other accommodations that were already seen as legitimate in the workplace.

> I did have, early on, a supervisor who called me just to say, "Well, what if they need more time than just their lunch hour and their break?" And I always remind them of the policy that says "Allow for work time flexibility for them to be able to do that." I said, "Now, just let me ask you this as a comparison question and that is, "Do you monitor how often your smokers go out and how long they stay out?" That will sometimes get their attention. Most of them say no. And I said, "Well, if you don't, then considering this is a healthy thing, whereas smoking is not a healthy thing, I'll ask that you be flexible."
>
> [035]

The political nature of the lactation accommodations is illustrated by how the concept of break time is sometimes seen as less legitimate for women-only activities (lactation) versus ones that likely include men workers (smoking). By challenging this manager's resistance to allowing flexible break times for lactating employees, she underscored an inequality in this exercise of management discretion.

A human resource specialist who had been put in charge of facilitating her organization's lactation accommodations described a confrontation she had with the head of the human resource office who worried that publicizing accommodation information would harm the organization's internal workings.

> They didn't want to list it in the [employee handbook]. Like, almost a don't-ask-don't-tell sorta thing, where we'd give it to the women but not, like, broadcast it exactly. I thought, that's crazy! We want our people to know! ... But, also, if *only* those nursing moms who come to us know, then someone else, maybe a woman who is going to go on [maternity] leave, or maybe that the manager of that woman who is going to go on [maternity] leave, [won't know about the lactation accommodations] and so the woman doesn't know and decides to not nurse because she's [not aware of the accommodations], but she could've! What [accommodations] we offer can affect what moms decide to do, so we want them, and their managers, to know about this stuff – even before they go on [maternity] leave. Even before they get pregnant. [132]

This human resource specialist's supervisor was afraid that spelling out the policy would lead to a flood of requests for lactation accommodations.

> [My supervisor] thought, if we got too many requests [for lactation accommodations], the supervisors would be upset – too many women leaving ... But I told her, doing this big will actually make our job easier. This is what we want ... Once we get the hang of this – set up the rooms, get supervisors on board, and so on – the more women the better. In fact, it's in our office's advantage to get more women to do it, because we're going to have to do it somewhat. We should offer it to everyone! And then it's all the easier as more [supervising managers and employees] get used to it.
> [132]

Her argument was successful, and her supervisor approved inclusion of full information about the lactation accommodations both in the information given to employees taking maternity leave and in the general employee handbook.

This logistical change in how the organization functioned was important because, as she had suggested, promotion of available lactation accommodations could have a synergistic effect: As more workers use these accommodations, more managers and co-workers will become aware of them; the more they are aware of them, the more lactating workers will make use of them. Greater publicity within the organization, she argued, can normalize workplace milk expression, making accommodations and requests for those accommodations easier.

The ultimate goal of the Lactation at Work Law, arguably, was to make lactation accommodations become an unremarkable part of the workplace. A human resource specialist in a small manufacturing company asserted that greater awareness of lactation accommodations would normalize and legitimate the issue within the organization's culture:

> In our management meetings and in our [internal management newsletters], I've highlighted the benefits of accommodating our breastfeeding members. I also do this in [all-employee] newsletters. I do this so our moms know about this, but also everyone knows about this. The more it's out there, the more people know this is something some women are doing, the less stigma it will have and the better people will be [about easily adopting lactation accommodations].
>
> [111]

The efforts by this human resource specialist – whose company employed about half men and half women – highlight the potential for education on lactation accommodations to affect corporate culture over time, so that lactating employees could discuss their lactation needs more easily with co-workers and supervising managers. That, in turn, could further normalize and legitimize lactation accommodations.

In some workplaces, lactating employees would work together to share information among themselves, although creating greater awareness of available resources was not consistently successful. For example, when this nurse moved to the postpartum unit between the births of her first and second children, she discovered her hospital provided additional lactation resources.

> Where I work now, we actually have a lactation room: a room set up with breast pumps and stuff. I just bring my own [sanitary attachments] and don't even need to bring a pump with me to work! I never knew this existed until I got here. With [my first child], I always had to find a place to pump. Finding it was never a big problem, and [my supervisor] was always helpful in finding a place, but it wasn't always the same place week after week, and I always had to go get my own pump and haul it with me. This is so much better now! . . . I've told [two women from my old unit, who returned from maternity leave, wanting to express milk] about this. They were thrilled, but they wouldn't have known [if I hadn't told them] . . . And then they knew other [lactating employees, and I made sure they] told them about these rooms!
>
> [W083]

Through greater dissemination of information about this resource these lactating employees were able to affect the culture of the organization.

Especially when management perceived lactation accommodations as being better than the lactating employees believed them to be, lactating employees needed to act affirmatively, alone or together, to improve the organizational culture, structure, or both. For example, a pharmaceutical factory human resource specialist, Interviewee #017, quoted elsewhere in this chapter, characterized that factory's work situation as ideal for lactating employees. Yet, employee Interviewee #W291, quoted shortly, noted that accommodations were not consistently available. She was quite successful in pumping at work because of the location of her work building and ability to implement a scheduling strategy, but she was concerned about the struggles of less fortunately placed lactating employees, so she shared her strategy with fellow lactating workers.

> Here we are in Cube Land so you can't do this at your desk . . . You do have to schedule in because depending on when it was or how many women in the area had kids, it could be very tight. I was incredible lucky when I was pumping because pretty much nobody in my building was also doing it . . . [But even then, I had to be careful and] keep count and schedule it ahead of time. I mean, it is competitive to get those rooms, but since you know that you are going to be pumping for an extended period of time well enough in advance [you must] try to get [in] around the same time every day. And so because there were three different room options, one room would be available every Tuesday morning and a different room would be available every Wednesday morning [and so on].
>
> [W291]

She knew lactating co-workers located elsewhere could not always access nearby lactation rooms and were left to scramble for unpopular times, schedule a room far from their work stations, or organize their own informal place to express milk.

Supportive co-workers could directly ameliorate insufficient accommodations, shifting the internal processes of their organizations. For example, this woman explains how she negotiated better physical space than what she actually needed herself in order to benefit other women in her unit.

> Meaning no disrespect to my current employer, the space provided was not good. They basically took what was a semi-empty office and said this is the space. I am fortunate enough to have my own office with fully tinted windows where I can simply leave the pump here in the room,

> shut the door, pump, and be done. There, in the space that they've designated, there's no sink. There weren't blinds. I had to fight to get blinds. One of the employees followed me [after] having her first child, and she doesn't have the same office set up that I do, and so she needed that space, so I had to fight to get some blinds and some other things. They designated a space without thinking it through. So we've helped them think it through [laughs].
>
> [W177]

Even non-lactating co-workers could transform the organization's culture and structure, and, thereby, improve lactation accommodations. For example, this educator at a nature conservatory explained that she was provided with a lactation room, but the culture of that workplace was that educators would often use their own break time to clean up after groups had left.

> The lactation room was in the basement. Not far, but not really convenient. The thing is, after groups go through, you have to clean up, and that can use up some or even all of your break time . . . I knew the law said I should get break time [to express milk]. She knew [that I was struggling with pumping milk] so she would just say, "Just go. Go. Go and I'll do your clean-up." And she'd make me go and basically clean up her room and my room at the times when I'd needed to pump.
>
> [W160]

Her co-worker adjusted the organization norm of each worker using her break time for her own clean up by taking on this part of the lactating employee's job.

LEGITIMACY AND COERCIVE MECHANISMS

Lactation accommodations gained legitimacy when human resource personnel presented them as mandatory. Accommodations could be mandated by legal threat but also by nonlegal pressures, such as the organization's fear of not being legitimate in its field if it did not satisfy the law.

Human Resource Personnel Using Coercive Mechanisms with Upper-Level Management

Particularly during the first wave of interviews, human resource personnel employed coercive mechanisms to impress upon their organizations' boards of directors and other upper-level management the importance and legitimacy of the changes mandated by the new law. Sometimes, their coercive mechanisms involved pressure from other organizations to embrace a certain law; other times they emphasized the organization's reputation in its field; and in other cases, they focused on formal adherence to the law's requirements.

Human resource officers could draw on managers' awareness of their mission to foster legitimacy for the law and the accommodations. For example, a human resource specialist at a car manufacturing plant explained lactating support in the following way:

> We are known as being family-friendly, as being a great place to work for all of the "extras" we provide – exercise room, discounted vacation [packages], yoga classes, leisure area. [The board] backed my [lactation accommodations] but they were hesitant regarding how much they wanted to publicize them. I said, "These [lactation accommodations] are in line with our reputation in the industry. This is part of our rep [utation]. Make it [broadly publicized] so everyone knows."
>
> [027]

Once this human resource officer overcame his factory's initial reluctance to promote its lactation accommodations, he was able to better affect the organization's internal workings and culture around lactation accommodations.

A human resource specialist from a manufacturing plant interviewed at Time One narrated how he approached his managing board and secured funding for two new wellness rooms:

> It's not that people don't want [to accommodate lactating employees], but it's hard to change how you do things. But now it's the law . . . This is a good law and we always support the law. And we support our employees. This law says that we have to support our employees in this way, and we will. This is what I told [my managing board]. They respond to that – to obeying the law.
>
> [081]

Invoking the law was not the only way that human resources personnel employed coercive mechanisms. Some organizations felt pressure to preserve their reputations within their field, as this human resource specialist at a large, urban law firm explained:

> [When broaching the topic with the committee of managing partners] I explained that we would look bad if we didn't adequately implement the law. I mean, we're a law firm. We know that this is now the law. But

> some of them wanted to wait and see if any of our [lactating] employees would really want [milk expression accommodations]. I felt he wanted to see if anyone said anything. Not complained, exactly, but see if anyone really needed us to do something . . . I said, "How can we do that? We're a law firm. How could we hold our heads up?"
>
> [174]

The threat of possible negative consequences – whether from the state or from pressure from peer organizations – nudged reluctant owners, board members, and top management toward effective legal compliance.

The human resource specialist just quoted (Interviewee #081) shifted his rhetoric to include managerial mechanisms, discussed shortly. The type of coercive mechanism that motivated him also changed over time: At Time One, he focused on the law's mandate. However, at Time Two, he emphasized field-level pressures and expectations:

> This law helps all of us; it's what everyone is doing now. [The lactation policies] help [the organization] by keeping morale up. And by helping new moms return back to work, it helps with turn-over and re-hiring. This has become expected. [Every organization] is making these changes, if they hadn't done so already.
>
> [081]

In this way, the legitimacy that legal compliance can bestow on an organization and its process and structures motivates the organization to comply with the industry norms and follow the new expectations that the law has created (Edelman and Suchman 1997).

Human Resource Personnel Using Coercive Mechanisms with Supervising Managers

The human resource specialists' job is not only to rally those in charge of their organizations to embrace new laws, but also to convince supervising managers of the legitimacy of the laws and the subsequent policies. Because many of the managerial benefits used to enlist the support of senior management are almost invisible to supervising managers (e.g., health insurance costs; temp-staffing salaries), human resource personnel have to present those benefits explicitly to supervising managers and frame them appropriately.

When the Lactation at Work Law was first passed, human resource specialists encouraged supervising managers to comply with the law by drawing on the legitimacy of the law's coercive power, just as they did with upper-level management. For example, a human resource specialist at a large university directly cited the law in order to convince those who allocated campus space to locate and provide lactation places:

> The law helped people like myself no matter where the worksite was, helped them have more of a legal backing when they were trying to help women pursue spaces, so I think the law helped in that respect … Before, before there was a law, it would basically be me having to plead the case for a woman as to why it would be important for this building deputy or whomever I was working with to help them find space. And now, I can say, "Well as an employer we have this rule that we have to follow, that we have to accommodate these women," and it seems to have a little more clout when it's they have to versus just doing it because they were willing to help me, which is how it kind of was in the past … Before, it was kind of me saying, "You know, I've had someone contact us, and it'd really help out if you could help me make accommodations for this woman," and pleading the case. [But now it's different because] a lot of people here at [this university] are black and white, and they wanna go by the book, so [citing the law] seems to resonate more.
>
> [004]

Earlier in the interview, when contrasting her current accommodation discussions to those that took place before the law was passed, she said, "We can't be pushing women into restrooms anymore." The new law gave her the legitimating language of rights to frame the accommodations as necessary, rather than having to rely on people's goodwill (see McCann 1994).

In this way, human resource specialists used the coercive power of a legal mandate to shift the discussion toward the legitimate need for lactation accommodations.

> Change is always hard. All [employee accommodations] can be hard to sell to [supervising managers]. Resources are limited. And people's capacity for awareness of other people's issues is limited. But this isn't just about moms breastfeeding their babies. I don't care what you think about breastfeeding, or whatever. Me, I don't care. But it's the law, and that's what I say [to supervising managers].
>
> [088]

By invoking the law, this human resource specialist framed the issue as being about legitimacy of the law, rather than breastfeeding. Citing the protection of the law not only made accommodation seem less optional; it also gave the issue of breastfeeding and lactation greater legitimacy.

Supervising Managers Using Coercive Mechanisms with Employees

Supervising managers engaged coercive mechanisms to enlist support – or at least acceptance – for lactation accommodations. For example, a restaurant manager invoked the coercive and legitimizing power of the law to communicate to employees that lactation accommodations were necessary.

> It's a hassle. Or it can be. Or, if not a hassle, it's one more thing to think about – scheduling around [when the lactating employee] has her pumping breaks. Sure, there's some grumbling sometimes [from co-workers]. But I told them, Look, it's the law. You might not like it, but we gotta do this.
>
> [130]

This supervising manager did not stipulate legal enforcement or penalty if they did not comply with the law. She didn't need to: The law designated lactation as a sufficiently legitimate activity to warrant accommodations.

Similarly, a supervising manager at a transportation company used the law's presence to communicate the legitimacy for what otherwise might be perceived as a private, personal issue:

> The guys didn't like to hear about it. Some of the women, too. They think it's a private thing, and, yeah, it is ... But the law says that [lactating employees] can do this private thing at work. So, that's that ... It might be a joke to some of the guys, but it's a real issue, real important to [my lactating employee]. And the law is there. So, it's gotta be important to us. Or at least we gotta treat it that way.
>
> [093]

For many employees – and possibly supervising managers themselves – legal enforcement was an abstract issue because of their role in their organizations. The force of law came less from the fear of legal consequences and more from its power to signal legitimacy and worthiness.

Employees Using Coercive Mechanisms with Management and Co-workers

Although other coercive mechanisms, such as pressure by organizations, had little resonance among employees, referencing the formal law remained a powerful way for workers to counter organizational reluctance to provide needed lactation accommodations, as the following quote from an office receptionist illustrates.

> Before I went on maternity leave, I talked to [my supervising manager]. I told him when I planned to come back and also that I planned to pump. And he said he wasn't sure they could let me do that. He said he wasn't sure they'd have any space for me to do that. I wasn't mean about it or anything, but I sort of shrugged and said, "Well, it is the law. There's a law that says you gotta." And he sort of went, "humph." And then when I came back [from maternity leave], I just went to [the human relations specialist] who found me a room ... I didn't talk to him about it again, but that was fine; I didn't really need to. Everything was fine then.
>
> [W025]

Although her reference to the law was unassertive and almost casual, by mentioning the law she informed her supervising manager that this was a legitimate, government-backed request that he was obligated to honor.

Other times, employees engaged coercive mechanisms to convey legitimacy to co-workers. The following data analysist grew frustrated after a co-worker did not respect the agreed-upon schedule:

> He would always "forget" when I was scheduled to pump. I mean, it's on our [shared electronic schedule]. He knew. And, at first, I'd be like, "Ah, would you mind? Ah, please could you?" And then I was like, f**k it. I was tired of his s**t. And I said, "Look. This is my right. This is the law. You better stop this." And he's like, "There's a law?" Like he didn't know. I don't know, maybe he didn't. But I'm like, "Yeah, it's the law." And he was better [about scheduling] after that. Nicer, even? I don't know? Maybe? I think he really thought this was just some dumb idea I had that I just pulled [out of thin air].
>
> [W067]

In this situation, the lactating worker invoked her legal rights to silence her obstreperous co-worker; by doing so she communicated the legitimacy of expressing breast milk at work.

When lactating employees lacked necessary support from management or co-workers, they could reference the law to elicit support and demonstrate the legitimacy of their requests. Sometimes such problems arose when management assumed that no accommodation assistance from the organization was needed, or that the assistance was trivial and insignificant. While lactation needs could be misunderstood, the coercive power of the law was readily understood and was useful for employees to assert the legitimacy of their needs.

This is demonstrated by contrasting interviews from the same university: #120 and W153. Interviewee #120 was a private university human resource specialist who was quoted earlier in this chapter about professors, saying "It's not a problem for them." Interviewee #W153, a lactating worker at the same university, an assistant professor with her own office and substantial control over her time, still struggled with sufficient accommodation regarding the sanctity of her pumping breaks:

> My office is my own, and my time, except when I'm teaching, is my own. The only thing was getting people to not schedule committee work over my pumping time. We use [an online scheduling software] so the administrative people knew, but my colleagues were the worst. They understood when I was teaching and they'd schedule some meeting right after that, and I kept saying that *that* is when I have to pump. It wasn't so bad, but I felt like I had to tell a couple people in particular very often. [A male colleague] really gave me a hard time about it sometimes. Finally, I told him, "Look, this is the law that my employer – that's you! – has to accommodate this. I'm sorry this is a *bit* inconvenient, but this is what I need and you need to work around it."
>
> [W153]

Although this professor had her private space (her own office) and sufficient time (a very flexible schedule), her lactation needs lacked sufficient legitimacy from some people, which led them to schedule committee meetings during her pumping times. Even though the woman had some organizational power, she was an untenured professor and lacked the job security that her senior colleagues enjoyed. As such, she still needed the law to legitimate her lactation needs.

LEGITIMACY AND MANAGERIALISM

Coercive mechanisms can only achieve limited progress. After the Lactation at Work Law was in force for a longer period of time, human resource personnel translated the law and its coercive power into managerial goals. In this way, the human resource personnel presented the legally mandated accommodations as legitimate and worthy of implementing – not through coercion, but because doing so was advantageous for the organization.

Managerializing among Upper-Level Management

Human resource specialists communicated the legitimacy of lactation accommodation to upper-level management by linking it to something that was already valued: managerial goals.

> Everything costs something. I had to explain [to senior management] how the costs were worth it, not just because of the [Lactation at Work Law] but because it helps us. [Senior management] thinks about ... turnover, and hiring, and sick days, and [insurance/medical] costs. Well, guess what? These [lactation] accommodations help all of that. This helps us. And I got authorization to [create a series of lactation rooms]. [111]

Similarly, the human resource specialist at a paper production factory, quoted next, explained that he translated compliance with lactation accommodations into financial benefits to the organization.

> I tell them it will help the employees, which will reduce turnover and our costs for hiring more people to replace the moms who don't come back, for example ... They understand reducing costs. Then they were on board, and I went forward [to create the new accommodations]. [134]

In this frame, the costs of lactation accommodations is offset by the direct, financial benefits. This managerial frame made compliance into something management should want to do because complying with the law would further management's goals.

Managerialization among Supervising Managers

Just as higher-level management responded to human resource specialists explaining compliance and lactation accommodations in terms of benefit to the organizations, so, were supervising managers similarly responsive. Quoted previously discussing how he framed compliance for upper management, here this human resource specialist explains how he used similar framing to convince supervising managers.

> No one likes to be told they got to do things differently now. To do something different. These [lactation accommodations] are no different. So you have to tell them. But tell them so they understand that it will help [the organization] and help them by not having to, say, have to train new employees when [would-be lactating employees never return from maternity leave]. And when they do return, they will have better morale. Be better employees. They get that ... Then they're more okay

> with being a bit more flexible with time, or finding the woman a place [for milk expression].
>
> [134]

Although members of upper management might be familiar with concerns about turnover and the costs of hiring new employees, supervising managers are less in touch with those issues, until the human resource personnel present the issue in terms of direct employee supervision, as this human resource specialist at a media company noted:

> You just have to explain it. Break it down so [supervising managers] see how they'll benefit. Because they don't always see the cost. They see that employee is . . . gone from her [cubicle] longer than expected or more often or what have you. They see [the hassle] to them as managers. So you have to explain it: Would you rather have to train a whole new employee? And then another? Or just be short some employees altogether?
>
> [135]

This quote from Time Two demonstrates the way one manager reframed compliance with the law into the goal of reducing turnover. This contrasts with his first interview where he focused on the coercive force of the law, saying, "It's the law now, so of course we follow it." [135]

Supervising managers also embraced these managerial goals, drawing on them to legitimize their responses to the law and lactation policies during their interviews. The supervising manager, quoted next, is from the same manufacturing organization as the human resource specialist #081, quoted previously. By Time Two, just as his human resource specialist did, he articulated the ways lactation accommodations served classic managerial benefits:

> [In the past three years] I've had three employees who were breastfeeding. We have a room for the moms who want to pump breast milk. It helps them and it's not a problem. It helps them come back and still have that connection to their babies. So it helps with moral, with turnover, so the moms can come back to work. That's good so we don't have to hire and train someone else.
>
> [083]

Elsewhere in the interview, this manager explained how the necessary accommodations were easy for him to implement, because the room the lactating workers used was within the area where they all worked.

Accessing it demanded little travel time and easy, informal coordination among those workers who needed the space. In addition, one of his lactating employees (Interviewee #078), quoted in this chapter, had a private office. Because his organization could easily satisfy these women's needs for private space, the only remaining concern was granting sufficient legitimacy to warrant the company providing adequate flexibility in granting break times for successful milk expression.

Another supervising manager, a news director at a local television station, specifically referenced management's goal of reducing employee turnover and absenteeism, saying that lactation accommodations helped with retention and attendance:

> We want our good people to stay in the news business. I think too many good newswomen have to quit the job because they just can't do both. They can't be a journalist and a mother, they think. This is a practical matter, that these new mothers don't have sickly babies. The baby will be healthier if they continue nursing, if the mother continues nursing. It's a fact. The mothers that don't nurse, that's a fact, that babies aren't as healthy. So that's a practical matter. I don't need my employees having to take sick days because they have a sick child. If they have to, they have to, but hopefully this would help eliminate or cut back on some of that.
>
> [011]

She framed legal compliance as helping not just her lactating employees, but also her business's operating goals. The company installed a lactation room with accoutrements that helped both her employees and her business, such as a computer, so that the women could express milk while using the Internet to research their projects.

In contrast to the cases explored in Chapter 6, this supervising manager references child health, but not for its own sake. She mentions that breastfed babies are healthier because parents of healthier kids take fewer sick days. In her view, the children's health is "a practical matter."

Similarly, this human resource specialist at a large law firm focuses on the goal of retaining workers:

> I do a lot of work with regards to retention of attorneys. We make a huge investment in attorneys when we hire them here, especially if they come through our summer program, and that return on investment, when you hire an attorney, starts to bear fruit two, three, four years, you know, into their work here. Because it's a huge learning curve . . . So, you know, we

> view it as a really key retention issue ... It was an initial outlay of resources but it has already paid dividends in less than a year.
>
> [034]

This "huge investment" was paid back, not only in terms of retention of experienced employees, but also because they could offer that experience to the firm's clients.

Lactating employees, as well, invoke managerial goals, especially reduced turnover and absenteeism, to gain legitimacy for their needed accommodations.

> We were planning who would be in charge of [an upcoming conference]. I reminded [my boss and co-workers] that I'd still need to break to pump ... my boss says something like, "This is an important time for [the company]. We all have to pull together." Or something. Like, I'm not being a good team member if I need to pump at [the conference]?! So I say – and I thought this was really good – I tell him that it's hard for nursing moms to be away from their babies for several days and I realize that I'll need to do *more* pumping, not less, at [the conference], so maybe it would be easier if I stayed back. I apologized, but also reminded him, that, you know, this was harder for me and all that ... He mellowed out after that.
>
> [W012]

Framing her need to pump as an organizational choice helped her communicate to her supervisors that pumping actually furthered her employer's goals, helping to establish its legitimacy.

Other workers were able to draw on management's concerns about staff turnover. A grade school teacher in a growing school district reminded her principal that she had remained in the workplace while other mother-employees had left the school.

> I told him, "Remember [a former employee]? She took maternity leave and never came back. That could have been me, but here I am. But that can change ... I could leave tomorrow. I could take [time out of the work force]." I basically told him that if [pumping milk at work] became too hard, I might leave ... And he didn't like that.
>
> [W154]

Because staffing was a struggle for this principal – and a common organizational concern generally – he responded to the teacher's threat to leave by implementing the lactation accommodation she needed: a floating teacher's aide to cover for her when she needed her afternoon milk-expression break.

MANAGERIAL GOALS PRESERVING CORE OPERATIONS

Managerialization transforms legal ideals, such as greater equality, into managerial goals, such as reduced turnover, to preserve the core operations of organizations. Aligning compliance with the law with the mission of the organization furthers this objective. At times, interviewees in this study articulated a synergy between the goals of the Lactation at Work Law and employees' understanding of the organization's core operations

An overlap between the law and an organization's mission is illustrated by the following quote from a human resource administrator at a large, urban hospital:

> How good a [health and wellness center] would we be if we didn't support our employees staying healthy. Breastfeeding helps them, and it also helps their babies stay healthy. We're in the business of health. If I told my nurses, "Too bad, you can't breastfeed 'cause you can't pump, so you better switch to formula, we'd be being a complete hypocrite." [Interviewer: Does someone's pumping ever get in the way of patient care?] Well, sure, but not really. No more than if you have to return a phone call, or take a bathroom break. We adjust and cover for each other as need be.
>
> [161]

Because the need to express breast milk was framed as legitimate, even though it could be disruptive, those disruptions were understood as congruent with the organization's core mission of promoting health and, by extension, lactation.

Like the human resource personnel in this study, the supervising managers communicated the legitimacy of lactation accommodations by linking them to the organization's mission. For example, a supervising manager at a public hospital focused on the hospital's commitment to health when she argued for successful lactation accommodations.

> We know lactation. Our birthing wing is highly regarded. We take excellent care of our postpartum patients and have earned certification as [a pro-breastfeeding hospital]. Supporting breastfeeding is part of who we are, so of course we do this for our employees, too.
>
> [073]

Another supervising nurse at a larger hospital explained that the hospital's identity was one of promoting the health of its community, so lactation support was already part of its mission, informally. Once the Lactation at Work Law was passed, those informal lactation accommodations were formalized and publicized so that more people were aware of them.

> We did not have a policy before [the law was passed] just a standard practice. Now we [formalized] it a little bit . . . What we are is a hospital. We are about health and helping people, so we were already [supporting lactation]. But now we have handouts and [include it in maternity leave and other employee] information so everyone knows we do this. But we've always done it . . . How could we not [support our lactating employees]? . . . We can't take care of patients if we don't take care of our employees.
>
> [018]

Formalizing and promoting the accommodations that were already in place was another subtle yet substantial effect of the new law. Organizations that promoted information about lactation facilities helped lactating workers overcome what could have been a significant hurdle. Some organizations, such as large hospitals, already had excellent lactation facilities available, but many lactating workers (and their supervising managers) were unaware of these resources, such as Interviewee W083, quoted toward the end of this chapter.

MANAGERIALIZATION BY LACTATING EMPLOYEES

Lactating employees, too, would connect lactation support to their workplaces' core operations. By emphasizing the overlap of mission and workplace lactation, these lactating employees made compelling arguments for their needed accommodations. This alignment of missions echoed rationales expressed by human resource personnel and supervising managers, except that now these comparisons were being made in order to challenge management.

This is illustrated by comparing the statement of Interviewees #161 and W143. The hospital human resource specialist quoted earlier explained the importance of the lactation accommodations by referencing the organization's mission: health and wellness. This same rhetoric was used by one of that hospital's nurses to secure a more accessible lactation room:

> We do have an ethic of covering for each other if you need to step off the floor. But, I mean, we're often just barely [sufficiently] staffed, if that, so if I have to go far to [reach the designated lactation room], I'll be gone

> for too long. This is a hospital, so in many ways it's great – we have, literally, hospital-grade pumps to use and all that. But if it takes too long to go that far, I can't take that long of a break. I told my [supervising manager] that I couldn't make it [to the lactation room] and back in time. It was hurting my health, my stress, and I was worried about it affecting our care on the floor. She talked to [a building manager] and got me a place at the end of our floor.
>
> [W143]

By invoking her organization's mission of care, her request for a more convenient location to pump had greater legitimacy and was granted swift attention.

SUMMARY

In understanding how the process of managerialization led to effective accommodations for lactating women working in the organizations discussed in this chapter, three important concepts emerge: flexible scheduling, private space, and the legitimacy of workplace milk expression and its accommodations. Some organizations already provided private space and flexible breaks, and in those organizations the specific legitimacy of workplace pumping was a relative nonissue because it was subsumed in the broader issue of workers having control over their break time. Other organizations lacked some or all these elements for some or all of their members, but key people worked to establish, create, or improve them sufficiently.

Necessary changes to spaces and break schedules were predicated on lactation accommodations having adequate legitimacy. When legitimacy was lacking, organizational actors worked to heighten the legitimacy of expressing milk and its accommodations. They used various means: comparison to established, legitimate personal activities, such as smoking; communication, including human resource specialists disseminating information about the accommodations and workers sharing information among themselves; and coercion, especially calling upon the coercive power of the law, but also using the coercive power of the organization's reputation and the force of field norms. Workplace lactation also gained legitimacy through the process of managerialization itself. For those who worked to strengthen the legitimacy of workplace milk pumping and its accommodations, managerialization became a tool for furthering that legitimacy. This particular use of managerialization implies the existence of a different cultural tool kit from the one described in the previous chapter (Swidler 1986).

Although past civil rights research predicts managerialization of the law, this chapter's surprising findings directly challenge the extant literature by demonstrating that managerialization actually resulted in effective compliance with the Lactation at Work Law in many cases. The data of the previous chapter – and, indeed, most law and society studies – demonstrate a substantial gap between the formal law and the lesser protection experienced by individuals in practice. In contrast to other studies that have found that translating legal mandates into managerial goals resulted in compliance that was only symbolic, the organizations discussed in this chapter managerialized the law; yet they also produced effective, substantive changes.

These findings suggest that the scholars should resist automatically dismissing the process of managerialization as a means for successful workplace reforms; this chapter demonstrates that under specific conditions personnel can call upon the process to create substantive accommodations.

The goals of the Lactation at Work Law were advanced because the accommodations the law mandates are sufficiently concrete such that people can easily assess and discuss them. This contrasts with many civil rights laws that convey vague mandates, such as "equal opportunity." Even if people disagree about whether accommodations are adequate, the parameters of the discussion are clear. For example, people can debate whether a lactation room is easily accessible or not, but the fact that its accessibility hinges on how far the lactating employee must travel – and how difficult it is for her to consistently gain entry – would not be controversial.

The most consistent success for lactating workers gaining accommodations occurred where an organization's preexisting culture and structure supported the substance of the legal mandates. Organizations with a permissive culture around schedules were more likely to be sufficiently flexible about lactating employees' breaks to express milk. Similarly, organizations whose physical structures allocated individual offices to most employees were less likely to have employees who needed separate spaces to express milk.

In addition to cultural and structural resources, workplace milk expression needed to be seen as a legitimate endeavor, accepted as part of the organizational culture. The new law codified and protected this legitimacy. Actors throughout the organization needed to recognize this legitimacy – from upper-level management to lactating employees and their co-workers. In workplaces where breastfeeding and pumping lacked legitimacy, even those lactation accommodations with ample time and accessible space were not successful.

The reframing of the justice focus of the law into managerial goals occurred in several steps, and, in this instance, furthered the success of the Lactation at Work Law in creating effective accommodations. Once the law was passed, human resource personnel attended conferences to learn about the law. They returned to their organizations and persuaded upper management to dedicate sufficient resources to comply with the law. Then they developed a rhetoric to convince their supervising managers that they should support these new lactation-at-work policies. This was important because even though the law provides leverage for human resource personnel, it is not enough to compel full compliance, as is evidenced by the resistant managers of Chapter 3. Finally, the human resource personnel translate compliance into managerial frames and communicate those ideas to managers, who pass them on to their employees. When all these elements line up, lactating employees benefit. But the managerial frame alone is not always sufficient to create a true lactation-friendly workplace.

CHAPTER FIVE

ALLIES ALREADY

Supportive Human Resource Specialists and Supervising Managers

When I had my first child at [another company], sometimes I'd pump [my breast milk] in the ladies' room. Once in a while, I pumped in my car. There just wasn't any place to pump ... This [second] baby I had after the law changed. [The workplace] gave me my own key to a small room on the same floor as where I was working. [HR staff person on lactation issues, Gary] was so great. He really went out of his way to help. He found the room, he got me my own key, he would check in with me, like "Do you need anything more in [the lactation room]?" I was very supported.

Alysha, order processor for a large manufacturing company

This was something I had tried to get going ... I actually submitted a proposal about this to [upper management] as part of another report ... Basically, they said I could do it, but didn't authorize me to take over any space, or any additional funds to do it ... Then after the law, I pulled that part of the report, made it its own thing. And this time, I could say, "Look! This is the law! We've got to do this. We either just barely do it, or do it well." And I convinced them to do it well, to give me more money to buy some things, to demand some rooms ... We help our employees to stop bad behavior – stop smoking, lose weight – but here we're helping our employees, that is, our mom employees, to actually do *a healthy behavior.*

Gary, Alysha's supportive HR staffer and father of two breastfed children

PUMPING RIGHTS AND MANAGERIAL "LACTIVISM"

How did the Lactation at Work Law affect people who were already predisposed to support it? In organizations throughout this study, some individual supervising managers and human resource supervisors supported the goals of the new Lactation at Work Law before it was even passed. These "Allies Already" advocated for accommodation of lactating employees' needs, often surpassing what the law mandated. They valued their employees' efforts to breastfeed and understood the hurdles lactating women faced when expressing milk at work.

The law enabled them to challenge their embeddedness within their organizations, balancing it with their strong pro-lactation values. The Lactation at Work Law facilitated a focus on these values, providing a context for human resource personnel and supervising managers to move beyond their organizations' established norms and become what DiMaggio would call "institutional entrepreneurs" for lactation accommodations, actors who advocate for organizational change when they have sufficient resources and recognize an "opportunity to realize interests that they value highly" (1988: 14). These Allies Already of lactating workers championed full and swift compliance, sometimes even surpassing the accommodations mandated by the law.

Their use of the law as leverage to compel swift compliance, often compliance beyond what the law stipulated, stands a stark contrast to members of management discussed in earlier chapters, who complied only by producing those accommodations that the law specified or changes that were easy for their organizations to implement due to preexisting cultural or physical structures.

The allies of the lactating employees in this chapter were different. Because they were knowledgeable about, and committed to, the issue of breastfeeding, they were able to overcome the norms and structures of their organizations to spark real change (DiMaggio 1988). These institutional entrepreneurs advocated for swift compliance with the law, often speedily implementing full compliance in their organizations.

Because of their ready advocacy, these Allies Already were able to step up even before the lactating employee needed to come forward. By mobilizing to have accommodation plans and policies in place right after the law was passed, these allies created workplaces with available lactation accommodations. This meant that employees who wished to express milk at work could benefit from their organization's compliance with the law without having to assert their right and demand change from their organizations – their allies had already done this for them.

Empathy and the Proximity to Pumping Milk

Some managers and human resource specialists who were lactation Allies Already had expressed milk at work themselves. Having done so, they were aware of some of the difficulties of pumping at work. Thus, their relationship to the issue of expressing milk at work extended past sympathy and compassion with employees' struggles to include genuine empathy and greater comprehension of the issue (Madeira 2006).

Their personal decision to pump also demonstrates their ideological commitment to breastfeeding. For example, this human resource specialist had expressed milk at work more than a decade ago (prior to any Lactation at Work Law), demonstrating her commitment to the issue, as well as her firsthand knowledge:

> I had trouble finding spaces that worked in order to do the pump. I didn't have an office at the time. I was in a cubicle. So I tried to use other people's offices, and [management] didn't like that. So ultimately what I ended up doing is that I went into a closet, which housed our records. It was not a lot of room. I had to put a little sticky [note] on the door to tell people not to enter, and I sat down on a little foot stool and plugged into an outlet that was in there. [Interviewer: Doesn't sound very comfortable.] No, it wasn't ... Going through it myself, I understand what a necessity it is. You know, to be able to support that [milk expression and breastfeeding], too, and the bonding between a mother and a child. And just supporting the fact [of] being working women, they need this ... They need this in order to be successful in their jobs as well as their personal lives.
>
> [023]

Her own experiences with breastfeeding and pumping contributed to her understanding of the difficulty of milk expression at work. By considering employees' personal lives, in addition to their time at work, this human resource specialist was thinking beyond the norms of managerialism to consider other, nonorganizational values.

The news director at a local television station, quoted next, had pumped milk for her own children, and tried to support her employees who also wished to express milk at work.

> There was an empty office upstairs in the sales area, and it first started out as a place where people who weren't feeling well could lie down ...

> We call it The Quiet Room . . . When one of our employees came [back from maternity leave] . . . I let her have the key [to the Quiet Room] for about two months, three months, while she went up there twice a day. The other thing I did, it didn't have a working computer in the Quiet Room. I got one set up so she could even sit at the computer and still read the wires or you know, chip away at her show – she was a producer – while pumping. So that she wasn't just not doing anything, but she could actually still keep up with what was going on. So I got that computer installed up there.
>
> [011]

This supervising manager was proud of her own efforts on behalf of her lactating employees. Yet, simply setting up the space was not the extent of the advocacy work she needed to do. She also had to engage in politics within her office to protect the lactating employee's pumping breaks:

> Sometimes, [someone] would be looking for her and she'd be on a pumping break. Just happens that way sometimes. They'd be like, "She's gone again!" Especially this [one employee]. I'd say, "Yes, she's stepped away to do something important: She's taking care of her baby while still being at work." She's still working. And she's still caring for her baby. I'd hear that stuff and I would try not to let it pass [without challenging it].
>
> (011]

As a mom who had pumped breast milk, this supervising manager shared the status of lactating worker and was empathetic about the need for a convenient place to pump. As a newsperson, she also understood the importance of not wasting time or being away from the wire services for too long. She initiated changes that addressed both sets of needs. By doing so, she went beyond the norms of managerialization and challenged the prevailing organizational culture by asserting the importance of other, potentially competing values.

Most other Allies Already had not been nursing mothers themselves. Instead, they had been educated about lactation and milk expression and sensitized to the value of breastfeeding because their wives, daughters, daughters-in-law, other relatives, or close friends had breastfed. These secondhand experiences had given them greater knowledge, heightened awareness, and empathy for employees struggling to successfully express milk at work. For example, a hotel manager whose wife had nursed was both cognizant of the value of breastfeeding and aware of the challenges of expressing milk at work because of his wife's unsuccessful attempt to do so.

> [Shortly before the Lactation at Work Law was passed, my wife and I had] just had our first son and she had gone back to work and they were going to allow her to take breaks to pump breast milk and she was able to do that. But after a couple weeks, it seemed like it became bothersome, like people were getting upset about it and it was some kind of burden and they didn't want to cover for her while she was on her break to do this, so ... she just, rather than deal with all that, she just stopped doing it. And we started bottle feeding our son.
>
> [015]

The effect of his secondhand experience illustrates how managers' personal experiences increased their empathy regarding the issue of lactation at work while also helping them question the assumption (demonstrated in Chapter 3) that managerial norms should take precedence over all else.

Other human resource personnel and supervising managers also explained that they had become early allies of lactating employees because they had witnessed family members or friends struggle with trying to combine working and breastfeeding. For example, a middle school principal's experience-driven belief in the value of breastfeeding led him to offer practical solutions, such as floating staff – teacher assistants who, rather than assigned to a single classroom, rotate among many rooms – to help cover breaks. He even allowed lactating employees to use his office to pump when other rooms were in use.

> My wife nursed our children, which are now ages 2, 4, and 6 years old. I do encourage [those I supervise] to nurse. We provide a place. As a matter of fact, last year we had a teacher who used her prep period to pump ... I try to help them to nurse and pump. If I were a single guy, maybe, I would have a different viewpoint, but since my wife nursed, I understand the importance of it ... I think the law is a good policy. It is something good: It is healthy for the baby and mother and it is cheaper. It is better for the parents and it should be encouraged as much as possible ... Some managers may be uncomfortable because it is not something guys talk about. It is not something we think about – it's not something we think about if we do not have a wife. We just need to work together ... I am fortunate because my wife nursed, so I understand.
>
> [010]

As this principal explained elsewhere during the interview, in the coming year, 3 out of his 100 employees planned to express milk when they returned from their maternity leaves. At 3 percent of all employees, his school had one of the highest percentages of lactating employees in this study.

Like the school principal, who felt that being a man made his pro-lactation advocacy more unusual, others felt that male allies could be more effective advocates for lactating employees than women managers. For example, the next interviewee to be discussed explained that he was able to steer conversations away from potentially inappropriate discussions.

> [But for management] to be more welcoming to the idea and more accepting of it, you really need someone to champion the program and get it going, you know, and be all gung-ho about it. Preferably, I think – since the joking around really comes from men mostly, about breast milk and boobs and all that; you can probably picture what some people say – I think, it works out, it worked out very well that the champion in my case was a male.
>
> [015]

He believed that he was a more effective champion for lactation accommodations for his lactating employee because he was both an ally and one of the guys.

Other women, too, became allies, due to social proximity to breastfeeding rather than their own experiences. For example, she talked about her own family.

> I have two daughters-in-law, that both have breastfed grandsons, and the time that it takes, you know just listening to them and just seeing if it would apply to a work setting and stuff. But I think we're pretty [accommodating of lactation] . . . I think we work with people. There's that culture here to try and work with people, so it's not that big of a deal.
>
> [029]

She was sensitized to the difficulties of expressing milk at work, and as a result, she did not simply sympathize with her lactating employees' struggles; she also empathized with their needs and created effective support. Using her position in the human resources office, this interviewee had created four lactation stations about five years before the Indiana state law was passed. However, once the law was in place, she was able to mobilize additional resources to more than triple the number of lactation rooms available across the factory campuses.

Greater empathy stems from increased knowledge about an issue and also heightened compassion toward people who are struggling with an issue (see Glynn and Sen 2014). The personal experience or close social proximity of human resource specialists and supervising managers to the challenge of expressing breast milk at work contributed to both of these components of empathy. These Allies Already understood the physiology of lactation and the biological consequences of alternating between nursing and milk expression, including the risks of mastitis, the pain of milk-engorged breasts, the embarrassment of leaking breasts, and the need for continuous demand to maintain milk supply. This basic knowledge was a key component of their becoming allies to their lactating employees; their depth of understanding about the issue of milk expression at work motivated their advocacy and further legitimated the demands and assertions they made about their lactating employees' needs.

Scholarship by Reason, Millar, and Scales (2005) and by Briodo (1997) on racism, sexism, and heterosexism demonstrates the importance of in-group members' efforts to educate potential out-group allies. Teaching facts about social problems can create allies who would advocate against various forms of oppression. The extant research shows that such education can be formal, such as college courses, or informal, such as conversations (Broido 1997; Fingerhut 2011; Kokkonen and Karlsson 2017; Reason, Millar, and Scales 2005; Russell 2011).

In addition to being knowledgeable about lactation and pumping, Allies Already shared a belief in the value of nursing and breast milk. They considered breast milk as sufficiently superior to synthetic alternatives to warrant the additional hassles, stress, and discomfort it created for the mothers – and their workplaces. These lactating workers' allies' somewhat subversive normative views and understanding of the physiology of breastfeeding led them to see it as logical and right to enable lactating women to express milk at work.

These allies' values were influenced by their close social ties with family and friends who had breastfed, including some who had sought to express milk at work. This dynamic recalls Russell's (2011) and Fingerhut's (2011) findings that heterosexual people's friendships with members of the LGBTQ community increased their sensitivity to heterosexism and homophobia. Casey and Smith's study illustrates this same experience in men whose commitment to fight male violence against women increased as their social networks sensitized them to the issue (2010).

The empathy and knowledge base of these human resource specialists and supervising managers led them to become Allies Already who were ready and willing to mobilize for lactation accommodations as soon as the law came into force. They did not need to be coerced by the law. Nor did they need to be convinced that accommodations mandated by the law would benefit their organization – in fact, they demonstrated a willingness to compromise managerial priorities for the sake of an issue they saw as more important. Instead, they were able to use the law to further accommodations that they already supported, as the next section discusses.

THE LAW AS A TOOL FOR SWIFT COMPLIANCE

As Edelman and Suchman explain, laws do not create change through pure coercion. Laws alter the normative value of innovations so that new practices can take hold in organizations (Edelman and Suchman 1997; Suchman and Edelman 1996). The Lactation at Work Law became a useful instrument for these supervising managers and human resource personnel to compel their organizations not only to create lactation accommodations, but also to do so with substantial alacrity.

The empathy these supervising managers and human resource personnel had toward their lactating employees motivated them to champion swift and full compliance with the law within their organizations. Many of these actors had wanted to create lactation accommodations before the law was passed. Some had raised the issue and had been met with resistance, and a few had won limited concessions.

The Lactation at Work Law gave these Allies Already a tool they could use to drive further change in their organizations. For example, a human resource specialist at a private university explained that, although her earlier efforts had been unsuccessful, once she had the law behind her, she could reframe lactation accommodations as legally necessary, rather than a benevolent action. In this way, her organization began to understand that accommodation was consistent with the organization's secondary goal of legal compliance and was worth pursuing.

> Actually, it was something we tried to do a few years ago, when I was doing primarily the wellness work and [my lactation accommodation ideas] didn't have a whole lot of [upper management] support, reason being space. Space is always an issue. So to give up space to be able to

> provide women a place to nurse or to pump. [It] was difficult to find people willing to give it up. And then, there was an Indiana law that passed last July, so, kind of after that came, I brought it up again, saying, now it's our responsibility to do this! It's no longer a nice thing to do; it's a legal requirement.
>
> [025]

The initial challenge to compliance did not change – space continued to be in short supply – but the new law made lactation accommodation a higher priority for her organization. Her coercion strategy of using the law to compel action by the organization harks back to the strategies described in Chapter 4. Nevertheless, this approach goes well beyond the use of legal compulsion and managerial goals described in that chapter.

The director of the human resources department in a large hospital explained that, while space shortages were a problem for her organization as well, the law now reframed lactating employees' needs as important.

> Now that there's a law [about lactation accommodation], it is easier now. No one listened, before. It just wasn't taken seriously. Before the law, we didn't have a way to show that it was important. The problem was available space and capital funding – no empty space available and no money to build the rooms. Any businesses that [are] big enough that will want to provide those spaces for mothers, they will run into those same challenges.
>
> [106]

This human relations director faced what was presented as an insurmountable problem: lack of space and money to create lactation accommodations. However, the passage of the Lactation at Work Law legitimated the issue of lactation at work, enabling this director to reframe the issue as an important priority, rather than being part of her own trivial, idiosyncratic agenda (e.g., McCann 1994).

> [The Lactation at Work Law] was passed and that was a game changer. The issue now was relevant, was important ... They said, "We can't" but then they said, "I guess we must," because now we can say that the law says we must. And so we did. Now they would listen.
>
> [106]

According to a human resource specialist in manufacturing, the Lactation at Work Law shifted the organization's norms by transforming lactation accommodation from being "a women's issue" into a legitimate concern for the organization as a whole:

> [In earlier years] I had talked about this, about the need to set up some places [for women to express milk]. I think it was seen as "a women's issue," and so it wasn't taken seriously, and I couldn't move anything forward. Now, [higher management] is interested. It's a real issue now, because the law says it's something to be taken seriously.
>
> [098]

Elsewhere, she explained that the passage of the law allowed her to quickly implement a fully compliant accommodation policy.

New laws attempt to reframe issues, often asserting a broader relevancy. Indeed, legislation does not simply create new law; it asserts clear normative declarations about what behavior is good and should be encouraged, and what is bad and ought to be condemned (Barnes and Burke 2012; Bernstein, Marshall, and Barclay 2009; Engel and Munger 1996, 2003; Gunningham, Kagan, and Thornton 2003; Kagan, Gunningham, and Thornton 2012). By signaling a shift in public norms and bringing forth a new understanding of a possibly under-considered, under-valued issue, the law creates new feelings of duty (McAdams 2017). Thus, the Lactation at Work Law legitimized workplace milk expression and proclaimed it worthy of legal protection.

Scholars have shown that issues tied to reproduction or the physical aspects of childcare are often framed as women's issues in the United States (see Glass and Fodor 2018).

Women's concerns are accorded secondary importance, situated behind concerns defined as more legitimate because they affect the entire society. This framing inhibits effective advocacy for these issues.

INTERNATIONAL APPRECIATION OF BREASTFEEDING

In contrast to the trivialization of breastfeeding in the United States, other countries frame breastfeeding as a practice with relevance to society as a whole, rather than casting it as a women's issue. For example, in Brazil, breastfeeding is considered so important that the government releases pro-breastfeeding PSAs on television and radio, and even includes pro-breastfeeding messages on utility bills. Brazil has established the largest nationwide network of breast-milk banks; breast-milk donations are picked up at the mother's home by special courier. Peru values breastfeeding enough to hold contests for nursing mothers, awarding prizes to those whose babies can nurse the longest time in a single sitting (Phelan 2015).

In Israel, public breastfeeding and workplace milk expression is protected because these acts are seen as contributing to the greater society. The Ministry of Health declared breastfeeding "not the mother's exclusive responsibly. It is society's responsibility" (Ministry of Health 2019: 1).

Not only does the government of the Philippines support breastfeeding through serious efforts like paid work breaks, and ubiquitous public lactation stations with handwashing, refrigeration, electrical outlets, and comfortable furniture; but it also organized lactating mothers into a Guinness contest. In 2005, 3,738 lactating women from across Manila brought their babies to the large local sports complex to simultaneously – at the mayor's cue – nurse their babies for one minute. This broke the previous record for simultaneous breastfeeding set in Berkeley, California, with a mere 1,135 mothers. The lactating women of the Philippines take seriously their responsibilities for the health of the community. When Typhoon Haiyan/Yolanda devasted the country in 2013, lactating women mobilized to donate breast milk to displaced women who could not nurse (Phelan 2015).

RIGHTS HOLDERS AND ALLIES ALREADY

When allies invoked the new Lactation at Work Law, the actual rights holders – the lactating employees – were able to step back. The allies used the language of rights and entitlements to compel accommodations without the affected employees having to appear to engage in any confrontation themselves. For example, the news director, quoted earlier (Interviewee #011), explained that she had been willing to speak up for her lactating employee's rights to an extent that the employee herself was not:

> I'd defend her. I'd defend what she was doing . . . She couldn't. It's hard to do that, but I could defend her. This was her right and the right thing to do.
>
> [011]

Research on various other rights – disability accommodations, racial desegregation, gender equity, etc. – demonstrates that rights holders might not engage the law because they view such actions, and possibly even each legal right itself, somewhat negatively.

Similarly, the hotel manager explained that his lactating employees were reluctant to assert themselves.

> They might mention [their lactation needs] to management somewhat apologetically. Or, I'd hear about someone's circumstances from [her] co-worker. But they were afraid to come forward [themselves]. I told them that this was an important thing they were doing and it was their right. But it was easier if I worked things out for them [to secure adequate break time to pump, etc.].
>
> [015]

He noticed that how lactation accommodations became framed could affect the employees' willingness to come forward to ask for necessary accommodations.

A human resource specialist who had weaned her daughter only the year before noted that when lactating employees framed requests for accommodations as helping them feed their babies, not as workers' rights nor as mothers' needs, they were more willing to advocate for themselves.

> I tell them that this is their right. I can speak to [their supervising managers] for them, but they can, too. They aren't asking for favors; they're wanting what they need to feed their babies . . . They seem more willing [to talk to managers about accommodations] when I say it like that; more women feel better about talking to their [supervising managers] then because they're not feeling like they're asking for a favor for themselves.
>
> [138]

By not framing a request for accommodations as a special favor, this Ally Already enabled her lactating employees to speak to their managers. She believed that refocusing the request on their providing food for their babies made them more able to come forward to their supervising managers. (The power of shifting the focus to the welfare of the employees' children is developed much further in Chapter 6).

Rights mobilization can be extremely difficult in that it involves awareness of the rights, a willingness to put oneself forward as deserving of those rights, and an ability to claim the right-given benefit for oneself (see Bumiller 1988; Engel and Munger 2003; McCann 1994; Trautner, Hatton, and Smith 2013). Because of the advocacy of the Allies Already on the employees' behalf, the rights holders avoid having to assert themselves.

Research on civil rights in other contexts has shown that rights holders may actually be discouraged from asserting their rights because doing so involves embracing the label of "victim." And some rights holders might also resist claiming their rights because they find it distasteful to use the law to force compliance.

Sometimes people whose rights have been violated prefer not to engage the law, even when they know it may help remedy their situation (see Barnes and Burke 2006; Bumiller 1988; Engel and Munger 2003; Levitsky 2008; McCann 1994; Trautner, Hatton, and Smith 2013; Young and Billings 2020). Members of groups that benefit from civil rights might associate the law with people other than themselves, with causes they do not fully embrace, or with an overly intrusive government (see Bumiller 1988; Engel and Munger 2003).

The advocacy by the Allies Already on behalf of their lactating employees – sometimes even before those employees requested accommodation – demonstrates how the law affected those organizational actors who were already predisposed to support it. The allies were able to use the law as a tool to counter the assumptions of managerialization and assert the worth of breastfeeding and workplace milk expression as a competing positive value.

The passage of the Lactation at Work Law gave Allies Already a tool to command the attention of their organizations. This tool provided legitimacy for the issue of workplace milk expression and helped them demand sufficient accommodation, even securing measures that went beyond basic compliance with the law.

Because the Allies Already often were more comfortable invoking the law than their lactating employees, the rights-bearing employees themselves could remain somewhat distanced from any struggles over accommodations. Similar to the way employing an attorney shifts the mental and emotional work of resolving the dispute to a "hired gun," these allies insulate the lactating employees from discussions, inquires, and confrontations that lactating employees describe in other chapters.

COMPLIANCE BEYOND THE LAW

While the process of managerialization discussed in Chapter 4 saw organizational actors focusing their efforts on getting their organizations to comply with the law, the Allies Already in this chapter went beyond simple compliance. They realized that the law's specifications might not fully meet all the needs of their lactating employees. They worked to ensure that their organizations implemented the law in ways that would truly address the law's underlying intent: to genuinely accommodate all lactating employees for workplace lactation success.

As empathetic allies, these lactation-accommodation institutional entrepreneurs understood both the organizational politics needed to secure accommodations and the human physiology at the root of the accommodations. They embraced pumping milk as a valued activity that they wanted to encourage and support. Thus, the Allies Already were both able to perceive unmet (and legally supported) needs of lactating employees. They were capable of improving accommodations so that their organizations facilitated workplace milk expression, even if that meant surpassing the level of accommodation mandated by law (see Barnes and Burke 2012; Kagan, Gunningham, and Thornton 2012).

Recognizing that the basic requirements of the law might be insufficient for some women's needs, the Allies Already mobilized to raise the level of accommodation until they felt the organizational response was appropriate, as the following quote from a university human relations specialist illustrates.

> I don't have a budget for workplace at all. But I do ask people to donate things to me, so I've gotten bulletin boards donated. There was some money left at the end of the year one time, and I was able to get some curtains to use in various places and a chair that we move around from place to place as needed. When we were doing away with a certain type of paper towel holder, I was able to get those so I could offer those to people in order to be able to have a paper towel holder in place in the nursing area for the nursing mothers.
>
> Sometimes I have been able to get us small tables from Surplus Supply; they do charge five dollars for anything that's minor, and I usually just pay for them myself and put them in place. If they need painting, I take them out and paint them so that they'll look nice. But we can usually get those tables for them to put a pump on. And people have donated bulletin boards to me so they can put up their child's picture.
>
> [035]

Although this human resource specialist never breastfed her children, she had close proximity to lactation issues because her daughter had breastfed. Her efforts to provide a comfortable place for milk expression went well beyond the law's minimum mandate. She and her co-workers decorated the lactation rooms with artwork and bulletin boards for the walls, curtains for the windows, freshly painted furniture, and lockers for women to store their pumping apparatus.

Earlier in the interview, she explained that she had wanted to create lactation rooms before the law was passed, but did not get much support from the human relations department. At that time, she had been reluctant to take on the building deputies who were in charge of allocating space in each building. However, once the law was passed, she quickly initiated a lactation policy and created lactation rooms across her campus, mobilizing university funds, volunteers' donations, and her own time and money.

The new law granted legitimacy to her efforts. The force of the law might have been sufficient to compel the organizations to adhere to the letter of the law, institutionalizing the exact requirements – but nothing more. However, the normative and expressive power of the law enabled the Allies Already to push for further accommodations, as a human resource specialist at another university explains:

> For a few different options [that I took] to the table with administration, I said, "We could either be legally compliant or we could really do this well and market this as a benefit that we offer to our employees." And, "By all means!" they all agreed, "We need to do this. We need to do it the right way." It's not about getting it done as fast as we can or as cheap, but doing it well so that people want to use it, and people appreciate the service that this provides them. So that was a very positive thing.
>
> [025]

With the legitimacy the law conferred, the human resources specialist was able to move her university to go beyond the basic, legally required accommodations and allocate more funding for the lactation accommodations because she was already sensitized to and informed about the issue the law addressed.

Sometimes the compliance beyond a law's requirements demanded substantial personal commitment. For example, the university human resources specialist whose daughter had breastfed (Interviewee #035) convinced her organization to not only create sufficient numbers of accessible lactation rooms, but also to make these rooms as inviting and pleasant as possible.

> It was important to me to make the room functional and attractive. We found some lockers on campus that nobody wanted anymore . . . [When our office was] getting some new furniture, we [donated an old] table . . . [which partly] is light blue so it goes with the artwork that is in there . . . We wanted to just say, "We care enough about you and want to encourage you to do this, so it is important for us to make this as nice as we can."
>
> [035]

Even though her office's mission was to serve employees' needs, she allowed the rooms to be used by students as well. Similarly, Interviewee #059, quoted next, offered her law firm's lactation room to not just employees but also to visitors:

> When a visiting counsel from another firm was coming over to do depositions and was in a position where she needed to actually pump, and wasn't quite sure how to approach the firm, so she went to the reception desk, and she was whispering. She's like, "Gosh I'm so embarrassed. I . . . do you have any place, a private space that I can, ah?" and she kind of hemmed and hawed until she got around to her point. Well, we were thrilled to be able to say, "You know, we actually have a room! We have a new mother's lounge dedicated for that. Let's take you back there!" And that was a huge selling point to that opposing counsel, that visitor and our guests, and we realized that it didn't need to be just for internal firm personnel. So we actually have that for use for anyone who comes into the firm, any new mother that needs that privacy to do so.
>
> [059]

Although the leaders of her firm knew that the law did not require them to provide the lactation room to visitors, they chose to accommodate them. In this way, the presence of the law was able create new practices as these lactation accommodations became understood as furthering the organization's secondary goal of being seen as welcoming of diverse needs (Albiston 2005).

The supervising manager at a large manufacturing plant, quoted next, had pumped milk at work herself. Although her organization provided rooms for expressing milk that were in basic compliance with the law, she found them difficult to locate. She took the initiative to create a flier that her human relations department distributed to women who returned from maternity leave, detailing exactly where to find the rooms where they could express milk.

> I worked with HR to build their brochure for nursing moms to make it much more easy. I wrote directions, specifically [explaining] how to walk to them from main spots because sometimes they're kind of hidden, because they'll be in more of closet-esque type locations that have a sink and a nice sitting area but they're not always easy to find, and especially if you're visiting another building and have a meeting there.
>
> [008]

Recognizing that substantial time spent searching for the lactation-approved rooms would detract from the time lactating employees had to express milk, she felt strongly that it was helpful and necessary to provide directions, even if doing so was not specifically stipulated by law.

These Allies Already helped leverage the Lactation at Work Law to exceed the minimum requirements and offer even greater accommodation than the law required. Accomplishing this often meant challenging managerial norms and sacrificing their own time, money, and effort. Their close proximity to breastfeeding and workplace milk expression made them knowledgeable and passionate about enacting these accommodations.

PROXIMITY, LEGITIMACY, AND EARLY MOBILIZATION

As soon as the Lactation at Work law was passed, allies in many industries were poised to comply with the law's mandates. They were well positioned and able to create organizational change that rose above the minimum threshold for compliance. Because these allies were motivated by their shared values regarding breastfeeding and their insights into the hurdles of milk expression, they were able to use the law to advocate for effective changes that challenged organizational norms regarding control of the employees' time, physical placement, and mental focus.

The coercive power of the law might have forced the organizations to adhere to the exact requirements of the letter of the law. However, the normative and expressive power of the law gave the Allies Already a tool to demand accommodations that went well beyond the legally prescribed minimum. By recognizing workplace milk expression as an activity important enough to warrant official, legal protection, the Lactation at Work Law created a normative shift that enabled the allies to generate organizational responses that went beyond mere compliance. In doing so, the Allies Already challenged managerial norms and priorities to focus not just on sufficient compliance but on effective accommodation for ongoing, successful workplace lactation and breastfeeding.

Importantly, all interviewees identified as Allies Already had personal or close secondhand experience with lactating at work. However, the reverse does not hold: Some human resource specialists and supervising managers, who had personal experience expressing milk at work, were not allies. People in that category still complied with the law to create adequate accommodations, often using what was easily available within the cultural and physical structures of their organizations, but they were not poised to comply when the law came into force, nor did they regularly exceed the law's basic requirements.

Of my 188 management interviewees, only three who had personal experience with lactation provided accommodations that, although legally compliant, were at least partially insufficient for one or more lactating employee. An example is this human resource supervisor:

> I was a lactating mom and had to go through it once myself, but I think it can be done as long as we keep, again, the employers' needs in focus as well. [021]

No managerial interviewee with close connections to lactating and pumping failed to provide at least this level of accommodation. It is possible, but unlikely, that I missed some managers with close secondhand experience who resisted making adequate accommodations. My interviews captured this by asking everyone about personal and spousal experiences with lactating and pumping, and although the interview protocol did not ask if a close friend or non-spouse family member had pumped, the open-ended nature of the interviews invited that information, which often emerged naturally. Significantly, none of the interviewees who provided insufficient accommodations reported that they had a close friend or relative who nursed. Additionally, the interviews with the lactating workers could have provided examples of management with personal or close experiences who insufficiently accommodated, but none did.

Thus, the data indicate that personal or close proximate experiences with lactation and milk expression are necessary to for people to become allies, but they might not be sufficient. This is an important point about causality: Exposure to breastfeeding experiences, struggles, and ideology were a critical component for supporting the law's accommodations before the law was even passed. The law then became the tool that those allies used. An important lesson here is that rights holders might benefit from greater organization compliance and accommodation if they work to identify and enlist the help of allies as soon as new legislation is enacted.

The swift mobilization by the Allies Already allowed for the lactating employees' rights to be secured without the employees themselves having to mobilize. However, as the next chapter demonstrates, this was not the only pathway for advocacy for lactating employees; workplace interactions can develop new allies.

Chapter 6 describes how some supervising managers became allies over time. For the most part, they were not converted because they empathized or felt solidarity with their lactating employees – like the Allies Already – but they saw breastfeeding and lactation accommodations as contributing to a healthier society. Through discussions about lactation with their employees, certain supervising managers become persuaded that support for lactation accommodation contributes to the greater good.

CHAPTER SIX

MORALIZING THE LAW

Listening in the Shadow of the Law and the Transformation of Supervising Managers

[The Lactation at Workplace] Law is important because it helps the women come back from maternity leave and be able to work and do the milk for her baby. She can come back sooner without so much time away from work ... The law helps the women come back so other people can focus on their own work and not do her job, too.

—Jack, a supervising manager at a manufacturing plant (Time One interview)

When I talked to him about [my need to pump milk at work] before I left for maternity leave, I swear he rolled his eyes. I mean, in a friendly way. But he was like, "Okay, whatever." So, I knew he didn't want to know about it ... But then I'd say things to him about [expressing milk]. Like, I'd tell him why I was doing it. Why I wanted my kid to have my milk, not just some formula. And, we sort of would talk about it. Not really talk, but I'd tell him stuff. I think he started listening. Well ... not just listening, but caring. Like he got it.

—Kristy, a lactating employee at the plant

The milk the moms pump, it isn't like regular milk. It has antibodies and fights infection, like ear infections, that babies get a lot. It's important that the babies have milk from the moms so they don't get sick. There's no other milk, anything, like it. It has to come from the mom and [the babies] have to have it to not get sick. We need to make that happen.

—Jack (Time Two interview)

This chapter discusses a different set of allies from those in Chapter 5. These allies are supervising managers who had *not* been Allies Already at Time One, but who became Morality-Motivated Advocates over time as they underwent a process of shifting how they understood the lactation accommodations. Unlike the allies of the last chapter who were both knowledgeable and supportive of pumping from the start, this chapter's advocates began focused on providing only accommodations required by law that furthered a managerial rationale. While the Allies Already of the previous chapter engaged various angles to argue for improved lactation accommodations, drawing on their direct or proximate knowledge of milk expression, this chapter's new allies eventually understood lactation accommodations through a moralization of the law that engaged concepts of children's health as a key motivation.

Educational conversations between lactating workers and their supervising managers shifted the managers' focus from managerial goals (such as how breastfed babies might require fewer sick days) to a moral focus that also included health-and-wellness goals, such the health of breastfed babies. Lactating workers often initiated discussions to secure the necessary accommodations and assert their rights under the law, but the conversations had the longer term benefit of creating "moral allies" (Becker 1963). The "moralization of the law" that occurred – that is, this broadening of the organizational attention to include the welfare of those outside the organization – constitutes a key shift in how compliance with the Lactation at Work Law was framed. As Morality-Motivated Advocates for adequate lactation accommodations, these supervising managers joined the Allies Already in becoming "institutional entrepreneurs" (DiMaggio 1988: 14) who were able to extend the focus of the organization beyond managerial needs.

This moralization of the Lactation at Work Law occurred after supervising managers began to consider the children's health benefits of breastfeeding and the role of workplace expression in maintaining breastfeeding. Through educational conversations with their lactating employees about lactation and milk expression, these supervising managers began to reframe their organizations' compliance. Initially, these supervising managers often saw the accommodations simply as regulations mandated by their organizations in response to legal mandates. Or, to the extent that they were aware of health benefits of breastfeeding, they saw the lactation accommodations as a means to key managerial ends. They knew that accommodations would reduce absenteeism and turnover and potentially boost morale. However, eventually some of the supervising managers came to understand the health benefits as important both for the sake of the health of their employees' children's health, and of society more generally. They embraced a concern that extended beyond the "economic rationale for wellness" (Kirkland 2014: 958).

The Lactation at Work Law – although no longer compelling compliance instrumentally through threat of force – remained an important component in how the lactating workers gained useful accommodations and substantive compliance. By its very presence, the law designated expressing milk at work to be sufficiently legitimate to warrant the attention of the law. Moreover, by mandating tangible accommodations, the law compelled discussion of whether accommodations were insufficient, thereby creating the social space for the educational conversations that led to the moralization of the law.

The relevant literature, however, does not predict the galvanizing effect of these educational discussions between employees and supervising managers. To the contrary, earlier studies often found supervising managers to be uncooperative and obdurate when it comes to meeting employee accommodation needs (e.g., Gwartney-Gibbs and Lach 1992; Hallden 2015; Hodson and Roscigno 2004; Kelly et al. 2014; Marshall 2003). This is not surprising since providing most accommodations – extra time, more space, etc. – has a direct impact on the remaining resources the supervising manager has to address other employee concerns and to accomplish the work of that organizational unit. Thus, on the one hand, one might expect supervising managers to be more likely than human resource specialists to become advocates, because human resource specialists lack the frequent contact with lactating employees that made these educational conversations possible, and supervising managers are the ones who affect the day-to-day work life of their employees. Yet, on the other hand, supervising managers bear the responsibility for the day-to-day functioning of their divisions, which makes their willingness to create accommodations quite surprising; they are the organizational actors who would bear the brunt of any negative consequences resulting from the accommodations. For example, the time and effort lactating employees spent pumping could directly affect these supervising managers, while any reduced productivity or inconvenience might be invisible to human resource specialists.

For this reason, many might expect that the supervising managers would have been less, rather than more, supportive of milk expression accommodations.

This is an example of how people's positions in organizations affect their responses to the law. Some extant research agrees, finding that organizational location affects the reaction to legal mandates (e.g., Gray and Silbey 2014). However, this finding is contrary to other findings that the institutional culture permeates organizations creating uniform legal responses consistently throughout organizations (e.g., Kagan, Gunningham, and Thornton 2012). In the case of the Lactation at Work Law, human resource personnel were positioned away from daily employee interactions; they were focused on crafting laws into organizational policies, and, consequently, did not moralize the law.

Ironically, perhaps, the workplaces where lactating employees had more difficulty were more likely to experience a shift from managerial objectives to embracing external, health-related goals. This is because lactating employees at more challenging workplaces needed to contact their supervising managers at each problem juncture to negotiate a solution – whether to sort out initial logistics, or to strategize solutions to new complications that arose. These discussions were more likely to become the educational conversations between employees and supervising managers that caused those managers to embrace the morality frame of protecting the health of children. As a result of compliance rationales that drew on morality external to the organizations, those workplace accommodations became more deeply engrained than they were when they referenced only managerial goals or legal mandates.

EDUCATIONAL CONVERSATIONS: FROM MANAGERIALIZATION TO CHILDREN'S HEALTH

Those supervising managers whose focus shifted from the law or managerial motivations to include a moral framework of children's health became Morality-Motivated Advocates for their lactating employees, drawing on health-focused rhetoric and implementing accommodations beyond the minimum requirements when necessary. The supervising managers went from – sometimes begrudgingly – just complying with the law at Time One to fully supporting lactation accommodations at Time Two, about five years later. During the second wave of interviews, about two-thirds of supervising managers who had not been Allies Already at Time One no longer described their understanding of the lactation accommodations exclusively through the lens of managerial needs, as they had done at Time One, and as human resource personnel continued to do. While the human resource personnel continued to maintain their focus solely on benefit to the organization, about two-thirds of the supervising managers had shifted to include a morality-based health-and-wellness understanding of the Lactation at Work Law to justify fully complying or even exceeding the mandates of the law.

This new focus on health and wellness was not simply a means to a managerial end (e.g., fewer sick kids results in fewer sick days of parents missing work), nor was it a strategic way to help their organizations. Instead, this seemed to be a focus on health for its own sake. For example, during his second interview, this supervising manager explained his focus on the health benefits of breastfeeding for the children of his staff:

> By breastfeeding the baby, the mother gets health benefits – like less cancer likelihood, and mental health benefits – but also the baby gets loads of health benefits: fewer infections, less allergies, less likely to be overweight, and on and on. It's not just about the employee and the law, but it's about the health of the babies. If they're breastfed, they'll be healthier and they can't be breastfed unless their moms pump the milk. So it's up to us, to me, to supervisors, to support those moms so that their babies can be healthy.
>
> [168]

This contrasts with the comments he made during his first interview:

> This is a good law. It helps employees return to work. They want to have a baby, but then also nurse them and do that for them. And this law helps them do both. They use their breaks to go off and do that. Otherwise, we lose employees and we need to hire and train someone else.
>
> [168]

His initial focus was on managerial benefits from the Lactation at Work Law and how it met goals beneficial to the organization, like reducing turnover.

One of his lactating employees explained that occasionally she struggled with finding a place to express her milk. When this happened, she would go to her manager to ask what space she should try next.

> Things would be going okay, and then something would happen. [Early on] I was pumping in [what is now a new employee's] office. That was

> great! Then, of course, [that employee] got hired. Then I was pumping in the back room, which was okay, but then someone put all the boxes [of materials for an upcoming initiative in the organization] in that room, and there was no more room for me! [laughs] So I had to keep going back to [my manager]: "Where should I go now? What room can I use now?" And each time, I'd sort of have to explain to him, not only that I'm still pumping, but why I am and why it's important . . . It's the natural food for a baby. It keeps them healthy. And it hurts [my breasts] if I don't pump when I have to! . . . [Manager] didn't know. Or maybe he didn't care. Until I told him about it.
>
> [W077]

Although each hurdle was a frustration for her, these frustrating moments also presented opportunities for her to discuss lactation with her supervising managers. That is, to engage in educational conversations.

Similarly, at Time One, this supervisor of office workers in a manufacturing organization said, fairly tersely, that the lactation accommodations were "good to help women. Sometimes it's a hassle when [current lactating employee] isn't there [because she's pumping]. But it's what we've gotta do . . . It's the law now." [157]

Because this employee's time away did create some difficulties, she had to talk with this supervising manager about lactation and milk expression:

> Sometimes, it just takes longer. You know? I mean, in the beginning, I guess, I was figuring out how to do everything, get everything set up, and then washed and taken down. I hadn't figured out I could just store [part of the equipment] in the fridge, and only wash it at the end. But, even later, sometimes my milk just took longer to really start. Or, I just wasn't moving so fast. Sometimes, it just took longer, and I had to explain to him that. I had to explain why it was worth it to get that last ounce, or, [expletive], just to do it at all . . . [Earlier in the interview:] I do it because it's good for my baby. It's the best food. It's the best food and the best I can give him . . . [and] it has good benefits for me, too, as a woman.
>
> [W080]

During her interview, she listed health benefits to both her child and herself, so she may have mentioned those benefits when she talked to her supervising manager, although she did not state this explicitly.

In fact, by Time Two, these educational conversations had been so effective that the manager [#157] permitted her extra time and more flexibility to successfully express milk; now he framed the accommodations as more than legal compliance and vital to supporting key health goals:

> If I help, say, I have a diabetic employee, do what he needs to do, then I've helped [just] him. But if I help one of our women pump the milk, I'm helping beyond just all of us here. [Interviewer: What do you mean?] I mean, I'm helping, well I'm not, I mean, the woman is, but I'm helping her help her baby, and then more women are helping their babies. I mean, I think of it as sort of helping the kids who will be the grown-ups of the next generation. You don't realize what that milk will do. But now I do.
>
> [157]

Without the law mandating accommodations, these lactating employees could not have commanded their managers' attention to reevaluate their understandings of breast milk and lactation accommodations.

Importantly, this shift to health goals could even include benefits of those outside and unrelated to the organization. For example, at Time One, this director of a county government office was focused on the benefits of the lactation accommodations to the organization and the employee; although he used the words "everyone is happy," he was referring to people within his organization:

> This is the right thing to do. Absolutely. Women come back to work. They miss their babies. This lets them keep up that connection. It's not easy, of course. We aren't really set up for that, but we find a place and we make it all work out so everyone is happy . . . There's this law.
>
> [147]

By the second wave of interviews, he believed that by supporting his lactating employees he was helping his country as a whole:

> We've learned that "breast is best." That wasn't the case when I had kids, but now we know that breastfed babies are healthier. That not only means that their moms will miss less work because of them. I mean, that's great for me! But it also means that they will grow up to be healthier kids and adults. That's good for all of us. For America. If I support my employees so they can nurse their kids, then that [benefit is] passed on to the whole next generation. We need a healthy country to be competitive in this whole global economy. That starts with their babies.
>
> [147]

This supervising manager's switch at Time Two to understanding that breastfeeding benefits people entirely outside the organization shows a substantial shift. Between the two interviews, this manager did not simply change his talk; he became a Morality-Motivated Advocate, successfully mobilizing for an additional lactation room near his employees' work area, even though a legally compliant room was available farther away.

Importantly, these conversations did not happen in a vacuum. The law created the organizational commitment. Arguably, the frame of health and wellness was first provided by the Lactation at Work Law, since this amendment to the FLSA came from the Affordable Care Act. Moreover, organizational knowledge that these accommodations were legally mandated bestowed legitimacy on the needs, which encouraged the supervising managers to engage and listen to what their lactating employees were saying. These supervising managers often voiced their awareness of the law during their first interviews, such as when manager #157 said, "It's the law now." However, the Lactation at Work Law, created space for conversations that deepened knowledge and facilitated effective compliance.

Employees' Stories on Educational Conversations

Many workers who did engage in educational discussions with their supervising managers described these discussions as difficult, at least initially. For example, this public grade school teacher described how she had to emotionally prepare before talking to her school's principal:

> Of course, I needed to talk with him about it. But, I mean, he's older and sort of standoff-ish, and, it's not that we're not friendly, but I just didn't want to, I don't know, say the wrong thing. The first time I went to tell him that I'd need a private place [to pump] I really had to steady myself. And then [once I had been pumping for a while] something would come up about [the space where I pumped] and I had to clear it with him, or I'd need something changed. And, whew! I just kept telling myself how important [pumping/breast milk] is. And so I told him, too. It was hard enough for me to go talk with him, so I guess I just told him everything I could.
>
> [W028]

The structure of her workplace, with her principal enjoying substantial power over her, created a great emotional hurdle for engaging him in an educational conversation.

Educational discussions sometimes posed risks to the lactating employees to the extent that they were challenging their managers' beliefs about motherhood, worker identity, physiology, and the division between home and work. Extant research shows that posing alternate understandings to powerful actors' beliefs – although critical to changing their opinions – might also anger or annoy them (Boyle and Corle 2010; Plumm and Terrance 2009). In less supportive work environments, these educational conversations could involve asserting one's dual parent-employee identity, defending one's parenting philosophies, and discussing one's anatomy in workplace contexts that could be intimidating, and, with a temperamental manager, truly dangerous.

By providing legitimacy and leverage, the law created space for the educational conversations – conversations that were important for effective, substantive compliance. The political importance of the law is critical because the law facilitates the educational conversations by enabling the women to remain at work, to continue to breastfeed, and to tell their stories. Critically, the law endows the educational conversations with legitimacy so that employees can talk with reticent, resistant, underinformed, and less helpful supervising managers about lactation.

Some lactating employees, like the restaurant employee discussed next, saw the law as a source of strength that confirmed the legitimacy of her needs and accommodations.

> I knew what the law said. I knew [the provided space] couldn't be a bathroom. I knew they had to let me do it. I knew I was right. [laughs] I just didn't know if [my manager] knew it! [laughs] But I knew the law, so I went ahead and asked for what I needed 'cause the law said so. [Interviewer: Did you mention the law to your manager?] No, the law never came up.
>
> [W065]

Even though the employee never directly mentioned the law to her supervising manager, her own knowledge that the law was there helped her ask for what she needed.

Similarly, this office worker in the transportation industry talks about how the law empowered her to ask for necessary accommodations.

> The law says the employer has to do certain things ... I read all about this before I came back [from maternity leave]. I don't always like asking for favors. But this was *the law* and so it wasn't really a favor.

> It was what the law said. I wasn't being demanding. I was just doing what the law said.
>
> [W063]

The law enabled her to speak up about what accommodations she needed because it helped her reframe the lactation accommodations as a legal entitlement, which had greater legitimacy, rather than as a favor, which would have made her feel like she was being "demanding."

In her interview, an accounting firm receptionist drew on the very presence of the Lactation at Work Law to validate her needs:

> It's the law. This isn't something I just made up in my head that I should have. The law says I should – any woman should – get [these accommodations]. Even though I never said, "You gotta do this because the law says so" I could have said [that]. [Lactation accommodations] are important. It's not just me. If it wasn't important, it wouldn't be a law.
>
> [W054]

Even though very few women in this study explicitly discussed the law with their supervising managers, the law had a substantial impact on their ability to ask for the accommodations they needed. These women knew that the law gave them the right to express milk at work and to secure certain accommodations from their employers. This knowledge of their legal rights shifted the onus from them onto the legal mandate; their requests were legal entitlements rather than special favors, which confirmed the validity of their needs.

Managers' Stories

Employees and supervising managers were aware of the power of these educational conversations. They observed the shift from management goals to a moralized focus on health benefits for children. For example, in his Time Two interview, a manager explained that his acceptance of his employees' pumping at work and his greater understanding of the health benefits of breastfeeding came directly as a result of discussions with his lactating workers:

> At first, I'll tell you, I thought it was gross. I mean, it's a bit like excrement – I mean, that's what I *used* to think. Now I understand how beneficial that milk is. I mean, it has antibodies that help the babies stay healthy and it helps with allergies and all sorts of other things. I had two women employees – they were both pregnant at the same time and they both nursed their kids. And they both pumped.

> And, at first, I just wanted them to go away and do what they had to do. But then they were telling me, like, why they were doing it. It wasn't easy for them. It was a lot of work but they believed that it was helping their babies be healthy. I really didn't understand that. I thought: milk is milk, but human milk is made especially for human babies – in fact, each mother's milk is made especially for her own baby. Man, it's like, how can you not give the baby that? You want healthy babies.
>
> [127]

This unmarried man started out with so little knowledge of breastfeeding that he described mothers' milk as repulsive. After conversations with his employees about why pumping and breastfeeding were important to them, he not only understood the health benefits; he became a supporter of breastfeeding. (However, he never used the terms "breastfeeding," "breast milk," or "breast" once during the entire interview, perhaps indicating that he still was a bit squeamish.)

Similarly, this supervising manager in manufacturing said that he had not understand the value of breast milk until his lactating employees taught him about it:

> At [my organization], we obey the law and we care about our employees, so of course we do whatever we have to do for everyone who [steps forward and says that s/he] needs something, needs some change, something for [the organization] to do. That's how I approach anything for an employee. Pumping the milk? I didn't really think about it, but, if I did, I didn't really want to think about it.
>
> It's, ah, "mother's milk." I don't know. I had just thought, these [accommodations] are something we gotta do. It's what they need, so it's good for employee morale and all ... But the milk is something different. It's good for the babies – really good. It's important for them ... I didn't know. I never knew that. Then the girls were talking to me. They'd say stuff. At first, I was, like, polite. But it was interesting, all the stuff the milk is good for. It's important because it does so much for the baby. I didn't know that.
>
> [121]

A principal, who shared that his wife had not breastfed any of their children, related that his employees taught him about the value of breast milk.

> My wife didn't nurse. I don't think people nursed so much then. But now we know that nursing is very important for the health of the baby. It's *critical*. But people didn't know that. I didn't know that.

> [Those lactating employees], they talked to me about it *a lot*. Not just to me, they talked about why pumping was important to other [employees], [as well as] to each other. I guess I needed to be told, because people don't know about pumping and nursing. But if you understand how critical it is for the babies' health, you understand how important it is to do.
>
> [093]

These supervising managers – whether they were originally indifferent, ignorant, or resentful – learned about more than breast milk and pumping from their employees. They were exposed to their lactating workers' values and commitment to breastfeeding. Over time, they were transformed into Morality-Motivated Advocates.

Employees' Stories

The lactating employees themselves also spoke of educating their supervising managers about the various benefits of breastfeeding, sometimes explicitly explaining why pumping at work was necessary in order to breastfeed at home and to be comfortable at work. These lactating workers shared their beliefs in the importance of breastfeeding and their dedication to this goal. For example, this office worker, who had struggled with getting sufficient space for milk expression, described how she had to explain to her manager the health reasons for breastfeeding.

> Before I left, while I was still there, but was pregnant, I said that I wanted to breastfeed. [Manager] was like, "Why?" I explained that breastfed babies are healthier – fewer ear aches, fewer colds, they don't develop allergies as much and so on. He almost didn't believe me.
>
> But we kept talking. And then I left [for the birth and maternity leave] and then I returned a week or so before I started again, and I reminded him that I was going to pump and what I had arranged. And he was like, "You're really going to do that?" And then I explained to him again why this was important to me. And then, like, a week or so later, I started back at work . . . Every so often, my pumping would come up. Not like he was bad about it, just like, "Oh, right, you've got to go pump again."
>
> And I'd say something about the benefits of it. I started to feel like he was a guy and he just didn't understand. And then – and I could hardly believe this – but I overheard him explaining to a co-worker about my pumping. They were scheduling a meeting; it was [a busy time for the company] and I think the other guy [didn't understand why I had to

> pump]. And [the manager] was actually explaining all the health benefits and why it was important! I cried. I was there in the hallway, and I had to turn around and go the other way [because I didn't want to be seen crying]. I couldn't believe it.
>
> [W068]

Her supervising manager's transformation surprised and touched her so much that she was moved to tears.

Other workers echoed this experience (although often with less emotion), explaining that they, too, had to educate their managers, often in order to secure adequate accommodations. Eventually, these educational conversations resulted in the managers becoming advocates. For example, this event planner with her town's Chamber of Commerce explained how the issue of expressing milk at work was a foreign concept to her manager, but once he understood her predicament, he arranged for her to have a more easily accessible location to pump.

> The management [is] mostly men, mostly older men, and, mostly men whose wives were able to stay at home. And they're much older than me, like 60s. So, not only have they not had to be around this for a really long time, but probably their wives never had to deal with trying to pump and work or take care of the kids and work. So, I think that, just that lack of experience [is a hurdle] ... I talked about, "So this is important." And they were kind of like, "Do whatever, we don't really want to talk about this stuff," but, you know, [they started to understand] ... Like, they got that this was important for my baby to be healthy ... [And it's important] for my health, too, for me not be in pain with too much milk. Or leaking. It's not a [trivial] issue.
>
> [W011]

Similarly, the mother quoted next was an office worker in a downtown firm with very little space available for pumping in private. She explained how she initially encountered resistance, but persevered and educated her supervising manager, who rallied to find her better space and granted her greater flexibility for lactation breaks:

> My manager's an older guy. I don't know if his wife nursed his kids or what, but he had no idea about breastfeeding or about pumping or any of it. I didn't lecture him, but I would mention some of the health benefits: how it helps the baby. After I'd been pumping for a few months, he told me – this was just after Thanksgiving – that he had been at his son and daughter-in-law's house in Ohio and she's pregnant and he said that he

> had told her what I had told him about breastfeeding and all that. And she wasn't sure that she could nurse since she was going back to work – she's a teacher, I think – and he said that he was all "Sure you can! [Interviewee] pumps all the time!" I don't think I pump "all the time," thanks, but I thought it was great that he was able to talk to his daughter-in-law about this.
>
> [W023]

This story illustrates the power of these employee-manager conversations about lactation. The influence of this employee's ongoing discussions with her supervising manager even extended to the manager's actions outside the workplace to his own family. The day-to-day interactions of supervising managers and lactating workers enabled critical discussions that educated these supervising managers about the health benefits of breastfeeding, the physiology of lactation, and the personal beliefs behind these employees' commitment to expressing milk at work.

Why No Shift for Human Resource Personnel?

In contrast to the supervising managers, the human resource personnel I interviewed did not shift their focus to children's health concerns, nor did they engage in moralization of the law. These human resource specialists – those who were not Allies Already during the first round of interviews – did not shift their attitudes or actions to encompass any belief that expressing milk or breastfeeding benefited society. The deviation between human resource professionals and some supervising managers in the second wave of interviews highlights key differences between these two somewhat similar groups with regard to employees and to the law.

First, human resource specialists spend substantial time working with supervising managers to implement the new policies and very little time interacting with employees. Unlike supervising managers, who have daily interactions with employees, human resource specialists continued to focus on managerial goals. They did not have as many educational conversations with workers and were not exposed to their pro-breastfeeding values. In addition, it was the duty of the human resource department to compel supervising managers to follow the letter of the law. In this case, they were charged with helping workers secure time and space for milk expression, meaning they often spent more time educating managers who were resistant to implementing the new polices. For this reason, their efforts were focused on convincing supervising managers to comply, not on receiving information or learning about workers' experiences, whether directly from the workers or supervising managers.

Second, human resource specialists were more focused on the law and how compliance could benefit the organization. Human resource specialists could not promote a public-spirited argument because they feared it would undermine their reputation of loyalty to the organization. In maintaining a focus on managerial goals, human resource personnel demonstrated that they were strategically addressing issues crucial to the organization (e.g., absenteeism), and were not idealistic activists overreaching their role – a role they conceptualize primarily as ensuring the organization's compliance with the law. The human resource specialist's professional field, therefore, is radically different from the supervising manager's: The human resource specialist focuses on the organization, its place with society, and its compliance with society's laws; they are not charged with addressing the day-to-day needs of workers. Because of this, they have much less daily contact with employees than supervising managers do (see Edelman, Fuller, and Mara-Ditra 2001; Marshall 2005; Suchman and Edelman 1996).

In contrast, supervising managers deal directly with the needs of their employees – whether they are accommodating or rejecting those needs. They are aware of which accommodations are used and to what extent that usage disrupts the ground-level workings of the organization. For example, if lactation breaks diminish employees' productivity, the supervising managers not only are aware of it, but are responsible for compensating for it. The human resource personnel are insulated from the ways accommodations are actualized, including possible hidden costs. Therefore, it is striking that so many supervising managers became Morality-Motivated Advocates, because of their proximity to these costs.

WHAT ENABLED AND DISABLED THESE EDUCATIONAL CONVERSATIONS?

What were the necessary conditions for the educational conversations that created the Morality-Motivated Advocates? The conversations depended on having workers who had enough power to be able to initiate the conversations, but not so much power that they did not need to have them. For this group of lactating employees, the law made these conversations possible.

The Law

The law was critical for these conversations to occur in four ways: First, the accommodations, when adequate, enabled these women to remain at work while lactating – neither stopping breastfeeding so that these educational conversations were no longer needed, nor resigning from their jobs so that they would no longer be present to have these conversations. Second, the law provided leverage for the employees, regardless of whether their educational conversations actually invoked the law or not. Third, the law's designation of practical accommodations (space and time) enabled employees to focus on specifics in order to launch their educational conversations and address whether those specific accommodations were adequate. Fourth, the law conferred legitimacy by validating workplace milk expression. This legitimacy both bolstered the confidence of these women to embark on these conversations, and made supervising managers more likely to be attentive rather than dismissive of the educational conversations.

First, an obvious, but often overlooked, reality about workplace requests and grievances is that they are seldom found in workplaces that are so difficult that workers who might present those requests and grievances have been driven out (see Hoffmann 2006). In the case of lactation accommodations, if a workplace makes milk expression too difficult, the woman will either stop trying to pump at work, possibly ceasing nursing and lactation altogether, or she will prioritize lactation over employment and quit. In those scenarios, no lactating employee remains who could discuss adequate accommodations. Thus, the law facilitates these dialogues in many ways, but first simply by enabling the lactating workers to remain at work and continue to express milk – neither quitting nor abandoning breastfeeding – so that these important conversations can occur.

Second, the law provided leverage and was a key structural component of the success of the educational conversations. The lactating workers' recognition that the law was in their "back pocket" helped them feel that they were not alone, and that they could use it to force organizational compliance. The law, and the specific rights it provided, could take on the burden of "being demanding" so the workers could purse their rights and request the accommodations they needed by simply invoking the authoritarian voice of the law. Thus, regardless of whether the lactating employees engaged in actual rights-talk with their managers or not, the presence of the law legitimizes these women's accommodation needs, allowing them to challenge the hegemonic view separating family duties from the workplace (Kostiner 2003).

Third, by mandating specific accommodations, the law provided a direct, tangible way to discuss what adequate accommodations would look like. Many civil rights laws include general proscriptions, such as "equal opportunity," but they rarely mandate specific accommodations. While the exact nature of the breaks and the precise locations of the places provided to the employees for their milk expression are not specified by the law, the presence of these two articulated accommodations opens the opportunity to discuss aspects of those accommodations. How inconvenient can a lactation room be to still be useable? How much variation in length of break can be adjusted? Why do these issues matter?

Finally, the law provided legitimacy. Knowledge of these accommodations being established by law confirmed their importance, as well as the activity they facilitate. These accommodations are not mere recommendations or suggestions, but mandates. Thus, the weight of the law confers importance onto the activity the law protects. By its very presence, the Lactation at Work Law signals that workplace milk expression is so valuable an endeavor that the state and federal governments passed laws to protect and encourage it. While a place to pump and time to do so are both critical to successful milk expression at work, without the legitimacy conferred by the law on the activity, far fewer women would have negotiated adequate accommodations. More crucially, without the legitimacy bestowed by the law, far fewer women would have the temerity to engage in the educational conversations with their supervising managers to discuss their accommodations.

Worker Power: Enough, but Not Too Much

A sizeable minority of the supervising managers at Time Two did not moralize the law. They maintained their earlier focus on managerial goals as a rationale for understanding the importance of compliance. The reason that managerial conversion was not uniform is because educational conversations did not uniformly occur.

Not all lactating workers successfully educated their supervising managers. A substantial minority did not need to have these conversations; others could not have them. These dialogues often were difficult. In many ways, lactating employees' burden of explaining the importance and benefits of breastfeeding to supervising managers is similar to the that of many minority groups (see Herring 2009; Royster 2003).

Not all the lactating employees who attempted to have these educational conversations met with success. For example, this administrative assistant in a physical science department at a large university described her attempts to talk with her supervisor:

> [The department chair] would get upset when I was gone for too long, or if I took a break when he was expecting me to be there, or, maybe not expecting, but wanted me for something. I'd explain how I had to pump. I just had to. Like, once I leaked [unexpressed breast milk] all over myself. I had to wear a sweater over myself for the rest of the day that another girl lent me. He saw that. I'd say, "I have to pump." Sometimes, I'd say something like, "This is something I need to do for [my baby]." And he'd just shake his head, like, "Whatever!"
>
> [W040]

Her manager never assisted in improving her lactation accommodations, and during both interviews he expressed the belief that the accommodations were not a problem for him, and that his employees were doing fine and had no complaints.

Without educational conversations with lactating employees, managers were unlikely to change from Time One to Time Two. These supervising managers continued to articulate managerial needs and assumed that basic compliance would provide adequate accommodation. They did not shift to a broader understanding that included the moral benefit of children's health as the key motivation for compliance.

The importance of sufficient power – such as access to supervising managers to engage in educational conversations – is an ongoing issue regarding workplace disputes (e.g., Abel 1982; Crenshaw 1988; Delgado et al. 1985; Edelman, Erlanger, and Lande 1993; Galanter 1974; Grillo 1991; Hoffmann 2001, 2005; Lazerson 1982; McEwen, Mather, and Maiman 1994; Sarat 1990; Silbey and Sarat 1989). In most workplaces, men hold the majority of management positions (Haveman and Beresford 2012). This was true for the organizations in this study, as well, further exacerbating the difficulty of these employee–manager discussions for some women.

The workers who initiated these critical conversations did so because they needed their managers' support. They lacked the autonomy to make changes in the workplace without their assistance. However, they also had sufficient standing with their supervising managers to make these conversations happen. That is, the employees who had these educational conversations had enough – but not too much – power. In some ways, this makes sense: Workers who easily acquired sufficient accommodations did not have to engage their supervising managers in any discussion in order to gain the space and time they needed. But those workers whose work conditions required accommodations for time or space needed to talk with their supervising managers in order to work out solutions. These talks could evolve into educational conversations.

The irony is that those managers whose lactating employees had no struggle and, therefore, no need to discuss milk expression with them, were less likely to shift from a managerial perspective to moralization of the law. In these organizations, the accommodations stipulated by the law were less likely to be ensconced in a morality-focused social fabric; they are less likely to remain stable once the law changes or managerial goals shift, and less likely to become reified as a part of workplace culture.

Sufficient Autonomy

Some lactating employees did not need to discuss lactation accommodations because their workplace arrangements already were sufficient, such as this professor at a large university with her own office, who could pump privately whenever she wanted:

> I could simply lock my door and pump when I wasn't teaching or in a meeting. I had a little "mini-fridge" in my office already, so I stored everything in there – the milk, the pump, all that, so I wouldn't have to clean it between pumpings. I have no idea if anyone even knew I was pumping. I'm certain my [department] chair didn't know. How would he?
>
> [W053]

Because she had control over her time and adequate privacy, she required little accommodation from her organization, and so rarely spoke with her supervising manager about lactation and the accommodations it necessitated.

Illustrating the power of autonomy in the workplace, this supervisor of city assessors contrasted her previous job with her current one.

> I have a great set-up here. I can pump whenever I want to because, basically, I decide what I do when. When I pump, I just shut my door. I could lock it, but no one would come in without asking permission first anyway. I have it great . . . In my last job, I had to stick to a schedule [of visiting locations throughout the city]. I was told where to go when. I mean, I could have asked for time to pump, but where would I have done it if I were on site? I can't imagine [my former supervising manager]

> would have appreciated me needing to go back to the office frequently to pump my milk. He'd be like [makes a confused and annoyed face]! It just wouldn't have worked [in my earlier job].
>
> [W049]

Similarly, this middle school guidance counselor explained that her flexible schedule and private office allowed her to not have to discuss her milk expression needs with anyone

> It's my own office. And I set the schedule. So if I need to be gone for, say, a dentist appointment, I just block that amount of time in to [scheduling program] and I don't have any students or meetings during that time. [When I was breastfeeding more, a few months ago], I would do the same thing for my [milk pumping] breaks. I just type it into the [scheduling] system.
>
> [W084]

Without the need to request accommodations for pumping, they did not have to wrestle with the legitimacy or appropriateness of their milk expression needs as other women in this study did.

These workers enjoyed sufficient autonomy that was already built into their jobs, their locations, and in their organizational hierarchies, in contrast with substantially disempowered workers who desperately needed the law to assert their rights. Workers with autonomy did not need to request provision of a place to pump, since they had easy access to places already. They did not need to negotiate time away from their usual work activities to pump because their schedules were sufficiently flexible that they could take pumping breaks as needed. Because they had sufficient autonomy of space and time, they did not need to concern themselves with the legitimacy of their request. Indeed, they did not need to make any formal requests, whether deemed legitimate or not, since asserting their rights in this situation was less crucial.

However, without needing to make formal requests, they also did not need to have educational conversations with their supervising managers – conversations that could result in those managers becoming allies. For example, the principal who served as supervising manager of the guidance counselor [W084] was only abstractly aware of the guidance counselor's decision to pump milk. The guidance counselor explained:

> It's a private decision. Each [lactating] employee does that however she thinks is best. [shrugs] [Interviewer asked about lactation accommodation.] We would, of course. We are supposed to [under the law] but no

> one has asked for them. I'm not going to set up some special new place [to express milk] if no one is going to use it ... [later] This [law] is important because it keeps the new moms from missing their babies and helps them come back [to work], instead of deciding to quit to be [at home] with their babies.
>
> [088]

Without the motivation of need, the employee did not engage in any educational conversations with her principal. His attitudes did not shift between Time One, when he expressed managerial goals, and Time Two. He did not work to improve lactation accommodations during that time. Without the benefit of those educational conversations, the supervising manager did not gain any understanding of breastfeeding that would have compelled him to moralize the Lactation at Work Law and embrace the societal goal of children's health.

Insufficient Power

Employees' status within the organization and within society had an impact on their success in facilitating educational conversations. Some lactating employees did not feel sufficiently secure in their organizations and institutional hierarchies to be able to have such discussions at all. In stark contrast to the circumstances of the aforementioned upper-middle class, PhD-educated professor, this department store clerk considered discussing adequate pumping accommodations with her supervising manager, but felt too powerless.

> I really don't talk to him. Ever. He talks *to* [the other clerks and me]. He makes it clear that he is in charge and we are not in charge. That's how it's been since I came here. So, no, I didn't ask him about helping me with [lactation accommodations]. I figured it out for myself. [HR?] No, I didn't talk to anyone.
>
> [W008]

She did not ask her supervising manager for assistance even though she often wasn't able to get away when she needed to pump and she frequently struggled to find a private space when she did get a lactation break. Most likely as a consequence of the infrequent milk expression at work, her milk supply plummeted soon after she began working. She stopped breastfeeding entirely after three months.

This manufacturing industry office worker described how little control she had over her time and her physical space.

> At first, I would pump in the back room, but then [my manager] or maybe his manager decided that that room needed to be available for other things. So then I went downstairs to the break room, but that took more time to get there, and I still had to set up [the pumping apparatus], and so what I ended up doing was I had to clock out when I left to pump and then clock back in again. [Interviewer: How did clocking out and back in affect your pay?] Well, it cut into my pay obviously, but I couldn't do it during just my break time. It's only 15 minutes. I just couldn't. [Interviewer: Did you explain that to your manager?] Did I explain it? No. How could I? What was I supposed to say?
>
> [W066]

Despite facing extreme barriers to workplace lactation, these women felt unable to discuss the difficulty with their supervising managers, much less educate them about the benefits of breast milk or share their values that made them want to commit to pumping at work.

Indeed, at Time Two, the supervising manager of Interviewee #W066, the office worker, was unchanged. She said at Time Two:

> [Supervising managers] were all told about the [change in the law]. It's important because it helps [lactating employees] transition back from their maternity leave. It makes it easier on them.
>
> [099]

She did not expand or improve the lactation accommodations beyond what had already been available, nor did she moralize the law to embrace a focus on children's health.

These lactating workers were unable to engage in educational conversations with their supervising managers because they lacked sufficient power within the organization. They existed at the bottom of organizations' hierarchies and had little access to supervising managers, such as Interviewee #W008, a store clerk. Without being able to easily talk with a supervising manager, educational conversations become not only less convenient, but also difficult to have at all. Another worker in this situation was Interviewee #W066, a lower-tier office worker, who could talk with her manager, but was not able to request improved accommodations for her milk expression. Without those educational conversations, these workers' supervising managers did not moralize the law by shifting to children's health motivations, nor did they improve accommodations to better facilitate workers' milk expression.

Ideal Worker Norm

In some cases, women did not engage in educational conversations because of their lack of organizational power, as just illustrated, while other women held back from initiating conversations because the activity of milk expression lacked sufficient legitimacy to counter pressure to appear focused exclusively on work. These women feared violating the Ideal Worker Norm, a conception that the perfect worker always puts the job first. Because they felt that lactation accommodations could separate them from other workers, they feared that requesting accommodations would harm their reputations. For example, this physical therapist at a large hospital thought asking for accommodations would harm her reputation as a "dependable" employee:

> It's important for people to respect you, to know that you work hard. [Interviewer: People like who?] Your managers, your co-workers. They depend on you. They need to be able to depend on you. To know that they can depend on you. And if you have to go away all the time [to express milk], then – even if you could still be there for them, still do the work – if they think you can't because you've gone away, then they think they won't be able to depend on you.
>
> [W043]

She worried that she would be perceived as unreliable if she left her work area regularly to express breast milk, so she tried to manage expressing only during her lunch break, which quickly resulted in painful mastitis, and, eventually, diminished her milk supply.

Even human resource personnel sometimes felt compelled to forego their own lactation needs in order to maintain an ideal-worker image. Because milk expression lacked sufficient legitimacy at her workplace, this worker did not avail herself of adequate time and space for pumping milk, and so she regularly skipped designated pumping times.

> I know that my struggles with being able to pump, and not pumping as long as I originally intended had nothing to do with the accommodations. It was everything to do with my workload. Everything to do with just being, you know, an active member of the workforce. It wasn't that I wasn't allowed; it wasn't that I wasn't encouraged. I just didn't. My daily routine did not allow me to step away at the appropriate times. The longer I came back to work, the less I got an opportunity to pump, but of course, now I'm not at all.
>
> [Yet] it's more than just the employer responsibility. [Not going to pump] was just my own psyche of wanting to be, right up there with the

> guys in terms of being an active, valued member of our company . . . I tried to do it three times a day. But that quickly became twice a day, which then became once a day. Keeping the supply up [laughs] and keeping that kind of regular schedule . . . But again, the nature of my work is: Any minute somebody pops in and the world is ending. And I've gotta [laughs] help them, and then all of a sudden, okay, I've missed that 10 o'clock [pumping] time, and now it's lunch time, you know?
>
> So I think it's just that, and again this is a personal thing not a company policy or anything, just trying to really maintain that balance. I had a very kind of idyllic situation, where I was supported by my colleagues and the work policy.
>
> [036]

Her description underlines how legitimacy is a critical third requirement for successful workplace milk expression, as I have discussed elsewhere. This woman had the space, and she could have taken the time, but milk expression always came second to her other workplace tasks. While, structurally, this workplace provided accommodations, a workplace culture that demands that this lactating worker "be right up there with the guys" does not recognize individual employee needs and devalues those accommodations. By extension, it also devalues the people who would avail themselves of those accommodations. The culture of her workplace made stopping to express milk anathema to being a good worker.

The experience of a woman who worked the supply room at a large hospital illustrates the pervasive power of the Ideal Worker mythology.

> [My supervising manager] was very supportive. I could have taken breaks whenever I needed them, but there just wasn't time. I mean, I could have taken the time, but I didn't want to make a fuss, didn't want to seem like the kind of person . . . who couldn't just get on with her job.
>
> [W037]

Her concern that making use of available structural accommodation would be seen as "mak[ing] a fuss" demonstrates how workplace lactation lacked legitimacy in the culture of the organization.

Similarly, the following host at a large restaurant chain worried that asking for what she needed to successfully express milk would make her seem less dedicated to her work, or that she was unable to do her job without help.

> I tried [to successfully express milk] without, you know, everyone knowing. I'd find spaces here and there, but I didn't want to ask for a

> [designated space] . . . So sometimes it would be a bathroom. Once in a while, I'd even go to my car [laughs]. I just didn't want people to know. I didn't want to stand out. I didn't want to be that guy who always needed something.
>
> [W060]

These women's concerns about not wanting to stand out or seem to be doing less for their jobs than co-workers, illustrate how, despite needing accommodations, they would not violate the expectation of the Ideal Worker norm. This demonstrates how, even when the organization provided the structure to enable the women to express milk, the prevailing culture may have prevented lactating employees from taking advantage of those accommodations.

By resisting asking for necessary accommodations, not only did they forego having successful milk-expression support, but they also missed the opportunity to discuss lactation-related issues with their supervising managers. This was true for the supervising manager of Interviewee #W043, the first worker quoted in this section. At Time Two, he said:

> It lets those women who are [lactating] moms make milk for their babies. It's not a problem. It hasn't been an issue at all. Any woman who wants can just take their break and [express milk]. We provide a fridge here, and they can use that, just like I would for my lunch. We haven't had any problems.
>
> [116]

As he had at Time One, at Time Two he only articulated managerial goals and had not taken any steps make much-needed lactation breaks possible for this employee. As with the women who could not have the educational conversations, these women, too, lost out on the opportunity to enable their supervising managers to moralize compliance with the law and improve their lactation accommodations.

HAS THIS PRODUCED A SUCCESSFUL LAW?

Reification of Lactation at Work

Over time, the Lactation at Work Law may fade in its importance. Pumping at work may become as unremarkable as employee bathroom breaks. Absorbing lactation norms into workplace culture will create more effective and lasting compliance with the law than legal coercion or managerialization. This normative shift described in this chapter might reify these accommodations within the organizational culture so that challenging them is no longer even considered.

By embracing a moral understanding of health, these Morality-Motivated Advocates might heighten the law's symbolic importance. This echoes Edelman's finding that certain ways of demonstrating legal compliance dominate organizational fields because "civil rights law interacts with public support for civil rights to produce a normative environment in which fair treatment of employees becomes increasingly valued and racial or gender disparities may be challenged as violations of that value" (Edelman 2005: 343). In this vein, the ideals of health may lead to a normative environment in which organizations have a moral duty to support lactating employees – not simply as an employee right, but as a duty to the health of those outside the organization (e.g., the employee's child and children in society generally). In other words, the Morality-Motivated Advocates contribute to the development of a health morality within the organization that may strengthen, rather than diminish, the law's function as a form of rights protection.

IMPLICATIONS OF CHILDREN-FOCUSED RHETORIC

In their educational conversations with their supervising managers, the lactating workers strove to explain the importance of lactation accommodations and their commitment to breastfeeding. They drew on a range of concepts – legal rights, benefits to the organization, benefits to their own health, and benefits to their children's health. The collection of interviews discussed throughout this book provides examples of all of these.

Yet, it was the increased awareness about the benefits of breastfeeding to children's health that appears to have had the greatest impact in creating new allies who rallied for improved lactation accommodations in comparing Time One and Time Two interviews. A children's health focus indicated that the other issues surrounding lactation accommodation could be de-emphasized by those supervising managers. Moralization of the law elevates children's health above maternal health, workers' rights, and managerial goals, arguing for accommodations even when they reduce productivity or profit, for example.

Notably, the Lactation at Work Law confers a right to the employee, not her child; yet, the fact that the lactating worker is expressing milk for someone else makes the accommodation request more powerful. Rhetorically, the children's health narrative makes this labor right feel like a different kind of right. The intuitive appeal – and the danger – of this discursive connotation is the cultural resonance about maternal care and women's roles. It creates a fictional right for the infant, and, although it is a powerful fiction, it lacks any grounding in law.

Additionally, a children's health focus enables managers to exacerbate the power imbalance between workers and management by allowing the organization to disregard other accommodations workers may need that are unrelated to lactation. That is, by focusing on the children's benefit, and by extension the mothers' needs, management could ignore broader conceptualizations of workers' needs that could imply that other accommodations might also be legitimate (Elliott and Bowen 2018). If the legitimacy of the health needs of lactating employees is diminished, their female bodily presence is removed from the discussion (Budig and England 2001; Fraser 2016; Williams 2000). Thus, by focusing on children's needs rather than workers' rights, manager-allies can articulate a motivation for greater accommodation that minimally challenges the workplace hierarchy.

However, less focus on the lactating workers' rights removes certain hurdles that other accommodation seekers wrestle with. Employees who request accommodations for other needs – such as disability modifications – usually engage rights talk as a main verbal strategy. Yet, the idea of rights may be stigmatized, because they have negative associations with intrusive government, oppressed minority groups, or causes that are unattractive to the rights holder herself (Albiston 2010; Barnes and Burke 2012; Chua and Engel 2019; Engel and Munger 2003; O'Brien 2005).

Moreover, rights talk demands the peculiar linguistic and emotional gymnastics of asserting difference in order to demand equitable treatment and declaring oneself as injured or victimized if insufficiently accommodated (Bumiller 1988; Engel and Munger 2003). Because the moralization of the law reframed whose rights were being asserted – now, the rights of the child – lactating employees could demand accommodations without actually having to claim rights for themselves, avoiding the difficulties faced by other groups seeking accommodation. Supervising managers' responsiveness to children's health issues allowed the lactating employees to avoid labeling themselves as outsiders or victims because their moralization of the law reframed the lactation accommodations from a labor-rights issue to one of maternal care and children's health.

The data themselves, however, are unclear regarding to what extent this focus on children's health indicates managers gravitating toward this mindset or whether managers are simply reflecting the viewpoints of their lactating employees. Understandably, very few women were able to recreate exactly what they said to their supervising managers in each interaction, and, when they raised multiple motivations, they might not recall which they most compellingly emphasized. This means we cannot know precisely what they said to managers, and, even more so, we cannot know what was *not* said. For example, we do not know if few, all, or some of the educational conversations included discussions of benefits beyond those of children's health, such as maternal physical and mental health, workplace accessibility, work life quality, or gender equality – or how forcefully each topic was presented during these educational conversations.

It is, therefore, possible that the women, themselves, emphasized children's health benefits more than the benefits to themselves, their rights, or other motivations. This would not be surprising, given that women tend to prioritize their children's needs over their own (see Apple 2006;Czarnecki 2015) and because US society is dominated by a capitalist hegemony with a lack of cultural legitimacy of workers' rights (Edelman 2016; Gramsci 1971; Roscigno and Wilson 2014). It also is possible that, even if their own health benefits or workplace rights were foremost in their minds, they might have downplayed those and emphasized the children's health benefits in either a deliberate or implied acceptance of the societal norm of women putting their children's well-being before their own (see Correll, Benard, and Paik 2007; Shdaimah and Palley 2010).

This uncertainty around the exact content of the educational conversations does not diminish the significance of the supervising managers' shift to moralization of the law. Previously, human resource personnel had presented to them legal and managerial rationales for the lactation accommodations – employee morale and mental health, workplace accessibility, equality-focused and nondiscriminatory policies. Indeed, during their first interviews, the supervising managers had mentioned many of these rationales.

The outcome of the educational conversations is what is most important: These supervising managers shifted their understanding of workplace lactation to include a morality focus based on children's health. This morality rhetoric broadens the target of the law, but also alters the original motivation. That the managers' transformation centered on reframing legally mandated accommodations in terms of arguments about children's health demonstrates the power of those educational conversations

The Conservative Bent of a Children's Health Focus

While the children's health focus serves as a counterbalance to the managerial norms, it can obscure the health concerns and the rights of the lactating workers. Women's ability to make claims on the organization based on their own needs and rights disappear amid consideration of children's health.

Since the goal of the Lactation at Work Law is to guarantee sufficiently effective lactation accommodations and, as a result, improved working conditions for lactating workers, an exploration of exactly *why* organizations create substantive accommodations might not seem important. In the immediate sense, and for the individual women whose ability to express milk at work had been threatened, understanding exactly why the accommodations are available might not seem critical. However, in the longer run, a greater understanding is essential for anyone concerned about policy, improved gender parity, and workplace equality.

If supervising managers are creating accommodations only for the bottom line – that is, for managerial goals – then this is a more precarious type of support. How actions affect an organization's bottom line can change, and, when that happens, necessary accommodations could disappear. Accommodations made for moral reasons are more stable. Additionally, morality-based motivations, like children's health, may be particularly critical when accommodations cannot align with managerial logic, such as pausing an entire work group or assembly line for a member's lactation break.

While moralization of the law through a focus on children's health goals might more deeply engrain and, over time, reify progressive organizational changes, this could have macro-political effects that are very regressive. Certainly initially, moralization of the law by importing concerns into the organization's culture will counterbalance the capitalist, profit focus of managerial norms. In the case of the Lactation at Work Law, the moral argument of children's health becomes this counterbalance – a counterbalance sufficiently powerful to make furthering children's health so important that it warranted sidelining organizational goals, such as efficiency.

Yet, not all morality-based counterbalances are necessarily good for maternal employment. Although the goals of the law are progressive – greater workplace equality for women, facilitation of home–work harmony, and support for employed mothers – the shift to prioritizing children's health is also a shift away from these lactating employees' rights as workers and as women. By amplifying children's health concerns, law-focused rights and equality concerns might disappear entirely from the discussion.

Extolling concern for children as articulated motivations to further women's rights, employment safety, or human rights issues more generally is not unprecedented. Concern for children and for women's mothering duties has been used to further women's education (e.g., Moehling and Thomasson 2012), suffrage (e.g., Morris 2017), government assistance (e.g., Lemaitre and Sandvik 2015), and other issues. Yet while this children-centered rhetoric could expand lactating employees' accommodations in the workplace – which would have the effect of furthering women's access to paid employment and of supporting work/family dual commitments, both arguably feminist goals – it also may entrench conservative gender roles and perpetuate a view of women's first duty as being to their families. Thus, concern for women's health or their employment rights may get lost and, over time, may result in regressive politics pushing women out of the workplace.

A natural progression of this children's health focus could mean that a law intended to help women stay in the workforce when they have children could become the beginning of women being forced out of paid employment because the health of the baby would take priority over the mother's employment. A children's health narrative could argue that if pumped milk is better than formula, then breastfed milk is better than pumped milk; and if occasional access to the mother's body while she is at work, as mediated by a bottle, is beneficial for the child, then constant and unmediated access to the mother's body – from her remaining at home with the child – would be even more valuable.

This children's health focus of managers may create better work environments for the lactating workers, but by diminishing awareness of maternal needs and equal rights it raises concerns that the primary goals of the law might fade. Thus, while this moralization of the law may further, and even entrench, the legislative goals of facilitating lactating workers' employment in the more immediate, its ultimate affect may be to reduce mothers' employment by forcing them back into their homes for the benefit of their children's health. This conservative view of gender roles may elevate children's health above the needs of mothers, and above the rights of those lactating workers.

The danger is that the Lactation at Work Law becomes moralized in terms of children's health, and no longer addresses workers' rights or women's rights. This interpretation is another shift away from a workers' rights framework – just as managerialization moved from workers' rights to managerial goals. In this case, the shift is immediately helpful for women – it helps meet their needs to balance work and motherhood and solidifies the law and its effectiveness – but, like managerialization, it places other concerns before workers' rights. Thus, while it helps lactating workers express milk at work, it does not further workers' rights more broadly.

In this way, if we ask, "Was the Lactation at Work Law successful?" the answer might be "yes," but a deeper assessment would reveal more nuance. The law did succeed in helping women assert a right to workplace milk expression. It asserts a particular right (although not articulated as a right) and decenters managerial goals somewhat. But if we ask "Did the law succeed as a workers' rights law? Did it add to workers' power over their own working conditions?" – that answer is a bit more complex. Workers now can assert this one right, but more broadly, what started as a workers' rights law has been reframed either in managerial terms or in public health terms. The health rhetoric downplays workers' rights as a legitimate way of understanding the law. The considerably weak discourse currently in the United States regarding workers' rights makes claiming a right without "being a burden" quite difficult, and so rights claiming often requires some other discourse in order to have deeper legitimacy (see Albiston 2005; Chua and Engel 2019; Hoffmann 2009; Trautner, Hatton, and Smith 2013). In the case of workplace milk expression rights, the other discourse is that of public health.

Arguably, this is hegemony in action: Capitalism grants small wins like this, but only in terms that keep its structures in place (Gramsci 1971). This translation of the law into public health goals allows the law to succeed at its immediate goal of helping women express milk at work, but fails at the separate goal of helping workers secure rights and generally gain cultural legitimacy. The "workers' rights" frame is still not strong enough to survive the process of institutionalization in a capitalist society.

CHAPTER SEVEN

CONCLUSION

The successful accommodations discussed in this study – creating effective policies and procedures that coexist with managerial goals, moralizing the law to focus on health concerns, and embracing the health goals immediately after a law was enacted – offer the possibility of positive workplace improvements. Key social policies were furthered by combining the symbolic, instrumental, and educative powers of the law with the force of evolving societal norms. The success of the Lactation at Work Law provides important contributions to the scholarship on how law and compliance work while also providing insight on how organizational structure and culture affect perceptions of possible accommodations.

A CONTINUUM OF COMPLIANCE

What interpretive frames do organizations use to legitimate compliance, and how do those frames affect the law's success, specifically, and workers' rights, more generally? Although the law is but one factor in how organizations create meaning and determine compliance, it is a vital component. This book explores how individuals can be critical of how the law and subsequent policies roll out in an organization while also demonstrating how the law structures those experiences. The law provides the context for individuals to generate change within the organizations, such as facilitating key educational conversations between employees and managers, or providing leverage for allies to push for accommodations beyond those specified by law.

Sometimes, new lactation-at-work policies were mostly symbolic, producing little real change. Other times, new organizational policies created substantive changes that directly improved the situations for the lactating employees. Sometimes the application of these policies evolved, with management understanding compliance first through a legal frame and then through managerialization. Some supervising managers adjusted accommodations over time as their understanding of their lactating workers' experiences and values grew.

For the purposes of discussion, this book presents the various levels of compliance as somewhat discrete; in actual practice, they represent more of a continuum of compliance and legitimacy. At the far end would be absolutely zero compliance, where management simply refuses any accommodation whatsoever; this is only theoretical as none such were found in this study. The next level is formal compliance where in practice the accommodations are so purely symbolic and ineffective that large numbers of employees face the choice between breastfeeding and keeping their jobs. Another step along the continuum sees lactating employees forced to choose between breastfeeding and sacrificing something, such as part of their pay, if they must clock out in order to have enough time to express milk. Further along this continuum are lactating employees who are able to express milk at work without substantial sacrifices, but who need to do some relational work to gain accommodations that are sufficient, such as negotiating with a supervisor or co-workers. The furthest end of the spectrum is full compliance, where lactating employees are fully supported in their need to express milk in the workplace. Here, milk-pumping breaks have become reified into the workplace culture, as unremarkable as smoking breaks; accommodations for breastfeeding present negligible social stigma, much like an employee with a broken leg whose ambulatory challenges must be addressed.

These chapters demonstrate the importance of legitimacy for successful workplace milk expression. Women need private spaces to pump milk and adequate time to do so, but the practice of milk expression must also have legitimacy. For example, even if a lactating employee had access to private space and sufficient break time, her situation may be untenable if her co-workers or supervisor sabotage her efforts, harass her for using that time or space, or demean the activity. The law not only demands the space and time, but also provides the legitimacy; its very presence implies that pumping breast milk is a legitimate workplace activity. While some co-workers and supervisors might initially be uncomfortable with workplace milk expression, conversations with lactating employees have been proven to change those reactions – conversations that the lactating employees can have under the color of law that they could not necessarily otherwise have.

Chapter 2 provides context for the subsequent chapters. Societal changes, such as enabling more mothers to maintain full-time employment, and technological changes, such as electric breast pumps, significantly changed the world in which the Lactation at Work Law approaches accommodations. Additionally, the political and legal terrain from which the Lactation at Work Law emerged is unlike earlier laws. Preceded by the Civil Rights Act of 1964 by several decades, and by the Americans with Disabilities Act by almost twenty years, the Lactation at Work Law is enacted in workplaces where employee accommodations are not novel and diversity of experience is increasingly appreciated.

Yet, as a US law, the Lactation at Work Law still runs up against short maternity leaves, scarcity of quality childcare, and infrequent and insufficient worksite family resources. In countries with longer maternity leave policies, accommodations for lactation at work are less necessary because lactating workers have less need to express milk if they return to their jobs after twelve months, rather than six weeks. Workplace milk-expression accommodations also would be less critical in countries with cultures of on-site childcare or sufficiently robust childcare options that allow for nursing children on-site. Rather than expressing milk alone, nursing children at midday is a viable midday option for many lactating workers. Despite these obstacles, in the United States, the Lactation at Work Law was hailed as protecting important rights for women workers and mandating necessary accommodations.

Chapter 3 depicts a less-than-rosy story. This chapter describes the more difficult worksites for lactating employees, dominated by companies that resist compliance by providing mere symbolic compliance. Organizations warped the justice-focused objectives of the law into management goals, resulting in accommodations that were often ineffective. This story is familiar in law-and-society research – more so than the more promising findings of subsequent chapters. In some ways, these data are not surprising. However, it is noteworthy that this is not the dominant story of this book. Rather, only a minority of the organizations included in this study addressed the law with only symbolic compliance.

Chapter 4 moves from the struggles of the previous chapter to examining how human resource managers engaged in managerialization to create not just symbolic compliance but successful accommodations. Human resource personnel face multiple challenges: They must legitimize their place within the organization to both top management and supervising managers while also maintaining their legitimacy within their field. Human resource leaders establish the legitimacy of their position by confirming the need for human resource personnel within the organization through their usefulness in orchestrating legal compliance. On the other hand, they must move the supervising managers to comply with the law, despite various inconveniences. As Chapter 3 shows, a key hurdle is the existence of resistant managers who defy accommodating lactation needs.

Therefore, the human resource personnel translate compliance with the Lactation at Work Law into a managerial frame and communicate this frame to managers. The success of this frame is evident in how their supervising managers echo these management-focused rationales – such as turnover, absenteeism, and morale – and further the managerialization.

This chapter also shows how managerialization is successful, itself, in creating real, effective changes within the organizations. Successful examples of employee accommodations gained through managerialization are seldom found in law-and-society research. This is an important contribution to the scholarly literature. The dimensions of managerialization that this study found are different from much of the equal opportunity literature. In addition to this study's more obvious contributions to the socio-legal literature, this project also sheds light on what managerialization looks like outside of the equal opportunity office, the usual focus of such studies. Chapter 4 shows what compliance looks like where managerialization is not simply symbolic, but substantive. This means that, in contrast to earlier studies, managerialization can be viewed with optimism because it has resulted in effective accommodation in some places.

Lactating employees appreciate the managerial frame, but the frame is not always enough to enable them to successfully rally for better accommodations. Managerialization creates successful lactation accommodations most effectively in those organizations where lactation needs were more easily accommodated due to preexisting factors, for example, where relaxed culture around flexible time allows for lactation breaks of adequate lengths or workplace structures provide most workers with many individual offices, making private space easily accessible (and when time and space are constrained, particularly when the practice of workplace milk expression lacks sufficient legitimacy, managerialization creates only symbolic compliance, as seen in Chapter 3).

Yet, even when managerialization produces substantive accommodations, a fully lactation-friendly workplace might require more than this. Chapters 5 and 6 demonstrate that accommodations are successful when the managerial response goes beyond mere compliance.

Chapter 5 focuses on inhabited institutionalism, looking beneath the field-level effects that most law-and-organization scholarship studies. This chapter shows how the law provides leverage for management to create change through institutional politics within organizations, even moving their organization's lactation accommodations beyond basic compliance with the law. Even before the Lactation at Work Law was passed, some organizations had human resource personnel and supervising managers who were already supportive of lactating employees' efforts to express milk at work. Before the law, however, they encountered resistance to lactation accommodations within their organizations. The law provides them with the instrument they need to persuade higher management to allocate resources for these accommodations.

The law not only provides this tool, however, it also – even more importantly – confers legitimacy on these accommodations and the practice of employee milk expression. Until the law was passed, these Allies Already had empathy and solidarity with their lactating employees: They identified with their situation due to their social proximity to breastfeeding and milk expression, and they had a sense of shared interests, a solidarity, around breastfeeding and milk expression that compelled them to take greater responsibility for successful lactation accommodations. While solidarity is different from empathy – the former is more about "I have your back," while the latter is more akin to "I get it; I know what you need" – together they motivated these allies to become "institutional entrepreneurs" (DiMaggio 1988) and utilize the law to champion the needs of lactating employees.

Chapter 6 shows how the law not only provides more leverage to lactating employees and allies, but also creates opportunities for critical educational conversations between lactating employees and their supervising managers. In this way, the law is changing the political dynamic. As lactating employees discussed why they needed certain accommodations and explained their decisions to nurse and express breast milk, their supervising managers listened and shifted their understanding of those activities. They moved from exclusively managerializing the law to adding a morality framework as motivation for legal compliance with the lactation accommodations.

This change is facilitated by educational conversations between the lactating employees and their supervising managers; communicating greater understanding about the need for milk expression, but also instilling values about breastfeeding. In several ways, the Lactation at Work Law enables these educational conversations to happen. First, by providing some accommodation, the law enables some women who would have quit their jobs to stay home and nurse to remain in their jobs, and it encourages those women who would have never attempted combining full employment with nursing and milk expression to do so; otherwise, these women would be sharing their stories with their supervising managers. Second, the presence of the law provides legitimation to milk expression at work; it communicates that this activity is sufficiently important to warrant legal protection. Third, the law provides a vocabulary for beginning the educational conversations; by mandating specific accommodations (non-bathroom private space, break time, etc.), the law helps women begin those conversations by addressing their needs and the corresponding accommodations. The law opens up space for those educational conversations, and those conversations are important for meaningful compliance so that, for example, a supervising manager understands why a room designated for milk expression across campus meets the legal requirements but was insufficient.

HIERARCHICAL AND SOCIOECONOMIC POWER

How the law and the lactation accommodations framed the lactating employees' milk-expression experiences varies by the power and status the employee possesses. For example, some of the lactating workers quoted in this study who had the most successful milk-expression experiences were university professors. These women had substantial control over almost all of their time and usually had private, locking offices. Moreover, they also enjoyed the privilege of working from home regularly if they wished. This ample control over their space and time, with little oversight, meant they could pump milk easily and seldom referenced the Lactation at Work law.

Others at their same institutions had very different experiences. Office workers, laboratory assistants, and graduate students in this study were much more likely to mention the Lactation at Work law. They rarely had private offices. They generally had less control over their time throughout the day. Not surprisingly, they struggled more with pumping milk. Conversely, some advantages or disadvantages transcend industry and organization.

While not perfect correlation, the relationship between lactating employees' socioeconomic status and their lactation accommodations should be noted. As discussed in Chapter 3, employees' class initially affects what accommodations they need, while also affecting how they might be able to negotiate better, more effective accommodations. The jobs of lower socioeconomic status employees are less likely to include private offices and control over schedules. Without such benefits, those lactating employees' managers need to support the legitimacy of their lactating needs by providing sufficient break time and accessible private pumping places.

In addition to having greater need for the accommodations mandated by the law, low-status workers may have more challenges in securing better accommodations when the initial provisions are inadequate or when once-adequate accommodations change. Because of their unequal class status in relation to their supervising managers and to human resource personnel, these working-class employees might not be able to easily raise issues informally or to formally invoke the law. Critically, working-class employees may also not be sufficiently financially secure to opt to quit their jobs if the accommodations prove insufficient.

In contrast, employees with higher socioeconomic status may enjoy more of a peer relationship with similarly higher-status supervising managers and human resource personnel (and may even be management themselves). Without that class chasm, these lactating employees would be better able to mobilize their legal rights and become more successful at resolving issues informally. Moreover, if their organizations do not support their milk-expression needs, they have greater financial stability for leaving their jobs and the labor force entirely.

Nevertheless, the relationship between socioeconomic status and lactation resources is not determinative. Different occupations and positions within organizations are associated with various class statuses. For example, working-class assembly line workers do not have private offices, but neither do middle-class bank branch managers. Moreover, an assembly-line worker might be part of a strong pro-union shop and feel comfortable raising a formal grievance or approaching management with concerns, while the bank manager might feel social pressure to be constantly accessible to her employees such that she could rarely step away long enough to pump milk.

Many of the hurdles for lactating workers in the United States might not exist for similarly situated workers in other countries. Structurally, lactating employees experience both the workplace and the family differently in the United States. In countries with longer maternity or parental leaves, workplace lactation accommodations are less critical. When lactating employees have the option of remaining home for many months, often up to a year, their milk expression needs will be minimal compared to those employees who return after only six weeks. The lactating employee at twelve months post-birth most likely will only need to pump milk once during the work day, achievable during a lunch hour, and will have a more established milk supply, less likely harmed by an occasional missed lactation break. Employees in non-US workplaces may also have greater familiarity and comfort with bringing workplace problems to management.

Culturally, non-US countries have more relaxed relationships with issues around lactation. Public breastfeeding, nursing older children, and multigenerational and non-gendered discussion of breastfeeding in other cultures makes lactation issues less stigmatized and more easily addressed. Additionally, in the United States, the Ideal Worker model is often based on stereotypes of single men – people without family demands who focus on their jobs exclusively (Kelly et al. 2010). Other countries, however, embrace a broader view of work–family issues that assumes multiple demands for workers' time and attention.

WHY THE LAW MATTERS

This study demonstrates multiple pathways to compliance with the law. At times the threat of the law – however theoretical – was the impetus needed to create legally acceptable accommodations. More often, the educative or expressive powers of the law reinterpret the law's goals into other agendas, such as through managerialization or moralizing of the law. These were new mechanisms for compliance that legitimized the law's mandate, presenting compliance through other frames.

The law provides a context for people who wish to pursue lactation accommodations to execute and implement those organizational changes. The law creates leverage for lactating employees and the allies in Chapter 5 to enforce their beliefs. But the law also actually produces converts, and that's how the law is changing the political dynamic. The law provides the social space for the conversations between those lactating employees and their supervising managers, as in Chapter 6, to get to that point, as well.

A narrative of sharing stories – lactating workers talking about why they are pumping milk at work – causes a shift in the orientation of some supervising managers to the law and its accommodations. The law facilitates that storytelling, first by retaining women who would have dropped out of the workplace in order to nurse so they could tell their stories, and then by legitimating workplace milk expression and providing a vocabulary for discussing it so that discussion of the necessary accommodation happens, even if a supervising manager is a bit reluctant or a lactating employee is a bit shy.

Both the Allies Already of Chapter 5 and the Morality-Motivated Advocates of Chapter 6 are important supporters. Chapter 5's Allies Already are supporters at Time One, and Chapter 6's Morality-Motivated Advocates are Time Two supporters. While this study draws on rich data about the path of the Chapter 6 Morality-Motivated Advocates, similar knowledge is not available regarding the path for the Allies Already. Particularly in Chapter 6, the data show how the law operates politically within the organization. While legal change causes normative change, on the ground, change happens because of organizational politics.

Thus, the law brings about the three things lactating employees need: (1) space to pump, (2) time to do so, and (3) legitimacy for the act of milk expression at work. The law's very presence validates the employees' milk expression, compelling greater acceptance by managers as well as co-workers – and lactating employees can have educational conversations with those who are insufficiently accepting, conversations they would not necessarily have otherwise.

WHY WAS THE LACTATION AT WORK LAW SO SUCCESSFUL?

More so than other similar laws, the Lactation at Work Law was successful in creating effective change within organizations. Not only does this study show managerialization of law working, at times, to create substantive compliance with effective accommodations, but, sometimes when managerialization was insufficient – or when it did not produce as fully lactation-supportive workplace environment as would benefit employees – the law facilitated other mechanisms to further the lactation accommodations. By creating space for educational conversations between lactating employees and supervising managers, or providing leverage for lactation allies in management, the law provided vital contexts within the organization that resulted in effective social changes.

Specifics of the Lactation at Work Law

Such successful compliance is unusual in the breadth of law-and-society and law-and-organizations scholarship. While most scholarship in these areas finds that civil rights laws improve the workplace very little, the present study finds substantial improvement. What makes the Lactation at Work Law so effective? This may be an especially felicitous case for examining substantive compliance, for several reasons.

First, the Lactation at Work Law's mandate is sufficiently specific that compliance or noncompliance is fairly clear. Unlike other civil rights laws with vague dictates, such as equal employment opportunities, the requirements, such as a private room that is not a lavatory, are quite clear. This relative clarity and concreteness of the types of accommodations the law requires make the adequacy of compliance an easy discussion – even if individuals disagree on the adequacy, the contributing factors and the parameters of the accommodations are explicit.

Second, the concrete nature of the accommodation requirements makes the construction of oppositional rights' frames simpler than is the case with other, more vague civil rights laws. Lactating employees or their advocates can more easily reframe what is required in a way that makes the accommodations possible, in contrast with advocates supporting rights from less specific laws. Thus, these rights holders and their advocates can avoid framing necessary accommodations as "special preference" with the resistance and possible backlash other laws have experienced.

Third, organizations' "business logic" will calculate costs and benefits according to their perceptions of the legal requirements. The effects-orientation of the Lactation at Work Law makes assessment of the accommodations – whether internally by the organization or externally by administrative agencies or courts – more straightforward than for other laws.

Fourth, the Lactation at Work Law facilitates on-the-job interactions and negotiations about accommodations as opportunities for educational conversations between lactating employees and supervising managers. The law facilitates these conversations by requiring sufficiently concrete accommodations so that discussion of those accommodations' adequacy can become a springboard for conversations. Thus, although some lactating employees still did the work to engage in the educational conversations, the law does not leave the entire onus on the employees. Other civil rights laws might not have the effect of facilitating these direct conversations if the accommodations are more abstract and less articulated; in those cases, educational conversations might only occur if affected workers deliberately undertake such exchanges, which might require greater employee assertiveness.

The causal story here is that legal change causes normative change, but on the ground this happens through organizational politics (see Pedriana and Stryker 2017; Stryker 2007). In practice, human resource personnel do not have to be educated themselves. Their job is to focus on those in management who are resistant. They must ensure that managers do what needs to be done even when managers are reluctant.

However, when managers do enact accommodations, employees convince some of those supervising managers to think about lactation differently. Thus, human resource personnel make managers create the accommodations but do not actually interact with the employees themselves. The law empowers employees, then, to discuss the accommodations with supervising managers, and that interaction changes some of those managers' attitudes. Human resource personnel do not change because they are otherwise occupied trying to convince resistant management to comply. They never actually hear employees' lactation stories.

Minimized Negative Stigma

Much previous research on civil rights has found that claiming one's rights can carry a negative stigma. That is, to qualify as a claimant, one must identify as different from others who do not need the law's protection, and then make a claim to join the group that includes people who have not been mistreated. In this way, the extant scholarship has demonstrated that invoking one's rights involves putting oneself forward as different and mistreated, but asserting one's sameness with the well-treated group. This duality – sameness yet victimhood – can attach a stigma to rights mobilization that inhibits employees from accessing workplace accommodations to which they are entitled (see Bumiller 1988; Engel and Munger 2003).

In the case of the Lactation at Work Law, this was less of an issue for two reasons: First, advocates and allies were willing to step forward to help workers secure lactation accommodations. This meant that the rights holders, the lactating employees, were not the only voice in their organizations to demand these accommodations.

Second, accommodation for workplace milk expression can also be framed as a right for the employees' children. In this way, even when the official rights holder, the woman, requests accommodation, she is able to frame it as fighting for the benefit of another, not for herself alone. In this way, workplace lactation rights and the subsequent accommodations could be pursued without the stigma that other studies have identified with rights mobilization. The lactating employee is able to claim lactation accommodations without feeling the stigma other employees feel when they are claiming rights. Lactating workers have no need to embrace a frame as being excluded, worry about perceptions of selfishness, or wrestle with victimhood status. Instead, the Lactation at Work Law enables very different kinds of rights talk – the rights of the child, not the rights of the employee herself. From this perspective, the legal subject is not any one individual, but the subject might be a relational figure. To distinguish between workers' rights, mothers' rights, parents' rights, and community rights might create various false binaries. A more accurate understanding might be to conceptualize the law and the rights holder more as a relational self, with the law's benefits extending beyond the official rights holder.

THE LACTATION AT WORK LAW AND THE ADA

The Lactation at Work Law appears to be more successful than other civil rights laws, including the Americans with Disabilities Act (ADA). While these two laws are somewhat similar, their content and, crucially, their historic sequence are quite different. When the ADA was introduced, business resistance was significant. The ADA was so contentious, in part, because it was the first time employers were told they must do more than avoid discriminating as an abstract goal; instead, the ADA demanded that organizations had to accommodate different levels of ability.

Thus, the ADA broke new ground, clearing a path for the Lactation at Work Law. The ADA demanded that employers reconceptualize what the organization truly needed from employees to successfully perform various jobs. In doing so, it began decoupling employer preference from actual organizational need (Engel and Munger 2003). This idea of accommodation was not as contentious or stigmatizing by the time the Lactation at Work Law was introduced. Thus, the Lactation at Work Law builds on the ADA's success.

The ADA mounted steeper cultural and structural inclines than the Lactation at Work Law because it introduced workplace accommodations on a level that organizations had not previously had to address. By the time of the Lactation at Work Law, workplace accommodations were not a foreign concept. In this way, the law becomes both an instigator of social change as well as the *result* of social change, because the Lactation at Work Law benefited from the cultural shifts begun by the ADA and other laws that preceded it.

However, unlike the ADA, the accommodations addressed by the Lactation at Work Law deal not just with the body, but with bodily fluids and functions. Milk expression and nursing are often done in private in the United States (but this is less the norm in other countries, see Chapter 2). This could make discussions of accommodations more difficult, and, possibly, more stigmatized.

Yet, also unlike the ADA, the immediate benefit from the accommodations is not solely to the employee. The secondary beneficiaries of the lactation – the employees' children – shift how applicable rights talk and discussion of accommodations unfold. Because lactation accommodations benefit someone other than the rights holder, advocacy – even by the rights holder herself – can occur on behalf of someone else. This not only affects the dynamics of asserting those rights, but affects the framing of the accommodations, as discussed.

STUDYING EFFECTIVE LAWS

The provision of milk-expression accommodations may lead to a range of further progress for workers' rights. For example, discussions about the benefits of breastmilk might develop into examining on-site childcare options so that women could nurse at work rather than pumping milk or quitting altogether, or of extended family leave so that both on-site care and workplace lactation accommodations would be less critical. Such policies would be complemented by other labor and civil rights reforms, including public and easily accessible childcare; rights for migrant domestic workers; coverage for workers in for-profit nursing homes, hospitals, and childcare centers; and unconditional basic income and health care access. Thus, just as the moralization of the law could be broadened to create policies for on-site childcare or longer maternity leaves, organizations could shift from a pro-capitalist orientation to a pro-worker orientation, or even a pro-community focus altogether.

Other countries have adopted such approaches, such as longer leaves, expanded childcare options, and other family-friendly policies. Australia provides 172 weeks of publicly funded parental leave. Sweden provides government-subsidized childcare, with parents paying the equivalent of $83 monthly for full-time care. Peru provides lactating workers with an hour each day of paid time to leave work to breastfeed their infants (see Chapter 2 for more discussion).

METHODOLOGICAL INNOVATION: WHO AND WHEN, AND AGAIN

The substantial contributions to the theoretical terrain and scholarly understanding of the law and organizational change would not be possible without the creative methodological design of this study. By using a two-wave methodology, I was able to examine whether and how orientations to the law and lactation accommodations shifted over time. While the extant literature asserts that such changes happened, much of that research drew on retrospective recollections from what would, in this immediate study, be called Time Two, rather than actual data collection at Time One, as well as Time Two.

In particular, the longitudinal aspect of this research provides an important contrast to extant research. By studying this law at Time One, this research avoids a particular bias almost unavoidable in most law and society scholarship: that of the problematic case identification. Socio-legal projects often begin with the question "What's an interesting law to study?" This question is answered by identifying a law that has become problematic in some way. This inherently focuses research at what this study considers Time Two.

More critically, this means that nearly all research looks at problematic laws, focusing scholarship on laws that are not functioning as well as they might be expected to function.

Since most research gathers data only at Time Two and focuses on laws that are not working, legal scholarship has a bias toward unsuccessful legislation. In this way, part of the virtue of the longitudinal design is the increased likelihood that the research will uncover what ultimately might become a successful, even iconic, law – a law that is effective and, therefore, less remarkable from a law-in-action perspective. It is useful to study such a law at a point when its success was not a foregone conclusion. That enables the development of better theory regarding which laws work, more so than research that simply studies what does not work and, arguably, samples on the dependent variable.

Additionally, by interviewing matched sets of organizational actors – human resource personnel, supervising managers, and lactating employees – within the same organization, this study provides a detailed look at how organizational mechanisms are experienced at different places within an organization. For example, unlike most other scholarship in this area that focuses on managerial actors, this study demonstrates how the affected employee experiences managerialization of the law. Much extant research in this area has focused on human resource personnel, occasionally including others in management, while the employee perspective is left completely outside of the focus of study.

EMPIRICAL SURPRISES AND EXPANDING THEORY

Extant theory predicts that managerialization leads to substantive failure. This case shows that it can actually lead to success. In this study, specific circumstances facilitated that success: organizational structure that facilitated private places for milk expression, organizational culture that allowed for flexibility in employees' time at work, and legitimacy within the organization of lactation at work. This suggests refining the theory of managerialization of the law to include the possibility that it can be a pathway to substantive success. In certain circumstances, managerialization can create effective, not merely symbolic, accommodations.

In exploring how human resource specialists and supervising managers approached the Lactation at Work law shortly after it was implemented, this study confirms that management-focused frames and the managerialization of law are often how human resource personnel interpret legal regulations. Managerialism has been seen in extant literature. But what is surprising in this study is the discovery that managerialism actually leads to effective accommodations. This means managerialism should not be automatically dismissed because it can be a path toward substantive compliance.

These data also suggest that middle managers wield an often overlooked amount of power in mediating how their organizations' formal policy becomes translated into day-to-day reality. As managers with ongoing, daily contact with workers, they are the ones who translate policy into reality. Conversely, they also are the ones who are able to learn from their employees to understand how policy needs to be altered or improved. This means that employees should engage supervising managers to help secure adequate accommodations.

In addition, this study shows that management might alter its approaches to providing time and space for workers. Organizations might become less rigid in managerial control of workers' time. For example, they might expand the possibilities for working remotely from home. Organizations might also dedicate more physical space to individual employees' private or personal matters. Small rooms, possibly cleaned between uses, would enable not only workplace milk expression but also medication injections or ingestion, meditation and prayer, and confidential phone calls. Including more concrete requirements about where accommodations are located, how much time must be allowed, etc. may reduce ambiguities and heighten the possibility of substantive, rather than symbolic, compliance. The findings of this study underline that even when physical space is allocated and control over time is relaxed, the employee accommodation must also be seen as legitimate within the organization.

The data suggest that much of the Lactation at Work Law's success lies in its ability to embrace certain types of relational aspects of the law, creating advocates through educational conversations and mobilizing allies already on the ground. In addition, this law has concrete compliance mechanisms that enabled educational conversations and legitimized the demands of those allies already in place. This law also addresses a complicated physical need for lactation accommodation that involves important secondary parties as well as preconceived concepts of the private–public divide.

BROADER IMPLICATIONS

This study's findings are applicable across a wide range of employment circumstances due to a very diverse sample of participants – drawn from 11 industries and 113 organizations. Despite this diversity of sample, the data demonstrated no meaningful variation by industry, most likely because employee needs were similar across industries.

For example, a receptionist who usually must remain at her desk for lunch and other breaks (a common practice), needs similar time and space accommodations whether she works in a textiles factory or a law firm. Thus, this book's findings regarding managerial response to the Lactation at Work law are applicable across industries and organizations, as well.

Additionally, individual interviewees varied by worker status and job category throughout all industries studied. Higher-status workers in factories, department stores, and hospitals, for example, who were somewhat advanced in their organizations' hierarchies, were more likely to have more control over their time. Even if they had minimum control over their work time – such as most hospital workers in this study – they still were more likely to have private offices. The advantages of time, space, or both were seen across industries. This indicates the broader applicability of these findings. That is, the results discussed in this book are not limited only to white-collar firms, large-production factories, or educational institutions, for example, but transcend industry type.

While this book examines a particular legal focus – the right to express breast milk in the workplace – its findings apply to many other areas. Organizational changes discussed here – such as more flexible time, greater access to private spaces when needed, legitimacy of workers' needs – would benefit many more employees other than those who are lactating. Ability, or "disability," is itself a fluid category, with employees who need certain accommodations at one point not needing those accommodations later, or requiring different accommodations at some other time. Although specific accommodations focused on certain needs are more easily addressed by the law than more general concepts, issue-specific accommodations often can benefit others whom the law had not intended to target. For example, the larger stalls in public toilets were initially mandated to accommodate wheelchairs. However, the additional space also helps parents who wish to take their strollers, walking children, or body-attached babies with them into the stall. Thus, a greater readiness to embrace accommodations for lactating workers might also result in workplace structures that could ameliorate the needs of differently situated workers, such as those needing private prayer space.

LEGITIMATION PROCESSES

Neo-institutionalist organizational theory explains that practices become taken for granted and reified – that is, institutionalized – as organizations respond to isomorphism within their legal environment: pressure from other organizations and society ("coercive isomorphism"), from efforts to copy what other organizations are doing ("mimetic isomorphism"), and from emerging norms established by professional networking and education ("normative isomorphism") (DiMaggio and Powell 1983; Powell and DiMaggio 1991). Most prevalently in Time One interviews, these interviewees voiced coercive isomorphic pressures: The new law mandated that accommodations for lactating employees had to be made. However, the human resource personnel also exhibited mimetic isomorphism in talking about "the new norm," "the new industry standard," and "becoming what's expected" when explaining how they decided what their organizations needed to do to be in compliance with the Lactation at Work law. Additionally, human resource specialists illustrated normative isomorphism in discussing the ethical value of the law and in explaining that providing Lactation at Work accommodations is what "good" organizations "ought" to do.

By examining organizations' reactions to the Lactation at Work Law, social change within organizations is seen as not just a field-level legitimation process, but also a within-organization legitimation process that is both strategic and political. Organizational politics "involves individual, group, and organizational actors mobilizing material and symbolic resources to influence authoritative decision-making in accord with their perceived interests and values" (Stryker 2000: 179).

The Lactation at Work Law provides key resources – both leverage and values – that organizational actors utilize in intra-organizational politics. As Stryker and others have noted, organizational change needs legitimacy to be successful – although legitimacy can be established in a variety of ways (Stryker 2000; Suchman 1995). Stryker emphasizes that logics that may effectively "produce legitimacy through one mechanism for one audience will also delegitimate through this or some other mechanism for another audience" (Stryker 2000: 219).

Thus, because different types of logics appeal to different actors – either within fields or within organizations – competing logics can result. Multiple competing logics can destabilize the institutional logics. At times, organizational actors might entertain more than one logic, with none being sufficiently ensconced to not be challenged and simply taken for granted, resulting in de-legitimization. When institutional logics conflict with some organizational actors' values, then those people are more likely to mobilize against that logic.

This dynamic appears with the Lactation at Work Law, particularly within Chapters 5 and 6. The introduction of the Lactation at Work Law destabilized the dominant logic in many organizations providing minimal, if any accommodation, for workplace milk expression. Advocates for lactating employees, as well as the employees themselves, used this opportunity to mobilize against the prevailing norm and push for full compliance, and often compliance well beyond the legally mandated accommodations.

In particular, these data illustrate how organizational politics capitalize on issues of cognitive legitimacy (Stryker 2000; Suchman 1995). In contrast to the organizational self-interest of the managerialization rationales, lactation advocates and lactating employees frame lactation accommodations as desirable and consistent with support from norms outside the organization itself. Facing competing logics and alternative approaches to understanding compliance with the Lactation at Work Law, advocates and lactating employees benefited from the legitimacy the law bestowed on workplace milk expression. This heightened legitimacy enhanced acceptance of lactation accommodations and framed them as being necessary or inevitable.

THE WORKER'S INITIATIVE, ADVOCATES, AND COMPLIANCE

The success of the Lactation at Work Law in expanding employees' rights is mitigated by the importance of the individual worker's agency and ability to present her needs for lactation accommodation. Although some organizations have preexisting lactation rooms – especially if they had lactating employees earlier – most organizations do not mobilize accommodations until an employee requests them. This puts the burden on the employee to step forward, mobilize, and explain what she needs for lactation accommodation (and possibly why). While this might be very effective and might be emotionally satisfying for some employees, other employees might benefit significantly if someone else were making the argument on their behalf. This is particularly true for those employees who lack sufficient power to have the educational conversations with their supervising managers.

Human Resource Personnel

In some ways, the organizations' human resource professionals might serve well in this role. They are accustomed to explaining laws and policies to managers. Additionally, human resource personnel often are sufficiently distanced from the employee's worksite that they can be seen as impartial advocates.

Yet, human resource professionals are unlikely to take on such an advocacy role. For a human resource professional, making a public-spirited argument might be quite harmful, both professionally and in terms of their future effectiveness in the organization. Articulating ideologically pro-worker sentiments could undermine upper management's assessment of their loyalty to the organization. Human resource personnel maintain their legitimacy and power within their organizations by demonstrating their worth to management and the organizations' missions, which rarely include workers' greater needs.

The value of the human resource office is that it deals with issues that are crucial to the organization, such as absenteeism. Being perceived as "starry-eyed do-gooders" would characterize human resource professionals as focused on more than simply what is best for their organizations. Much extant research on human resource professionals suggests that the hardest part of human resource professionals' jobs is convincing top management that it should make certain changes to comply with the law. The best way to do that is to make the business case to ownership or higher-level management. For these reasons, many human resource professionals might focus only on managerial arguments and would hesitate to be more proactive on behalf of individual employees.

The human resource personnel in this study who were proactively advocating for lactating employees' rights were fully fledged allies, willing to move beyond the usual constraints of their positions. However, in most organizations, the impetus lies with the lactating employee herself. If she is constrained in any way, lacks sufficient power or access, or is for any other reason unable to assert her lactating needs, the Lactation at Work Law will not expand her lactation-related civil rights.

Advocates and Empathy

To be sure, the Allies Already of Chapter 5 and the Morality-Motivated Advocates of Chapter 6 are basically Time One and Time Two advocates. One could argue that both groups empathize with the lactating employees – due to social proximity to the issue, the impact of educational conversations, or possibly other mechanisms not identified by these data. However, it is difficult to determine if it was empathy that led people to be allies, although the assumption seems safe to make.

How did those people who are Allies Already gain those experiences of close social proximity? Quite possibly, they learned about the importance and health benefits of breastfeeding because of their own experiences or those of a family member or friend. Maybe they had the same kinds of experiences as Time Two Morality-Motivated Advocates, even if they did not articulate that in the interviews. Conversely, the supervising managers who talk about the health benefits in order to comply beyond the law's mandate need to have some empathy – for those supervising managers, the health benefits are still the motivation, but the empathy is still necessary to be effective.

The health benefit motivations may be at the heart of support from both Allies Already and Morality-Motivated Advocates. These two groups might not be very different. They may appear in different forms yet still exist on the same spectrum. What is critical here is that the behavior of allies and advocates is learned, so those organizational actors who wish to further social change and institute new policies need to dedicate themselves to persuasion efforts to generate support for new accommodations.

When advocates at work are present and willing to support the affected employees, they could (a) be mobilized to put a new law in place, (b) push for accommodations before the law is passed, and (c) have conversations with resistant co-workers and managers on behalf of the employee. Therefore, a critical message for employees needing certain accommodations is: Don't assume you are alone. Instead, look around for allies already on the ground.

Moreover, simply because some people at work are not advocates initially, this does not mean they will remain obstacles; they, too, can become advocates. The data demonstrate the importance of advocates, and persuasion is an important way to get advocates on one's side.

Every organization might have allies and advocates who want to support a new law and its implementation. The challenge for human resource personnel and lactating employees alike who want to further compliance is to determine who these allies and advocates are. This could be most crucial for laws and policies more controversial than workplace milk expression.

COMPLIANCE AND BEYOND COMPLIANCE

In addition to simply complying with the law's requirements, organizations can move beyond compliance, as Chapters 5 and 6 demonstrate – both

Allies Already and Morality-Motivated Advocates becoming beyond-compliance advocates. For example, while the law mandates a private room, some organizations moved beyond compliance to beautify the room, adding aesthetic touches. Other organizations added additional conveniences to the lactations rooms, making them more functional, increasing their lactating employees' efficiency, whether it was adding storage lockers for greater break-time efficiency, or adding computers and internet access for enhanced productivity on the job.

On a larger level, an organization could move further beyond compliance to greater accommodation of parents more generally. This could involve innovations in the workplace, such as on-site childcare; in scheduling work time, such as greater flexibility in when work is performed; or in legitimating a range of family needs, including elder care, care for siblings, or for unrelated loved ones. In this way, greater accommodation for lactating workers could lead to a broader understanding of accommodation in a variety of situations.

Furthermore, organizations could move beyond compliance to actually rethinking some of the ideal worker myths. This could create a broader cultural change beyond just more accommodations, but truly rethinking the logic of the workplace. It would incorporate the strides in accommodations made by other laws, such as the ADA and FMLA, but would also permit flexibility from scheduled working hours for other activities such as educational self-enrichment or breastfeeding at home. In this way, workplace lactation becomes just one area in a much larger project of multifaceted change. This would be a "beyond compliance" that could move beyond the law entirely – an entirely new approach to social change.

In this way, compliance and beyond-compliance can be viewed along a continuum, with the following points arrayed: (1) formal compliance in which accommodations are formally provided but not always substantively adequate. This is where we see symbolic compliance; (2) fully empowered accommodation, in which the accommodations are improved beyond the bare necessities required by law. Lactation spaces are comfortable and designed to enhance workers' efficiency; (3) generalized accommodation beyond the actually protected group. In other words, supporting healthy babies generally, or supporting other workers' health needs that require them to have a private space, etc.; (4) a deeper, cultural shift to more worker-friendly workplaces, with generalized norms of flexibility and sustainable time commitment to all employees.

WORKERS' RIGHTS, CAPITALISM, AND POWER

The incorporation of the law into the organization – whether through managerialization or moralization of the law – may extend the law's reach beyond the basic mandated accommodations. This may contribute both to the lasting power of those changes as well as increasing accessibility of those changes as these accommodations, over time, may become part of the fabric of the organization – entrenched and unquestioned. However, this actually may undermine the very goals that the law championed by depoliticizing the workplace accommodations, and shifting the focus away from workers and rights and toward management's and babies' needs.

Capitalism and Managerial Logic

US hyper-capitalism embraces the stance that everyone should be working. This makes the assertion of managerial logic as a frame for lactation accommodations very understandable. With the stance that everyone should be working, and that being a responsible adult means working outside the home, then public policies that would allow lactating mothers to be home with their children to nurse in person are highly unlikely.

Thus, the Lactation at Work Law is about workplace lactation rooms and long-enough breaks, but not about time at home and longer maternity leaves. The managerialization of the law – and possibly the moralization of the law – has a definitively capitalist aspect. While the overall goal is harmonizing work–family conflicts, by addressing this issue of work/family conflict with exclusively workplace accommodation, managerialization emphasizes the economic perspective.

The managerial logic behind the Lactation at Work Law allows organizations to continue to use lactating employees' skills rather than enabling lactating employees to stay home. This is a good option for business; however, it may not be the ideal for many families. Paid leave, for example, might be better for families and their children; it would foster bonding and better relationships. In this way, the neoliberal argument is not that breastfeeding is such an important maternal duty that women should be able to stay home with their babies, but that it is such an important duty that it will be accommodated at work.

Pro-Capital or Pro-Woman?

In some ways, the Lactation at Work Law continues the neoliberal capitalist trend of shifting the burden of social reproduction onto individual women. For these reasons, some would assert that, rather than being actually pro-mother, pro-woman, or pro-worker, the Lactation at Work Law might better be characterized as pro-capital or pro-organization, with its pro-women impacts as more tangential to its capitalist goals. Indeed, initiatives like workplace lactation accommodation would be less needed if the burden for childcare and lactation were not understood as exclusively the problem of the lactating employee. Yet, as is common in neoliberal capitalism, the Lactation at Work Law offloads the work of social reproduction onto individuals while simultaneously extracting from those individuals the resources they require to sustain social reproduction (time, energy, mental health, physical health, etc.).

In this way, the Lactation at Work Law can be seen as an outgrowth of neoliberalism, which brings more women into the paid workforce. This greater presence of women in the labor market is often framed as "progressive" and facilitative of personal and financial empowerment; yet the result of separating family and work is to "externaliz[e] carework onto families and communities while diminishing their capacity to perform it" (Fraser 2016: 112). Although hailed as helping working mothers, the Lactation at Work Law actually might have the effect of subjugating the needs of the family to that of the company by making the lactating worker's physical presence at work primary.

Moreover, the Lactation at Work Law might inhibit more substantial workplace changes and beneficial societal reforms. That is, by facilitating lactating workers' ability to express milk at work but not improving other aspects of the work–family situation, the law actually could be a road block on the path to greater social change, or the law might improve enough aspects of the lactating employees' experience that the companies will not arrive at better solutions. For example, by enabling workplace milk expression, the Lactation at Work Law simply might be perpetuating an already suboptimum situation for mother-employees: the lack of adequate maternity leave.

On the one hand, lactation policies enable women to combine milk expression and employment; however, these policies also reinforce a double responsibility for working mothers, as exemplified by the image of the woman using a hands-free, double breast pump while typing at her computer. "In the absence of a sustainable institutionalization of the production/reproduction division, [the employer] shoehorned social reproduction responsibilities into the interstices and crevices of lives that capital insists must be dedicated first and foremost to accumulation" (Fraser and Jaeggi 2018: 87). Legislation that would be truly pro-women and pro-worker would recognize that pumping and breastfeeding are labor – both physically taxing and time-consuming; resulting accommodations would provide options of how and where to engage in lactation, including the option of face-to-face breastfeeding at worksite childcare, sufficient break time to travel to where their children are to nurse in person, or long enough family leave that breastfeeding or milk expression at work is no longer an issue.

RACE AND CLASS INEQUALITIES

Legislation such as the Lactation at Work Law arguably comes at the intersection of relatively successful feminism and the somewhat conservative US welfare state. On the one hand, feminism emphasized that careers are as important to women as to men, and as important as motherhood. Workplace lactation accommodations could be the preference over on-site childcare and longer parental leaves for those employees who truly choose to return to work quickly and prefer midday milk pumping to nursing.

On the other hand, the conservative welfare state reminds us that, even with the Family Medical Leave Act, there is no state financial support for parents staying home with their children; lactating mothers will not be paid for staying home. While professional women might elect to stay in the workplace out of vocational passion or concern for how stints away from the workforce might affect their career trajectories, working-class women, who could take long maternity leaves or hiatuses from employment without missing out on much vocational fulfillment or harm to their career advancement, must also remain in the workforce. Working-class women must come back even to *non-fulfilling* jobs.

Thus, the Lactation at Work Law may have the unintended effect of entrenching racial and class hierarchies. Due to differences in employment situations of working-class women and women of color, the "right" to pump at work will not always be realized and may continue to perpetuate race and class inequalities. Working-class and nonwhite women are more likely to work jobs not covered by the Lactation at Work Law and with unpaid break time, while middle-class and white women more often have positions at organizations covered by the law and for which lactation accommodations can easily be made, such as private offices and flexible schedules. Women who need to express breast milk but who lack sufficient paid break time – because the employer is too small to be covered by the law; because the industry does not provide paid breaks; because the employee works a collection of part-time jobs without any one job substantial enough to offer lactation breaks; or because the woman needs more time than her fifteen-minute paid break – are forced either to take a pay cut or not pump.

Women in already low-wage positions cannot afford pay cuts, yet lactating women cannot afford to skip pumping time without immediately experiencing discomfort and pain and decreases in their milk supply. Class and race disparities are then exacerbated because the women who would be forced to take unpaid break time, go part time, or forego employment altogether in order to continue to breastfeed, are the very women who are least likely to be able to do so. These women then must choose between financially supporting their families or providing breast milk to their children.

THE "IDEAL WORKER"

Sometimes, the "ideal worker" norm was so prevalent in the workplace culture of lactating employees that women were unable to avail themselves of the lactation accommodations their organizations provided. Not wanting to be seen as less committed than their co-workers, these women could not take the time or access the spaces available for workplace milk expression. This means that even when lactating workers have organizational support for breastfeeding, their milk expression might not be successful. True success might require a cultural shift not only around the issue of workplace lactation, but around what constitutes a good employee.

Even the shifts by those supervising managers discussed in Chapter 6 to moralize the law based on concerns for healthy children do not truly challenge this ideal. Managers can be supportive because of this moralization; yet the lactating worker might feel she must not take time to pump in order to be a good worker. Even if, like the workers in Chapters 4–6, she has strong advocates and adequate time and space, she still might not avail herself of lactation accommodations because it would risk her reputation as an ideal worker.

Although some barriers to using available lactation accommodations are structural, the difficulties caused by the ideal worker norm are not. For example, when a factory provides adequate lactation rooms, but it cannot stop the production line for someone to go pump, that is a structural problem. However, other barriers result from the ideal worker norm being culturally entrenched, such as the professional worker who said she could not stop people from knocking on her door and demanding her time or the restaurant manager who needed to continually help her servers. In these examples, management provided the structure but the lactating employee alone could not change the culture to overcome the power of the ideal worker norm.

RETALIATION AND REGRESSIVE POSSIBILITIES

The possibility of discrimination or retaliation against workers availing themselves of their employment rights, including those under the Lactation at Work Law, always looms as a possibility. The dominant trope in US culture that caregiving for family members is a personal responsibility (see Levitsky 2014) – that is, not the responsibility of employers, the state, or another entity – further heightens the possibility of workplace discrimination for family responsibilities. Thus, while the community health concept was a powerful rhetoric in Chapter 6, the extant literature has also documented much discrimination against caregivers (see e.g., Weisshaar 2017).

Additionally, the macro-politics of this law are potentially regressive in that its arguments could be carried forward to easily create a conservative maternalism. The public policy behind the Lactation at Work Law is philosophically complex. While the importance of breastfeeding is an effective rhetoric to create and motivate advocates for lactation accommodations, this rhetoric also begets a materialist argument that could be politically pernicious because it furthers the concept that women's primary responsibility is to their children. Such an argument to management could result in a perception that women are primarily mothers, and so are lesser workers. Or even that they should not be workers at all.

CONSERVATIVISM AND MATERNAL DUTY

The prescription to set up laws to play on moral appeals suggests a conservativism in law and social change. In the case of the Lactation at Work Law, the law works because of the association between women and babies. But when laws are being written to promote social change, a delicate balance exists in pushing a change while appealing to people who are conservative and hold conservative values. Laws might tap into values that mobilize tradition and morality but change the expectations that people have of how those values are put into practice.

This poses the possibility that progressive change might be possible by connecting with the familiar to generate change. Since people's minds connect with the familiar, laws might have more success when their accommodations resonate with preexisting familiar morality. Ironically, appeals to familiarity may be useful to spark change more generally.

Moreover, the rhetoric about children's health as a motivation for these lactation accommodations may ultimately result in the opposite of the law's goal. The benefit to the health of the lactating employees' children could be seen as engaging a conservative pro-family frame. Sociology has demonstrated that efforts at social change can gain significant advantages from using conservative frames to rally for their issues. These frames are both familiar and powerful.

The rights the Lactation at Work Law give to necessary space, time, and legitimacy for successful workplace milk expression embrace a quite conservative frame. By shifting the discussion away from the worker and her rights and toward the idea of infant health, the accommodations assume a very traditionalist trope of maternal care and duty. If taken to its logical end, this focus would argue not for greater inclusion of lactating employees into the workplace, but for compelling more of these workers to remain at home with their nurslings.

The conservative trope about the importance of mothers caring for babies, therefore, will not be brought to its next logical steps by asserting that lactating employees would best serve their children and the next generation by exiting the workforce entirely or leaving the workplace regularly to nurse in person. The law and subsequent policy does not assert that maternal duty is so important that these mothers should stay home. Rather, it says the workplace must make accommodations because of the primacy of maternal duty.

Interestingly, the prescription that laws should essentially play on effective moral appeals – a possible implication of this study – suggests a sort of conservativism in law and social change: The Lactation at Work Law is successful due to the conventional, conservative argument about mothers and babies. Given the correlation between conservativism and power, laws written in this way overlook that their very goals are actually anathema to many of the actors who are needed as allies to create that social change. Thus, this poses the question: Although the

Lactation at Work Law is effective, does it ultimately undermine our capacity to change some of these conservative cultural expectations? The challenge for progressively oriented laws is to devise ways to capitalize on abstract general values in ways that mobilize tradition, but change the concrete expectations that go along with those traditions.

Some might say the issue is not the tropes of maternal care themselves; they are not actually "conservative" but simply "familiar." A law such as the Lactation at Work Law attempts to drive social change in a new direction, but people's minds work incrementally in terms of what they can process politically. Part of the power of enacting conventionalism – whether regarding the Lactation at Work Law, same-sex marriage, or other similar legislation – is that it actually opens up conversations that transform how people think. Thus, the challenge might not be conservative back-sliding but the resilience of "familiarity" that thwarts new civil rights, since civil rights laws, by their very focus, are aimed at expanding what the public will come to accept as familiar.

EXTERNAL GOALS, OTHER NEEDS, AND RECURSIVITY

The success of the Lactation at Work Law suggests possibilities for other workplace accommodation issues. Although employees needing other workplace accommodation might not have a children's health rationale, many other moral principles might be engaged. Those employees could create educational conversations about other benefits to society, beyond those within the organization. The effectiveness of the Lactation at Work Law presents the possibility that employees in other contexts seeking different accommodations might be able to deduce what moral principles are relevant to their circumstances and use those to transform managerial logic over time in order to push the organization beyond symbolic compliance.

Chapter 6 demonstrates that empathy can be learned and developed. Educational conversations and the creation of moral allies can bring moral and ethical frames – such as health and wellness – into the organizational context. This has great significance for many groups that seek improved workplace accommodations or that wish, more generally, to improve society's acceptance. This study raises the possibility that groups might be able to educate others about substantive facts while also communicating norms and beliefs to effect change.

Moreover, the recursivity of the issue of workplace lactation accommodations may have a powerful cumulative effect. That is, in the case of workplace milk expression, the more employees choose to breastfeed and pump milk in the workplace, the more people who are exposed to the practice, mothers' motivations, and the necessary accommodations. The more people are exposed to pumping – that is, the more co-workers and managers have experience with it – the greater legitimacy it will enjoy. As a result, more employees will elect to breastfeed and express milk at work. This snowball effect of increasing exposure, growing support, and greater participation in the activity could extend to many other workplace accommodation issues.

FUTURE RESEARCH

Future research must study compliance at multiple levels and relationally. This project is about a regulatory law that has been successful in part due to its ability to embrace the relational aspect of the law, and because its compliance mechanisms created space for educational conversations by having substantive requirements. Future research might test the prevalence of the processes identified here.

How the law was interpreted and the way subsequent rules were applied did not vary by industry, by state or federal law, nor is it based on the percentage of women employees in an organization or within management. This finding is in contrast to others' findings (Bobbitt-Zeher 2011; DeCoster, Estes, and Mueller 1999; Stainback, Ratliff, and Roscigno 2011). A study using a probability sample might quantify the extent of moralization of the Lactation at Work Law with laws that vary in the extent to which health goals are their focus. Geographic areas, known for progressive and pro-health orientations, might be surveyed, as well as those areas where health goals are regularly placed behind other business goals and employee rights are most hard-fought.

This study did not include fast food businesses, despite substantial efforts. This might be an industry with the greatest managerial resistance and the most difficulty in locating private spaces for milk expression. Future research might look at this industry, which, in addition to having limited physical space, also is a key job source for the precariat – those workers with minimal job security and whose hours and pay are subject to management discretion more so than other sectors.

Multiple Paths for Compliance

This study found three different paths to successful compliance with the Lactation at Work Law. Sometimes managerialization produced successful lactation accommodations. Other times, allies had to rally to make the accommodations successful, often relying on the law to compel compliance and bestow legitimacy on workplace milk expression. A subsection of supervising managers shifted from managerialization of the law to include moralization of the law, often not only meeting the basics of compliance but reaching beyond basic compliance. Future research should explore which sequences are more effective than others. In particular, future waves of data at the same organizations might illuminate which mechanisms create the longest lasting organizational change.

As Wallace asserts, "the relationship between cultural values and specific, work-based ideologies is complicated" (2004: 3). The words and actions of lactating workers were not sufficient to shift all supervising managers to understanding the benefits of breastfeeding enough to embrace a moral framework. A few supervising managers continued to resist compliance or engage in mere symbolic compliance. In addition, some supervising managers who had embraced the new law by understanding how it furthered managerial goals created successful accommodations only in so far as they fit within the organizations' preexisting structure and culture; they did not shift to emphasize health-and-wellness aspects, but stayed focused only on conventional managerial goals and basic legal compliance. Although not the focus of this book, their presence underlines that legal compliance is a complex topic requiring much research. Clearly, education and persuasion are important to creating advocates. And the law opens up those spaces for educational conversations for those not already advocates. However, more research is needed to determine how educational conversations work to persuade people and what the exact psychosocial mechanisms are.

Peer Support or Resistance

Future research should more deeply explore the effects of co-workers' actions and attitudes. Extant research disagrees regarding directionality and dynamics of organizational change, especially the role of lower-hierarchy supervising managers and employees. While some scholars assert that management sets the cultural tone and drives change, others suggest that change will not happen unless employees challenge supervising managers who tend to cling to the established ways (see Kellogg 2009, 2014; Meyerson and Martin 1987). Although this study did not systematically sample co-workers or peers in the workplace, interviewee comments suggest that co-workers could impede or facilitate successful lactation at work.

This may be an important component of the politics of beyond-compliance. Politics within organizations and among co-workers should be studied further. Building on extant research such as that of Kellogg and co-authors that focuses on organizational politics (Kellogg 2009, 2011, 2014), future research could explore how co-workers might be "cooperators" versus "active advocates" or "subtle saboteurs."

However, more work needs to be done on the impact of co-workers. Future research could build on these findings to uncover the exact mechanisms through which peers facilitate and impede the success of milk expression or other organizational changes or accommodations. Management may, in fact, drive initial organizational change efforts, and so must be fully on board for successful change. Yet, perhaps some organizational change involves more differentiated and oppositional workplace culture, in which co-workers must be won over on their own terms; that without peer-level support, managerial support will make little difference. This presents an area for more research, something to be fleshed out in the future.

Missing Reports of Resistance

One reason why these data may tell a more positive story than might be anticipated is that those organizations, human resource personnel, and supervising managers who were most resistant to accommodating breastfeeding women simply refused to participate in this study. Indeed, more women agreed to participate in the study than I could match with human resource personnel and supervising managers. Additionally, those women who had particularly negative experiences with expressing milk in the workplace may not have been willing to participate and revisit difficult times in their past. Moreover, potential employee interviewees who worked in organizations with significant resistance might never have tried to express milk at work or, perhaps, did not attempt to breastfeed beyond the first few weeks postpartum. Other potential lactating employees may have entirely quit their jobs after giving birth, also never attempting to express milk at work, perceiving this to be too difficult at their workplaces.

These possibilities mean that the organizations with the most resistance might not have been captured by this study. Future research might attempt to capture these potentially missing data. Recruiting women immediately after giving birth, or even while still pregnant, could include some of these missing perspectives, although those who never considered workplace milk expression would still remain absent.

Additional Laws and Moral Principals

To better understand where organizations fall on the resistant/purely symbolic-compliance/substantive-accommodations spectrum, it will be useful to study other contexts. Future research could explore what happens with other civil rights and workplace accommodation laws as additional concrete manifestations of more abstract concepts or processes. This study examined the moralization of the law with a powerful moral principle: children's health. How might other moral principles in the communities in which organizations function affect legal compliance? Which organizational actors are in the positions to invoke such moral principles? Which will always be confined by business logic?

Conversely, this moral principle of children's health might be examined in other contexts. That research could explore such questions as: What factors affect the cultural resonance of the nurturing "mother duty"? How do educational efforts and ally-creating outreach affect the resonance of moral principles in these ways? Are there ways to tap into abstract general values in ways that mobilize conservative traditions, but modify the concrete expectations that go along with those traditions to create progressive change?

External Environments

Organizations are embedded in larger cultural contexts. Some of these are the specific contexts of individual professions, like the human resource profession. Others are the more general cultural contexts, created by the media as well as by people's lived communities. Beliefs shift over time based on people's experiences inside and outside the workplace. This study found relatively little change within the human resource profession and that most people who experienced change in their views of lactation described those changes as resulting from workplace conversations. Future research should be attentive to these larger contexts, particularly when studying lactation in other settings and when studying other legal reforms that may be affected more by external environments than by the organizational environment.

Changing Norms: The "Ideal Worker" and the Co-worker

The law and society literature often frames compliance as being the only way to spark social change, with resistance against legal compliance being a main hurdle. Yet, this study shows that the ideal worker norm has thwarted seemingly sufficient accommodations from producing effective practices of workplace milk expression. The prevalence of the "ideal worker" trope impairs people's ability to utilize available accommodations and to mobilize their rights.

Specifically, the concept of an ideal worker whose focus is exclusively on her job problematized some lactating workers' use of available accommodations. This meant that even when management provided sufficient space and adequate time, lactating workers might not assert their needs and use accommodations provided because they have internalized these expectations. This underlines that employees success in workplace milk expression also depends on the larger cultural environments surrounding the lactating employee. The ways that management and co-workers – and even other lactating employees – contribute to this internalized culture and its ramifications require more research as well.

Future studies should pursue a fuller exploration of peer culture. They should explore what reinforces versus what changes workplace norms. Workplace support groups and other mechanisms of potential cultural change at the workplace are potential strategies to change co-worker/peer culture.

APPENDIX A – FEDERAL AND STATE LACTATION AT WORK LAWS

THE FEDERAL LAW

Section 7 of the Fair Labor Standards Act of 1938 (29 U.S.C. 207) is amended by adding at the end the following:

(r)(1) An employer shall provide—

A a reasonable break time for an employee to express breast milk for her nursing child for 1 year after the child's birth each time such employee has need to express the milk; and

B a place, other than a bathroom, that is shielded from view and free from intrusion from coworkers and the public, which may be used by an employee to express breast milk.

(2) An employer shall not be required to compensate an employee receiving reasonable break time under paragraph (1) for any work time spent for such purpose.

(3) An employer that employs less than 50 employees shall not be subject to the requirements of this subsection, if such requirements would impose an undue hardship by causing the employer significant difficulty or expense when considered in relation to the size, financial resources, nature, or structure of the employer's business.

(4) Nothing in this subsection shall preempt a State law that provides greater protections to employees than the protections provided for under this subsection (Federal Lactation at Work Law 2010).

THE INDIANA LAW

Ind. Code § 5-10-6-2 and § 22-2-14-2 (2008)

As used in this chapter, "employer" means a person or entity that employs twenty-five (25) or more employees.

IC 5-10-6-2

Sec. 2. (a) The state and political subdivisions of the state shall provide reasonable paid break time each day to an employee who needs to express breast milk for the employee's infant child. The break time must, if possible, run concurrently with any break time already provided to the employee. The state and political subdivisions are not required to provide break time under this section if providing break time would unduly disrupt the operations of the state or political subdivisions.

(b) The state and political subdivisions of the state shall make reasonable efforts to provide a room or other location, other than a toilet stall, in close proximity to the work area, where an employee described in subsection (a) can express the employee's breast milk in privacy. The state and political subdivisions shall make reasonable efforts to provide a refrigerator or other cold storage space for keeping milk that has been expressed. The state or a political subdivision is not liable if the state or political subdivision makes a reasonable effort to comply with this subsection.

IC 22-2-14-2

Employer provide private location where employees can express milk; employer provide cold storage for expressed milk; employer not liable.

Sec. 2. (a) To the extent reasonably possible, an employer shall provide a private location, other than a toilet stall, where an employee can express the employee's breast milk in privacy during any period away from the employee's assigned duties.

(b) To the extent reasonably possible, an employer shall:

(1) provide a refrigerator or other cold storage space for keeping milk that has been expressed; or

(2) allow the employee to provide the employee's own portable cold storage device for keeping milk that has been expressed until the end of the employee's work day.

(c) Except in cases of willful misconduct, gross negligence, or bad faith, an employer is not liable for any harm caused by or arising from either of the following that occur on the employer's premises:

(1) The expressing of an employee's breast milk.

(2) The storage of expressed milk.

APPENDIX B – METHODOLOGY AND RESEARCH STRATEGY

The goal of this study was to understand how organizations applied the Lactation at Work Law over time. To do this, I investigated the perspectives of three kinds of organizational actors in relation to federal and Indiana law at two time periods approximately five years apart. To capture key organizational perspectives on the law, I triangulated the data by interviewing three categories of organizational actors: (1) human resource personnel, who crafted the law into policy; (2) supervising managers, who applied the policies to employees' workdays; and (3) the lactating employees whose daily needs to express milk are the focus of these laws and policies. To capture variation with governing bodies at different levels of government, I studied one state-level and one federal law. Since past scholarship in this area theorizes that changes in how organizational responses to certain laws evolve over time, I began open-ended interviews shortly after each Lactation at Work Law was in force, and then conducted as many follow-up interviews as possible approximately five years later, once the organizations had time to make organizational changes to implement the new Lactation at Work law. Specifically, interviews with human resource personnel and supervising managers were repeated four to six years later.[1] Since this study required many hours of interviews, all of which were transcribed, I am grateful that the data collection for the first wave of interviews was supported by the National Science Foundation, grant SES-0853534.

SAMPLING

This project draws on interviews with 173 employees who were expressing breast milk at work, 97 human resource specialists, and 93 supervising

[1] Sometimes, the supervising manager or the human resource specialist was not available for both waves of interviews. For some of the Indiana firms, often only a supervising manager or a human resource specialist was available for either interview. Although I usually interviewed only one employee in each organization, occasionally more than one area of an organization had a milk-expressing employee available; in those organizations, I interviewed more than one employee and each lactating worker's supervising manager whenever possible.

managers. As much as possible, I matched each employee interviewee with a human resource specialist and a supervising manager interviewee from the same organization. Approximately a third of the organizations were from Indiana, responding to the state-level law, and two-thirds were from Wisconsin, after the passage of federal legislation.

These interviewees were draw from 113 businesses and 10 industries – construction, dining/hotel/tourism, education, finance, government, health/medical, manufacturing, media, retail, and transportation – as well as from professional firms. I selected these industries because they provided a mix of businesses to include variation in manufacturing and service sectors (since characteristics of jobs and worksites could affect the ease with which organizations implemented lactation accommodations), variation in gender composition (since a higher density of women workers could affect need for lactation accommodations); and variation in entry costs (since lactating workers might be reluctant to quit if they might not be able to reenter the same or similar jobs).

I selected organizations to include a robust, diverse sample of organizations and industries. Initially, some were included because a lactating employee responded to my flier asking for interview volunteers; then I would contact her supervising manager and her organization's human resource specialist. I distributed electronic and hard-copy fliers to various support and discussion groups (online and in person) as well as conducting informal outreach through social contacts. The flier read, "If you have ever pumped breast milk at your workplace, please consider sharing your insights and experiences with Professor Elizabeth Hoffmann at Purdue University. Dr. Hoffmann is interested in learning from moms who used to pump at work, are currently pumping at work, started pumping at work but had to stop, or had planned to pump at work but were unable to do so. Dr. Hoffmann would like to include as many different perspectives as possible." I then provided email and phone contact information. Employee interviewees also heard about my study through word of mouth and contacted me directly.

Other times, the sequence would be reversed: I would seek out businesses using public listings of companies, along with some convenience sampling (for

TABLE A.1 Interviewees

	Lactating Workers	Supervising Managers	Human Resource Specialists	Total
Indiana	81	27	33	141
Wisconsin	92	66	62	220
Total	173	93	95	361

example, if a research assistant or acquaintance knew someone at particular organization). I would usually begin interviewing the human resource specialist and ask for the particular specialist responsible for lactation accommodations, if the human resource department employed many specialists. If the organization had employed a lactating employee since the new law took effect, then I would interview that woman as well as her supervising manager.

Human relation specialists were those working in human resource departments, or similar employee benefit departments, who oversaw their organizations' interpretations and applications of new policies. Supervising managers were those who directly oversaw workers and engaged in activities such as performance evaluation, scheduling, and assignments. For example, in hospitals, these manager-supervisors were clinic or division managers; in school systems, these managers were principals; in the tourism and finance industries, these were the general managers for a specific hotel or bank, respectively.

In 2009, I began interviewing lactating employees, human resource personnel, and supervising managers in Indiana to learn how businesses were interpreting and applying the new state law. I chose Indiana because, at the time this study began, it had just passed a lactation-at-work law. Additionally, I reside in Indiana, so this was a particularly accessible state.

Approximately four to six years later, I reinterviewed a portion of those same human resource specialists and supervising managers to see if their interpretations, practices, or viewpoints had changed after living with this new law for several years. To capture the effects of the 2010 federal Lactation at Work law, in 2011, I expanded the study to Wisconsin, a state that had no state-level Lactation at Work Law. In 2015–16, I reinterviewed those Wisconsin human resource specialists and supervising managers.

Thus, for Wisconsin, the federal Lactation at Work law was a new law covering a new workplace issue, just as the state-level law had been new for Indiana. I chose Wisconsin for its cultural similarity to Indiana; both are central Midwestern states with similar racial and ethnic demographics. These Wisconsin interviews were done initially to explore how organizations responded differently to federal laws than to state-level laws addressing the same goals; yet, I did not find any meaningful differences between the Indiana and Wisconsin interviews.

Although I tried to capture as full a range of perspectives as possible, some voices might not be included in this study. For example, I tried to include the perspectives of women who never tried to pump, for whatever reason, but I did not have any such volunteers. This means that those organizations that might be the most inhospitable for lactating women might not appear in these data. I also lack the perspective of those women who did not return to work following the birth of their children, even though I deliberately solicited for such interviewees. While the decision to exit the paid workforce might have nothing to do with real or perceived workplace lactation accommodations, it could; that experience, too, does not appear in this data set.

Additionally, since I wanted each business to include at least one interviewee from management and one lactating employee in at least one of the waves, some interviews were dropped from this project. For example, when a woman interviewee either did not wish me to contact the human resource or supervising manager at her organization, or neither one of these actors were willing to be interviewed ever, I dropped her interview from this study. Conversely, some human resource personnel were willing to talk with me, but their organization never had an actual lactating employee I could interview. They, too, were dropped from the study.

METHODS

A key benefit of qualitative research is the high validity possible (Hind 2007; Lévi-Strauss 1969). The researcher does not simply read off a survey, but asks initial questions and then probes the responses to understand the fuller, more complete situation. Thus, "the researcher is able to understand the greater context, to obtain a large overview, and can triangulate the accounts of differently situated interviewees with various bases of knowledge" (Hoffmann 2008: 274).

The interviews ranged from twenty minutes to just under two hours, with most lasting between thirty and ninety minutes. Interviews with human resource personnel and supervising managers generally occurred during the workday. Interviews with lactating employees often took place in the evenings or on weekends. All interviews were recorded and transcribed. Thus, all quotations used in this article are direct quotes, although I edited some to make them more readable by removing filler words ("ah," "um," "like," etc.), repeated words, and such.

The decision to sample from both supervising managers and human relation specialists was strategic. While compliance professionals – for example, human resource specialists – interpret the law and craft policy in response to those laws, the mid-level manager-supervisors are the ones who directly transform these policies into day-to-day workplace reality. Thus, this study draws on data from the human resource personnel who write policies as well as from the supervising managers whose practices apply those policies.

The interviews focused on understandings and application of the new Lactation at Work Law. Questions included inquiries about how they complied with the new law; how they explained it to others outside the organization; how they learned about the law; and how they would explain the law to subordinates or peers within the organization. Most questions were general or open-ended, but some, especially follow-up questions, were more direct.

With the help of research assistants, I coded the transcribed interviews, using the qualitative data software NVivo, for various themes. Sometimes these themes were responses to specific questions (e.g., "What sort of internal publications to do you use to communicate about this law?" "What would an employee do if she felt she needed different accommodations for pumping breast milk?" "What could she do if she didn't receive the accommodation she requested?"). However, many others were extracted from the responses of interviewees to broader questions (e.g., "How would you explain the law to someone else in the same industry?" "What would you change about this law if you could just snap your fingers and it would be different?" "How would you handle an employee who ... ?") or to follow up questions regarding other responses. Thus, many codes were not the result of a direct question or set of questions intended to measure a particular phenomenon, but were produced by careful analysis of interviewees' various responses.

Some coding was very straightforward. For example, I categorized management respondents who were lactation advocates at Time One as Allies Already. To qualify for his label, interviews at Time One had to contain pro–breastfeeding, pro–milk expression, and/or pro–lactating worker language and descriptions of actions the interviewee had taken to ensure effective lactation accommodations.

Other topics were more ambiguous. For example, interviewees received the label of Morality-Motivated Advocates if they drew on various health and wellness rhetorics in explaining their compliance and lactation accommodation at all. This did not need to be the sole rhetoric used in discussing accommodations. Indeed, some supervising managers drew on more than one rhetoric; they might have discussed moralizing the law but also articulated managerialization motivations. In that example, those supervising managers might be speaking not just about their organizational role and the benefit to management, but also about the larger societal situation and how lactation benefits it. In this example, if they spoke about the health benefits beyond their organization, even if they also mentioned the benefit of lower turnover, they were still labeled as Morality-Motivated Advocates.

Additionally, attitudes regarding the moralization of the law were somewhat arrayed along a continuum of intensity. Some supervising managers were more fervent supporters of breastfeeding and workplace lactation than others. However, I decided against presenting variations and degrees of converts-to-the-cause sentiments. Thus, although some supervising managers felt more strongly than others, I presented this code as a binary – supervising managers moralized the law or they did not – in order to maintain a useful, concise discussion.

Finally, all researchers must acknowledge the possibility that respondents were trying to provide those answers that they thought the interviewer wanted. As always, this must be a consideration, particularly for Time Two interviews when more rapport might have been established and respondents might have developed a greater understanding of my project. Nevertheless, Time Two interviews did not all have the same types of responses; only a portion of the supervising managers moralized the law, for example. Even if those replies included feigned enthusiasm for breastfeeding, such replies still indicate that the respondent was more in touch with the morality-based arguments of breastfeeding and the concurrent health rhetoric than those respondents who did not engage that language at all. This, in itself, is meaningful and worthy of note.

REFERENCES

CHAPTER 1

Agocs, Tricia, Debra Langan, and Carrie B. Sanders. 2015. "Police Mothers at Home: Police Work and Danger-Protection Parenting Practices." *Gender & Society* 29(2):265–89.

Albiston, Catherine R. 2005. "Bargaining in the Shadow of Social Institutions: Competing Discourses and Social Change in Workplace Mobilization of Civil Rights." *Law & Society Review* 39(1):11–49.

2007. "Institutional Perspectives on Law, Work, and Family." *Annual Review of Law & Social Science* 3:397–426.

2010. *Institutional Inequality and the Mobilization of the Family and Medical Leave Act: Rights on Leave*. Cambridge: Cambridge University Press.

American Academy of Pediatrics. 2015. *Your Baby's First Year*. New York: Bantam.

Beauregard, Alexandra. 2014. "Fairness Perceptions of Work–Life Balance Initiative: Effects on Counterproductive Work Behaviour." *British Journal of Management* 25(4):772–89.

Berger, Peter L. and Thomas Luckmann. 1966. *The Social Construction of Reality: A Treatise in the Sociology of Knowledge*. Garden City, NY: Doubleday.

Budig, Michelle J., Joya Misra, and Irene Boeckmann. 2016. "Work–Family Policy Trade-Offs for Mothers? Unpacking the Cross-National Variation in Motherhood Earnings Penalties." *Work and Occupation* 43(2):119–77.

Dobbin, Frank and Erin L. Kelly. 2007. "How to Stop Harassment: Professional Construction of Legal Compliance in Organizations." *American Journal of Sociology* 112(4):1203–43.

Edelman, Lauren B. 1992. "Legal Ambiguity and Symbolic Structures: Organizational Mediation of Civil Rights Law." *American Journal of Sociology* 97(6):1531–76.

Edelman, Lauren B., Christopher Uggen, and Howard S. Erlanger. 1999. "The Endogeneity of Legal Regulation: Grievance Procedures as Rational Myth." *American Journal of Sociology* 105(2):406–54.

Edelman, Lauren B., Howard S. Erlanger, and John Lande. 1993. "Internal Dispute Resolution: The Transformation of Civil Rights in the Workplace." *Law and Society Review* 27(3):497–534.

1999. "When the 'Haves' Hold Court: Speculations on the Organizational Internalization of Law." *Law & Society Review* 33(4): 941–991.

Edelman, Lauren B. and Mark C. Suchman. 1997. "The Legal Environments of Organizations." *Annual Review of Sociology* 23:479–515.

Edelman, Lauren B., Sally Riggs Fuller, and Iona Mara-Ditra. 2001. "Diversity Rhetoric and the Managerialization of Law." *American Journal of Sociology* 106(6):1589–641.

Edelman, Lauren B., Scott R. Eliason, Virgina Mellema, Linda H. Krieger, and Catherine R. Albiston. 2011. "When Organizations Rule: Judicial Deference to Institutionalized Employment Structures." *American Journal of Sociology* 117(3):888–954.

Fair Labor Standards Act of 1938 Article (29 U.S.C. 207) Section 7, Amended (2010). Patient Protection and Affordable Care Act, P.L. 111–48. (2010).

Fuller, Sally Riggs, Lauren B. Edelman, and Sharon F. Matusik. 2000. "Legal Readings: Employee Interpretation and Mobilization of Law." *Academy of Management Review* 25(1):200–16.

Gangl, Markus and Andrea Ziefle. 2015. "The Making of a Good Woman: Extended Parental Leave Entitlements and Mothers' Work Commitment in Germany." *American Journal of Sociology* 121(2):511–63.

Glass, Jennifer. 2004. "Blessing or Curse? Work-Family Policies and Mother's Wage Growth over Time." *Work and Occupations* 31(3):367–94.

Goldin, Claudia. 2006. "The Quiet Revolution That Transformed Women's Employment, Education, and Family." *The American Economic Review* 96(2):1–21.

Gray, Garry C. and Susan S. Silbey. 2014. "Governing Inside the Organization: Interpreting Regulation and Compliance." *American Journal of Sociology* 120(1):96–145.

Gusfield, Joseph. 1967. "Moral Passage: The Symbolic Process in Public Designations of Deviance." *Social Problems* 15:175–88.

Hind, Christine. 2007. "Multi-Sited Ethnography as a Middle Range Methodology for Contemporary STS." *Science, Technology & Human Values* 32(6):652–71.

Kelly, Erin L. 2003. "The Strange History of Employer-Sponsored Child Care: Interested Actors, Uncertainty, and the Transformation of Law in Organizational Fields." *American Journal of Sociology* 109(3):606–49.

2005. "Discrimination against Caregivers? Gendered Family Responsibilities, Employer Practices, and Work Rewards," in *Handbook of Employment Discrimination Research: Rights and Realities*, edited by R. L. Nelson and L. B. Nielsen. New York: Kluwer Academic Press, pp. 353–74.

Kelly, Erin L., Samantha K. Ammons, Kelly Chermack, and Phyllis Moen. 2010. "Gendered Challenge, Gendered Response." *Gender & Society* 24:281–303.

Kelly, Erin L. and Frank Dobbin. 1999. "Civil Rights Law at Work: Sex Discrimination and the Rise of Maternity Leave Policies." *American Journal of Sociology* 105(2):455–92.

Krieger, Linda Hamilton, Rachel Kahn Best, and Lauren B. Edelman. 2015. "When 'Best Practices' Win, Employees Lose: Symbolic Compliance and Judicial Inference in Federal Equal Employment Opportunity Cases." *Law & Social Inquiry* 40(2):342–71.

Lévi-Strauss, Claude. 1969. *The Elementary Structures of Kinship*. New York: Beacon Press.

McAdams, Richard H. 2017. *The Expressive Powers of Law: Theories and Limits*. Cambridge, MA: Harvard University Press.

Meyer, John W. and Brian Rowan. 1977. "Institutionalized Organizations: Formal Structure as Myth and Ceremony." *American Journal of Sociology* 83:340–63.

Mohrbacher, Nancy. 2014. *Working and Breastfeeding Made Simple*. New York: Praeclarus Press.

Pedriana, Nicholas and Robin Stryker. 2017. "From Legal Doctrine to Social Transformation? Comparing U.S. Voting Rights, Equal Employment Opportunity, and Fair Housing Legislation." *American Journal of Sociology* 123(1):86–135.

Pedulla, David S. and Sarah Thebaud. 2015. "Can We Finish the Revolution? Gender, Work-Family Ideals, and Institutional Constraint." *American Sociological Review* 80(1):116–39.

Perlow, Leslie A. and Erin L. Kelly. 2014. "Toward a Model of Work Redesign for Better Work and Better Life." *Work and Occupations* 41(1):111–34.

Reynolds, Jeremy and Mathew May. 2014. "Religion, Motherhood, and the Spirit of Capitalism." *Social Currents* 1(2):173–88.

Roth, Louise Marie. 2004. "Engendering Inequality: Processes of Sex-Segregation on Wall Street." *Sociological Forum* 19(2):203–28.

Stryker, Robin. 2007. "Half Empty, Half Full, or Neither: Law, Inequality, and Social Change in Capitalist Democracies." *Annual Review of Law & Social Science* 2007(3):69–97.

Waldfogel, Jane. 2001. *Unbending Gender: Why Family and Work Conflict and What to Do About It*. Oxford: Oxford University Press.

Whittington, Kjersten Bunker. 2011. "Mothers of Invention? Gender, Motherhood, and New Dimensions of Productivity in the Science Profession." *Work and Occupations* 38(3):417–56.

Williams, Joan C. 2000. *Unbending Gender: Why Work and Family Conflict and What to Do About It*. Oxford: Oxford University Press.

Woodward, Jennifer. 2015. "Making Rights Work: Legal Mobilization at the Agency Level." *Law & Society Review* 49(3):691–723.

World Health Organization. 2002. *The Optimal Duration of Exclusive Breastfeeding: A Systematic Review*. New York: World Health Organization.

CHAPTER 2

Abbott Nutrition Information Centre. 2013. *Research Update: Prevalence of Breastfeeding in Singapore*. Centros: Abbott Nutrition Information Centre.

Abel, Richard L. 1982. "The Contradictions of Informal Justice," in *The Politics of Informal Justice*, edited by R. L. Abel. New York: Academic Press.

Adams, Jerome M. 2017. "Breastfeeding and Infant Mortality in Indiana: Changing the Culture and Saving Lives: A Model for Other States." *Breastfeeding Medicine* 12(8):456–58.

Agocs, Tricia, Debra Langan, and Carrie B. Sanders. 2015. "Police Mothers at Home: Police Work and Danger-Protection Parenting Practices." *Gender & Society* 29(2):265–89.

Albiston, Catherine R. 2005. "Bargaining in the Shadow of Social Institutions: Competing Discourses and Social Change in Workplace Mobilization of Civil Rights." *Law & Society Review* 39(1):11–49.

2007. "Institutional Perspectives on Law, Work, and Family." *Annual Review of Law & Social Science* 3:397–426.

2010. *Institutional Inequality and the Mobilization of the Family and Medical Leave Act: Rights on Leave*. Cambridge: Cambridge University Press.

Albiston, Catherine R. and Lindsey Trimble O'Connor. 2016. "Just Leave." *Harvard Journal of Law & Gender* 39(1):1–65.

Alhabas, Maryam Suliman. 2016. "Breastfeeding among Working Mothers in Saudi Arabia." Dissertation for Master of Science in Public Health in Health Promotion, Education, and Behavior, The Norman J. Arnold School of Public Health University of South Carolina, Columbia, South Carolina.

Allers, Kimberly Seals. 2017. *The Big Letdown: How Medicine, Big Business, and Feminism Undermine Breastfeeding*. New York: St. Martin's Press

Alvarez, Lizette. 2003. "Norway Leads Industrial Nations Back to Breast-Feeding." *The New York Times*.

American Academy of Pediatrics. 2005. "Policy Statement." *Pediatrics* 115(2):496–506.

Assi, Tina-Marie, Efe Atabay, Alison Earle, S. Jody Heymann, Gabriella Kranz, Gonzalo Moreno, Arijit Nandi, Amy Raub, Ilona Vincent, and Elise Marie Vaughan Winfrey. 2014. *Global Findings on Breastfeeding Breaks at Work*. Los Angeles: WORLD Policy Analysis Center and MACHEquity.

Asta, Elizabeth L. and Tammi Vacha-Haase. 2013. "Heterosexual Ally Development in Counseling Psychologists: Experiences, Training, and Advocacy." *The Counseling Psychologist* 41(4):493–529.

Barnes, Jeb and Thomas F. Burke. 2006. "The Diffusion of Rights: From Law on the Books to Organizational Rights Practices." *Law & Society Review* 40(3):493–523.

2012. "Making Way: Legal Mobilization, Organizational Response, and Wheelchair Access." *Law & Society Review* 46(1):167–98.

Battilana, Julie. 2006. "Agency and Institutions: The Enabling Role of Individuals' Social Position." *Organization* 13(5):653–76.

Beauregard, Alexandra. 2014. "Fairness Perceptions of Work–Life Balance Initiative: Effects on Counterproductive Work Behaviour." *British Journal of Management* 25(4):772–89.

Becker, Howard S. 1963. *Outsiders: Studies in the Sociology of Deviance*. New York: Free Press.

Bentley, Margaret E., Deborah L. Dee, and Joan L. Jensen. 2003. "Breastfeeding among Low Income, African American Women: Power, Beliefs and Decision Making." *The Journal of Nutrition* 133(Spring):305–9.

Berger, Peter L. and Thomas Luckmann. 1966. *The Social Construction of Reality: A Treatise in the Sociology of Knowledge*. Garden City, NY: Doubleday.

Bernstein, Mary, Anna-Maria Marshall, and Scott Barclay. 2009. "The Challenge of Law: Sexual Orientation, Gender Identity, and Social Movements," in *Queer Mobilizations: LBGT Activists Confront the Law*, edited by S. Barclay, M. Bernstein, and A.-M. Marshall. New York: New York University Press, pp. 1–20.

Berrey, Ellen, Steve G. Hoffman, and Laura Beth Nielsen. 2012. "Situated Justice: A Contextual Analysis of Fairness and Inequality in Employment Discrimination Litigation." *Law & Society Review* 46(1):1–36.

Berrey, Ellen, Robert L. Nelson, and Laura Beth Nielsen. 2018. *Rights on Trial: How Workplace Discrimination Law Perpetuates Inequality*. Chicago: University of Chicago Press.

Bockhaven, Wouter Van, Paul Matthyssens, and Koen Vandenbempt. 2015. "Empowering the Underdog: Soft Power in the Development of Collective Institutional Entrepreneurship in Business Markets." *Industrial Marketing Management* 48:174–86.

Boone, Meghan. 2018a. "Lactation Law." *California Law Review* 106 (6):1827–84.

Boswell-Penc, Maia and Kate Boyer. 2007. "Expressing Anxiety? Breast Pump Usage in American Workplaces." *Gender, Place & Culture* 14(5):551–67.

Boyle, Elizabeth H. and Amelia C. Corle. 2010. "Law and Culture in a Global Context: Interventions to Eradicate Genital Cutting." *Annual Review of Law and Social Science* 6(1):195–215.

Budig, Michelle J., Joya Misra, and Irene Boeckmann. 2016. "Work–Family Policy Trade-Offs for Mothers? Unpacking the Cross-National Variation in Motherhood Earnings Penalties." *Work and Occupation* 43(2):119–77.

Bumiller, Kristin. 1988. *The Civil Rights Society: The Social Construction of Victims*. Baltimore: The John Hopkins University Press.

Calavita, Kitty and Valerie Jenness. 2013. "Inside the Pyramid of Disputes: Naming Problems and Filing Grievances in California Prisons." *Social Problems* 60(1):50–80.

Calero, Analía, Victoria Giroud-Castiella, and Artiom Sici. 2016. "Maternity Protection." International Labor Organization: Social Protection.

Cardarelli, Tina, Compliance Liaison for the Indiana Perinatal Network, interviewed by Elizabeth A. Hoffmann, August 3, 2016

Carreño, Sofia. 2019. "How Do Maternity Leaves Work in Latin America?" *Latin American Post*.

Choo, Tai Bee, Foo Ling Li, Gary Ong, and Mabel Yap. 2005. "Impact of Working Status on Breastfeeding in Singapore: Evidence from the National Breastfeeding Survey 2001." *European Journal of Public Health* 16(4):424–30.

Cohen, Mathilde and Yoriko Otomo. 2019. *Making Milk: The Past, Present and Future of Our Primary Food*. New York: Bloomsbury Academic.

Crenshaw, Kimberle. 1988. "Race, Reform and Retrenchment: Transformation and Legitimation in Antidiscrimination Law." *Harvard Law Review* 101:1131–387.

Deephouse, David L., Jonathan Bundy, Leigh Plunkett Tost, and Mark C. Suchman. 2017. "Organizational Legitimacy: Six Key Questions." *The SAGE Handbook of Organizational Institutionalism* 4(2):27–54.

Deephouse, David L. and Mark C. Suchman. 2008. "Legitimacy in Organizational Institutionalism," in *The Sage Handbook of Organizational Institutionalism*, edited by M. C. Suchman, pp. 77–91.

Delgado, Richard, Chris Dunn, Pamela Brown, Helena Lee, and David Hubbert. 1985. "Fairness and Formality: Minimizing the Risk of Prejudice in Alternative Dispute Resolution." *Wisconsin Law Review* 1985(6):1359–1404.

Department of Labor South Africa. 1998. *Code of Good Practice on the Protection of Employees during Pregnancy and after the Birth of a Child*, vol. 401. Geneva: International Labor Organization.

Desai, Sreedhari D. and Maryam Kouchaki. 2017. "Moral Symbols: A Necklace of Garlic against Unethical Requests." *Academy of Management* 60(2):7–28.

DiMaggio, Paul. 1988. "Interest and Agency in Institutional Theory," in *Institutional Patterns and Organizations*, edited by L. Zucker. Cambridge, MA: Ballinger, pp. 3–22.

DiMaggio, Paul and Walter Powell. 1983. "The Iron Cage Revisited: Institutional Isomorphism and Collective Rationality in Organizational Fields." *American Sociological Review* 48(2):147–60.

Dinour, Lauren M. and Yeon K. Bai. 2016. "Breastfeeding: The Illusion of Choice." *Women's Health Issues* 26(5):479–82.

Diwakar, Vidya, Michael Malcolm and George Naufal. 2017. *Violent Conflict and Breastfeeding: The Case of Iraq*. Bonn: IZA Institute of Labor Economics.

Dobbin, Frank and Erin L. Kelly. 2007. "How to Stop Harassment: Professional Construction of Legal Compliance in Organizations." *American Journal of Sociology* 112(4):1203–43.

Edelman, Lauren B. 1992. "Legal Ambiguity and Symbolic Structures: Organizational Mediation of Civil Rights Law." *American Journal of Sociology* 97(6):1531–76.

2005. "Law at Work: The Endogenous Construction of Civil Rights," in *Handbook of Employment Discrimination Research: Rights and Realities*, edited by R. L. Nelson and L. B. Nielsen. New York: Kluwer Academic Press, pp. 336–52.

2016. *Working Law: Courts, Corporations, and Symbolic Civil Rights*. Chicago: University of Chicago Press.

Edelman, Murray. 1967. *The Symbolic Uses of Politics*. Urbana-Champaign: University of Illinois Press.

Edelman, Lauren B., Christopher Uggen, and Howard S. Erlanger. 1999. "The Endogeneity of Legal Regulation: Grievance Procedures as Rational Myth." *American Journal of Sociology* 105(2):406–54.

Edelman, Lauren B., Howard S. Erlanger, and John Lande. 1993. "Internal Dispute Resolution: The Transformation of Civil Rights in the Workplace." *Law and Society Review* 27(3):497–534.

Edelman, Lauren B. and Mark C. Suchman. 1997. "The Legal Environments of Organizations." *Annual Review of Sociology* 23:479–515.

Edelman, Lauren B., Sally Riggs Fuller, and Iona Mara-Ditra. 2001. "Diversity Rhetoric and the Managerialization of Law." *American Journal of Sociology* 106(6):1589–641.

Elliott, Sinikka and Sarah Bowen. 2018. "Defending Motherhood: Morality, Responsibility, and Double Binds in Feeding Children." *Journal of Marriage and the Family* 80(2):499–520.

Engel, David M. and Frank W. Munger. 2003. *Rights of Inclusion: Law and Identity in the Life Stories of Americans with Disabilities*. Chicago: University of Chicago Press.

Ewick, Patricia and Susan S. Silbey. 1998. *The Common Place of Law*. Chicago: University of Chicago Press.

2003. "Narrating Social Structure: Stories of Resistance to Legal Authority." *American Journal of Sociology* 108(6):1328–72.

Fuller, Sally Riggs, Lauren B. Edelman, and Sharon F. Matusik. 2000. "Legal Readings: Employee Interpretation and Mobilization of Law." *Academy of Management Review* 25(1):200–16.

Galanter, Marc. 1974. "Why the 'Haves' Come out Ahead: Speculations on the Limits of Legal Change." *Law & Society Review* 9(1):95–127.

Gallagher, Mary and Yujeong Yang. 2017. "Getting Schooled: Legal Mobilization as an Educative Process." *Law & Social Inquiry* 42(1):163–94.

Galtry, Judith. 2000. "Extending the Bright Line: Feminism, Breastfeeding, and the Workplace in the United States." *Gender & Society* 14(2):295–317.

Gangl, Markus and Andrea Ziefle. 2015. "The Making of a Good Woman: Extended Parental Leave Entitlements and Mothers' Work Commitment in Germany." *American Journal of Sociology* 121(2):511–63.

Gelber, Katharine and Luke McNamara. 2015. "The Effects of Civil Hate Speech Laws: Lessons from Australia." *Law & Society Review* 49(3): 631–64

Glass, Jennifer. 2004. "Blessing or Curse? Work-Family Policies and Mother's Wage Growth over Time." *Work and Occupations* 31(3):367–94.

Goldin, Claudia. 2006. "The Quiet Revolution That Transformed Women's Employment, Education, and Family." *The American Economic Review* 96(2):1–21.

Grillo, Trina. 1991. "The Mediation Alternative: Process Dangers for Women." *Yale Law Journal* 100:1545–610.

Gunningham, Neil A., Robert A. Kagan, and Dorothy Thornton. 2003. *Shades of Green: Business, Regulation, and Environment*. Berkeley, CA: Stanford University Press.

Gusfield, Joseph. 1967. "Moral Passage: The Symbolic Process in Public Designations of Deviance." *Social Problems* 15(2):175–88.

Gwartney-Gibbs, Patricia A. and Denise H. Lach. 1992. "Workplace Dispute Resolution and Gender Inequality." *Sociological Practice* 3(2):79–96.

Halabi, Sam F. 2018. *Intellectual Property and the New International Economic Order: Oligopoly, Regulation, and Wealth Redistribution in the Global Knowledge Economy*. London: Cambridge University Press.

Hallden, Karin. 2015. "Taking Training to Task: Sex of the Immediate Supervisor and Men's and Women's Time in Initial On-the-Job Training." *Work and Occupations* 42(1):73–102.

Harrison, Jill Ann, Steven H. Lopez, and Andrew W. Martin. 2015. "Rethinking Organizational Decoupling: Fields, Power Struggles, and Work Routines." *Social Currents* 2(3):341–60.

Haveman, Heather A. and Lauren S. Beresford. 2012. "If You're So Smart, Why Aren't You the Boss? Explaining the Persistent Vertical Gender Gap in Management." *The Annals of the American Academy of Political and Social Science* 639(1):114–30.

Health Resources & Services Administration. 2015, "The Business Case for Breastfeeding," in *Maternal and Child Health*, U.S. Department of Health and Human Services. (www.womenshealth.gov/files/documents/bcfb_business-case-for-breastfeeding-for-business-managers.pdf).

Herring, Cedric. 2009. "Does Diversity Pay? Race, Gender, and the Business Case for Diversity." *American Sociological Review* 74:208–24.

Heymann, Jody, Amy Raub, and Alison Earle. 2013. "Breastfeeding Policy: A Globally Comparative Analysis." *Bulletin of the World Health Organization* 91(4):398–406.

Hicks, Jennifer. 2005. *Hirkani's Daughters: Women Who Scale Modern Mountains to Combine Breastfeeding and Working*. New York: La Leche League International.

Hochschild, Arlie Russell. 1997. *The Time Bind: When Work Becomes Home and Home Becomes Work*. New York: Metropolitan Books.

Hodson, Randy and Vincent J. Roscigno. 2004. "Organizational Success and Worker Dignity: Complementary or Contradictory?" *American Journal of Sociology* 110(3):672–708.

Hoffmann, Elizabeth A. 2001. "Confrontations and Compromise: Dispute Resolution at a Worker Cooperative Coal Mine." *Law & Social Inquiry* 26(3):555–96.

2003. "Legal Consciousness and Dispute Resolution: Different Disputing Behavior at Two Similar Taxicab Companies." *Law & Social Inquiry* 28(3):691–715.

2004. "Selective Sexual Harassment: How the Labeling of Token Workers Can Produce Different Workplace Environments for Similar Groups of Women." *Law and Human Behavior* 28(1):29–45.

2005. "Dispute Resolution in a Worker Cooperative: Formal Procedures and Procedural Justice." *Law & Society Review* 39(1):51–82.

2012. *Co-operative Workplace Dispute Resolution: Organizational Structure, Ownership, and Ideology*. New York: Routledge.

2019. "Allies Already Poised to Comply: How Social Proximity Affects Lactation-at-Work Law Compliance." *Law & Society Review* 53(3):791–822.

Hull, Kathleen E. 2016. "Legal Consciousness in Marginalized Groups: The Case of LGBT People." *Law & Social Inquiry* 41(3):551–72.

Inoue, Madoka, Colin W. Binns, Keiko Otsuka, Masamine Jimba, and Manami Matsubara. 2012. "Infant Feeding Practices and Breastfeeding Duration in Japan: A Review." *International Breastfeeding Journal* 7(15):1–15.

Jacobs, Andrew. 2018. "Opposition to Breast-Feeding Resolution." *New York Times*.

Jantzer, Amanda M., Jenn Anderson, and Rebecca A. Kuehl. 2018. "Breastfeeding Support in the Workplace: The Relationships among Breastfeeding Support, Work–Life Balance, and Job Satisfaction." *Journal of Human Lactation* 34(2):379–85.

Jia, Nan, Xiao-yuan Dong, and Yue-ping Song. 2018. "Paid Maternity Leave and Breastfeeding in Urban China." *Feminist Economics* 24(2):31–53.

Johnson, Cathryn. 2004. "Introduction: Legitimacy Processes in Organizations," in *Research in the Sociology of Organizations*, vol. 22, edited by C. Johnson. Amsterdam: Elsevier JAI, pp. 1–24.

Jones, Katherine M., Michael L. Power, John T. Queenan, and Jay Schulkin. 2015. "Racial and Ethnic Disparities in Breastfeeding." *Breastfeeding Medicine* 10(4):186–96.

Joyce, Kathryn. 2015. "The War over Breastfeeding." *The New Republic*.

Jung, Courtney. 2015. *Lactivism*. New York: Basic Books.

Kagan, Robert A., Neil Gunningham, and Dorothy Thornton. 2012. "Fear, Duty, and Regulatory Compliance: Lessons from Three Research Projects," in *Explaining Compliance: Business Responses to Regulation*, edited by C. Park and V. L. Nielsen. Northampton, MA: Edward Edgar, pp. 37–58.

Kelly, Erin L. 2003. "The Strange History of Employer-Sponsored Child Care: Interested Actors, Uncertainty, and the Transformation of Law in Organizational Fields." *American Journal of Sociology* 109(3):606–49.

2005. "Discrimination against Caregivers? Gendered Family Responsibilities, Employer Practices, and Work Rewards," in *Handbook of Employment Discrimination Research: Rights and Realities*, edited by R. L. Nelson and L. B. Nielsen. New York: Kluwer Academic Press, pp. 353–74.

Kelly, Erin L. and Frank Dobbin. 1999. "Civil Rights Law at Work: Sex Discrimination and the Rise of Maternity Leave Policies." *American Journal of Sociology* 105(2):455–92.

Kelly, Erin L., Phyllis Moen and Eric Tranby. 2011. "Changing Workplaces to Reduce Work-Family Conflict." *American Sociological Review* 76:265–30.

Kelly, Erin L., Phyllis Moen, J. Michael Oakes, Wen Fan, Cassandra Okechukwu, Kelly D. Davis, Leslie B. Hammer, Ellen Ernst Kossek, Rosalind Berkowitz King, Ginger C. Hanson, Frank Mierzwa, and Lynne M. Casper. 2014. "Changing Work and Work-Family Conflict: Evidence from the Work, Family, and Health Network." *American Sociological Review* 79(3):485–516.

Kelly, Erin L., Samantha K. Ammons, Kelly Chermack and Phyllis Moen. 2010. "Gendered Challenge, Gendered Response: Confronting the Ideal Worker Norm in a White-Collar Organization." *Gender & Society* 24(3):281–303.

Kim, Julia H., Jong C. Shin, and Sharon M. Donovan. 2019. "Effectiveness of Workplace Lactation Interventions on Breastfeeding Outcomes in the United States: An Updated Systematic Review." *Journal of Human Lactation* 35(1):100–13.

Kirkland, Anna. 2008. "Think of the Hippopotamus: Rights Consciousness in the Fat Acceptance Movement." *Law & Society Review* 43(2):397–431.

2014. "What Is Wellness Now." *Journal of Health Politics, Policy and Law* 39(5):957–70.

Kobayashi, Miki and Emiko Usui. 2017a. "Breastfeeding Practices and Parental Employment in Japan." *Review of Economics of the Household* 15(4):579–96.

Kol-Zchut. 2019. "Parenting Time," in *Kol Zchut*, edited by Sharon Hornstein. Tel Aviv: Kol Zchut, p. 4.

Kostiner, Idit. 2003. "Evaluating Legality: Toward a Cultural Approach to the Study of Law and Social Change." *Law and Society Review* 37(2):323–68.

Kozhimannil, Katy B., Judy Jou, Dwenda K. Gjerdingen, and Patricia M. McGovern. 2016. "Access to Workplace Accommodations to Support Breastfeeding after Passage of the Affordable Care Act." *Women's Health Issues* 26(1):6–13.

Lazerson, Mark H. 1982. "In the Halls of Justice, the Only Justice Is in the Halls," in *The Politics of Informal Justice*, edited by R. L. Abel. New York: Academic Press, pp. 45–69.

Lepore, Jill. 2009. "Baby Food." *The New Yorker*.

Levitsky, Sandra R. 2008. "'What Rights?' The Construction of Political Claims to American Health Care Entitlements." *Law and Society Review* 42(3):551–90.

2014. *Caring for Our Own: Why There Is No Political Demand for New American Social Welfare Rights*. New York: Oxford University Press.

Lindberg, L. 1996. "Women's Decisions about Breastfeeding and Maternal Employment." *Journal of Marriage and the Family* 58(1):239–51.

Lovell, George I. 2012. *This Is Not Civil Rights: Discovering Rights Talk in 1939 America*. Chicago: University of Chicago Press.

Lutter, Chessa K. and Ardythe L. Morrow. 2013. "Protection, Promotion, and Support and Global Trends in Breastfeeding." *American Society for Nutrition Advanced Nutrition* 4(2):213–19.

Macaulay, Stewart. 1963. "Non-contractual Relations in Business: A Preliminary Study." *American Sociological Review* 28:55–66.

Maloney, Carolyn B. June 11, 2009. *Congressional Record-House*.

Marshall, Anna-Maria. 2003. "Injustice Frames, Legality, and the Everyday Construction of Sexual Harassment." *Law & Social Inquiry* 28(3):659–89.

2005. "Idle Rights: Employees' Rights Consciousness and the Construction of Sexual Harassment Policies." *Law & Society Review* 39(1):83.

Marshall, Anna-Maria and Scott Barclay. 2003. "Introduction: In Their Own Words: How Ordinary People Construct the Legal World." *Law & Social Inquiry* 28(3):617–28.

Martin-Wiesner, Patricia. 2018. *A Policy-Friendly Environment for Breastfeeding: A Review of South Africa's Progress in Systematising Its International and National Responsibilities to Protect, Promote and Support*

Breastfeeding. Johannesburg: DST-NRF Centre of Excellence in Human Development, University of the Witwaterstrand.

Martucci, Jessica. 2015. *Back to the Breast: Natural Motherhood and Breastfeeding in America*. Chicago: University of Chicago Press.

Maternal and Child Health Bureau. April 30, 2019. "Breastfeeding State Laws." *National Conference of State Legislatures*.

May, Ashley. 2017. "Breastfeeding: Not a Single Country in the World Meets WHO, UNICEF Standards." *USA Today*.

McAdams, Richard H. 2017. *The Expressive Powers of Law: Theories and Limits*. Cambridge, MA: Harvard University Press.

McCann, Michael W. 1994. *Rights at Work: Pay Equity Reform and the Politics of Legal Mobilization*. Chicago: University Of Chicago Press.

McDowell, Margaret A., Chia-Yih Wang, and Jocelyn Kennedy-Stephenson. 2008. *Breastfeeding in the United States: Findings from the National Health and Nutrition Examination Surveys, 1999–2006*. U.S. Department of Health and Human Services, Centers for Disease Control and Prevention, National Center for Health Statistics.

McEwen, Craig A., Lynn Mather, and Richard J. Maiman. 1994. "Lawyers, Mediation, and the Management of Divorce Practice." *Law & Society Review* 28(1):149–86.

McKinney, Chelsea O., Jennifer Hahn-Holbrook, P. Lindsay Chase-Lansdale, Sharon L. Ramey, Julie Krohn, Maxine Reed-Vance, Tonse N. K. Raju, and Madeleine U. Shalowitz. 2016. "Racial and Ethnic Differences in Breastfeeding." *Pediatrics: Official Journal of the American Academy of Pediatrics* 138(2): 1–11.

Medela India. 2018. *Breastfeeding Challenges of Indian Moms: Research Report*. Gurgaon: Medela India Private Limited.

Menon, Lakshmi and Chris Mulford. 2007. *Innovative Initiatives: Supporting Working Women's Right to Breastfeed*. Malaysia: World Alliance for Breastfeeding Action.

Merkley, Jeffrey. June 11, 2009. *Congressional Record-Senate*.

Merry, Sally Engle. 1990. "The Discourses of Mediation and the Power of Naming." *Yale Journal of Law & the Humanities* 2(1):1–36.

Mexico News Daily. 2019. "Breastfeeding Is a Right,' Senator Says after Baby in Congress Draws Rebuke," *Mexico News Daily*.

Meyer, John W. and Brian Rowan. 1977. "Institutionalized Organizations: Formal Structure as Myth and Ceremony." *American Journal of Sociology* 83(2):340–63.

Ministry of Health, State of Israel. 2019, "Breastfeeding – Where and When It Suits You," Jerusalem: State of Israel. Retrieved April 29, 2019. (www.health.gov.il/English/Topics/Pregnancy/Childbirth/feeding/Pages/whenandwhere.aspx).

Ministry of Health and Family Welfare. 2017. *India Registers Significant Decline in Infant Mortality Rate (IMR) Major Drop in Birth Cohort and Infant Deaths*

Gender Gap Reducing: Big Boost to "Beti Bachao Beti Padhao." New Delhi: Press Information Bureau.

Mun, Eunmi and Mary C. Brinton. 2015. "Workplace Matters: The Use of Parental Leave Policy in Japan." *Work and Occupation* 42(3):335–69.

Nabbout, Mariam. 2019. "A Breakdown of Saudi Arabia's New 'Women in the Workplace' Initiative." *StepFeed.*

Nielsen, Laura Beth. 2000. "Situating Legal Consciousness: Experiences and Attitudes of Ordinary Citizens about Law and Street Harassment." *Law and Society Review* 34(4):1056–90.

2004. *License to Harass: Law, Hierarchy, and Offensive Public Speech.* Princeton, NJ: Princeton University Press.

Nielsen, Vibeke Lehmann and Christine Parker. 2012. "Mixed Motives: Economic, Social, and Normative Motivations in Business Compliance." *Law & Policy* 34(4):428–62.

Office on Women's Health. 2018. *Business Case for Breastfeeding.* Washington, DC: U.S. Department of Health and Human Services (last updated: October 26, 2018).

Oliveira, Danielle Soares de, Cristiano S. Boccolini, Eduardo Faestein, and Eiseu Verly. 2017. "Breastfeeding Duration and Associated Factors between 1960 and 2000." *Jornal de Pediatria* 93(2):130–35.

Olivetti, Claudia and Barbara Petrongolo. 2017. "The Economic Consequences of Family Policies: Lessons from a Century of Legislation in High-Income Countries." *Journal of Economic Perspectives* 31(1):205–30.

Orozco, Nicole Kennedy. 2010. "Pumping at Work: Protection from Lactation Discrimination in the Workplace." *Ohio State Law Journal* 71 (6):1281–316.

Palmer, Gabrielle. 2009. *The Politics of Breastfeeding.* New York: Pinter & Martin Ltd.

Papastavrou, Mark, S. M. Genitsaridi, E. Komodiki, S. Paliatsou, A. Kontogeorgou, and Nicoletta Iacovidou. 2015. "Breastfeeding in the Course of History." *Journal of Pediatrics and Neonatal Care* 2(6). doi: 10.15406/jpnc.2015.02.00096.

Pareek, Shatrughan. 2019. "Exclusive Breastfeeding in India: An Ultimate Need of Infants." *Journal of Nursing Practice Today* 6(1):4–6.

Patient Protection and Affordable Care Act, P.L. 111–48. (2010).

Pedriana, Nicholas and Robin Stryker. 1997. "Political Culture Wars 1960s Style: Equal Employment Opportunity-Affirmative Action Law and the Philadelphia Plan." *American Journal of Sociology* 103(3):633–91.

2017. "From Legal Doctrine to Social Transformation? Comparing U.S. Voting Rights, Equal Employment Opportunity, and Fair Housing Legislation." *American Journal of Sociology* 123(1):86–135.

Pedulla, David S. and Sarah Thebaud. 2015. "Can We Finish the Revolution? Gender, Work-Family Ideals, and Institutional Constraint." *American Sociological Review* 80(1):116–39.

Perlow, Leslie A. and Erin L. Kelly. 2014. "Toward a Model of Work Redesign for Better Work and Better Life." *Work and Occupations* 41(1):111–34.

Phelan, Jessica. 2015. "These Are the Best Places to Be a Breastfeeding Mother." *Public Radio International*, vol. 2019.

Plumm, Karyn M. and Cheryl A. Terrance. 2009. "Battered Women Who Kill: The Impact of Expert Testimony and Empathy Induction in the Courtroom." *Violence against Women* 15(1):186–205.

Pound, Roscoe. 1910. "Law in the Books and Law in Action." *American Law Review* 44:12–36.

Powell, Walter W. and Paul J. DiMaggio. 1991. *The New Institutionalism in Organizational Analysis*. Chicago: University of Chicago Press.

Rao, Hayagreeva, Calvin Morrill, and Mayer N. Zald. 2000. "Power Plays: How Social Movements and Collective Action Create New Organizational Forms." *Research in Organizational Behavior* 22(1):237–81.

Raymond, Leigh, S. Laurel Weldon, Daniel Kelly, Ximena B. Arriaga, and Ann Marie Clark. 2013. "Making Change: Norm-Based Strategies for Institutional Change to Address Intractable Problems." *Political Research Quarterly* 67(1):197–211.

Redding, Sharon R., Yan-Qiong Ouyang, and Ya Zhao. 2017. "Attitudes of Chinese Adults to Breastfeeding in Public: A Web-Based Survey." *Breastfeeding Medicine* 12(5):316–21.

Reynolds, Jeremy and Mathew May. 2014. "Religion, Motherhood, and the Spirit of Capitalism." *Social Currents* 1(2):173–88.

Rico. 2018. "Government Decrees Regulation for Breastfeeding Rooms in the Workplace." www.qcostarica.com.

Rose, Evan K. 2018. "The Rise and Fall of Female Labor Force Participation During World War II in the United States." *Journal of Economic History* 78(3):673–711.

Roth, Louise Marie. 2004. "Engendering Inequality: Processes of Sex-Segregation on Wall Street." *Sociological Forum* 19(2):203–28.

Royster, Deirdre A. 2003. *Race and the Invisible Hand: How White Networks Exclude Black Men from Blue-Collar Jobs*. Berkeley: University of California Press.

Rudavsky, Shari. 2008. "Law Aids Breast-Feeding Moms at Work." *The Indianapolis Star*.

Sarat, Austin. 1990. "'. . . The Law Is All Over': Power, Resistance and the Legal Consciousness of the Welfare Poor." *Yale Journal of Law & the Humanities* 2(343):343–79.

Scott, W. Richard and Gerald F. Davis. 2007. *Organizations and Organizing: Rational, Natural, and Open System Perspectives*. New York: Prentice Hall.

Shortall, Jessica. 2015. *Work. Pump. Repeat: The New Mom's Survival Guide to Breastfeeding and Going Back to Work*. New York: Harry N. Abrams.

Silbey, Susan and Austin Sarat. 1989. "Dispute Processing in Law and Legal Scholarship: From Institutional Critique to the Reconstruction of the Judicial Subject." *Denver University Law Review* 6(2):437–97.

Skitka, Linda J. and G. Scott Morgan. 2014. "The Social and Political Implications of Moral Conviction." *Political Psychology* 35(1):95–110.

Slim, Fundacion Carlos. 2015. *Women in Mexico Breastfeed Their Children*. Mexico City: Fundacion Carlos Slim.

Solomon, Stephen. 1981. "The Controversy over Infant Formula." *The New York Times Magazine*.

Soomro, J. A., Z. N. Shaikh, T. B. Saheer, and S. A. Bijarani. 2016. "Employers' Perspective of Workplace Breastfeeding Support in Karachi, Pakistan: A Cross-Sectional Study." *International Breastfeeding Journal* 11(1):24–32.

Stepan-Norris, Judith and Jasmine Kerriessey. 2016. "Enhancing Gender Equity in Academia: Lessons from the Advance Program." *Sociological Perspectives* 59(2):225–45.

Stevens, Emily E., Thelma E. Patrick, and Rita Pickler. 2009. "A History of Infant Feeding." *The Journal of Perinatal Education* 18(2):32–39.

Stryker, Robin. 1994. "Rules, Resources, and Legitimacy Processes: Some Implications for Social Conflict, Order, and Change." *American Journal of Sociology* 99(4):847–910.

2000. "Legitimacy Processes as Institutional Politics: Implications for Theory and Research in the Sociology of Organizations." *Research in the Sociology of Organizations* 17(1):179–223.

2001. "Disparate Impact and the Quota Debates: Law, Labor Market Sociology, and Equal Employment Policies." *The Sociological Quarterly* 42(1):13–46.

2007. "Half Empty, Half Full, or Neither: Law, Inequality, and Social Change in Capitalist Democracies." *Annual Review of Law & Social Science* 2007(3):69–97.

Stryker, Robin and Pamela Wald. 2009. "Redefining Compassion to Reform Welfare: How Supporters of 1990s US Federal Welfare Reform Aimed for the Moral High Ground." *Social Politics* 16(4):519–57.

Suchman, Mark C. 1995. "Managing Legitimacy: Strategic and Institutional Approaches." *Academy of Management Review* 20(3):571–610.

1997. "On Beyond Interest: Rational, Normative and Cognitive Perspectives in the Social Scientific Study of Law." *Wisconsin Law Review* 1997(3):475–501.

2003. "The Contract as Social Artifact." *Law & Society Review* 37(1) 91–142.

Suchman, Mark C. and Lauren B. Edelman. 1996. "Legal Rational Myths: The New Institutionalism and the Law and Society Tradition." *Law & Social Inquiry* 21(4):903–41.

Thulier, Diane. 2009. "Breastfeeding in America: A History of Influencing Factors." *Journal of Human Lactation* 25(1):85–94.

Trautner, Mary Nell, Erin Hatton, and Kelly E. Smith. 2013. "What Workers Want Depends: Legal Knowledge and the Desire for Workplace Change among Day Laborers." *Law & Policy* 35(4):319–40.

Unar-Munguía, Mishel, Dalia Stern, Monica Arantxa Colchero, and Teresita González de Cosío. 2019. "The Burden of Suboptimal Breastfeeding in Mexico: Maternal Health Outcomes and Costs." *Maternal and Child Nutrition* 15(1): 1–13.

United-Nations. 1989. *Convention on the Rights of the Child*. New York: United Nations.

Valk, Helga A. G. de, François Levrau, Jonas Loos, Karel Neels, Inge Pasteels, and Katrien Swartelé. 2014. *Family Policies*. Munkich: Population Europe Resource Finder & Archive (PERFAR).

Waldfogel, Jane. 2001. *Unbending Gender: Why Family and Work Conflict and What to Do about It*. New York: Oxford University Press.

Weber, Max. 1946. *From Max Weber: Essays in Sociology*. Translated by H. Gerth and C. W. Mills. New York: Oxford University Press.

Weinberg, Jill D. and Laura Beth Nielsen. 2012. "Examining Empathy: Discrimination, Experience, and Judicial Decision-Making." *Southern California Law Review* 85(2):313–39.

Welmer, Jan P. 1999. "Breastfeeding: Health and Economic Issues." *Food Review* 22(1):31–5.

Whittington, Kjersten Bunker. 2011. "Mothers of Invention? Gender, Motherhood, and New Dimensions of Productivity in the Science Profession." *Work and Occupations* 38(3):417–56.

Wiessinger, Diane, Diana West, and Teresa Pitman. 2010. *The Womanly Art of Breastfeeding*. New York: Ballantine Books.

Wijen, Frank and Shahzad Ansa. 2016. "Overcoming Inaction through Collective Institutional Entrepreneurship: Insights from Regime Theory." *Organization Studies* 28(7):1079–100.

Williams, Joan C. 2000. *Unbending Gender: Why Work and Family Conflict and What to Do about It*. Oxford: Oxford University Press.

Wolf, Jacqueline H. 2001. *Don't Kill Your Baby: Public Health and the Decline of Breastfeeding in the 19th and 20th Centuries*. Columbus: The Ohio University Press.

Woodward, Jennifer. 2015. "Making Rights Work: Legal Mobilization at the Agency Level." *Law & Society Review* 49(3):691–723.

World Health Organization. 2002. *The Optimal Duration of Exclusive Breastfeeding: A Systematic Review*. New York: World Health Organization.

2013. *Protecting Breastfeeding in Peru*. Geneva: World Health Organization.

WORLD Policy Analysis Center. 2019. *International Breastfeeding Protections*. Geneva.

Young, Kathryne M. 2014. "Everyone Knows the Game: Legitimacy and Legal Consciousness in the Hawaiian Cockfight." *Law & Society Review* 48(4):499–530.

Young, Kathryne M. and Katie R. Billings. 2020. "Legal Consciousness and Cultural Capital." *Law & Society Review* 54(1):33–65.

Zucker, Lynn G. 1977. "The Role of Institutionalization in Cultural Persistence." *American Sociological Review* 42(5):726–43.

CHAPTER 3

Albiston, Catherine R. 2005. "Bargaining in the Shadow of Social Institutions: Competing Discourses and Social Change in Workplace Mobilization of Civil Rights." *Law & Society Review* 39(1):11–49.

2010. *Institutional Inequality and the Mobilization of the Family and Medical Leave Act: Rights on Leave*. Cambridge: Cambridge University Press.

Foucault, Michel. 1980. *Power/Knowledge: Selected Interviews and Other Writings, 1972–1977*. New York: Pantheon.

Fraser, Nancy and Rahel Jaeggi. 2018. *Capitalism: A Conversation in Critical Theory*. New York: Polity.

Gerstel, Naomi and Dan Clawson. 2014. "Class Advantage and the Gender Divide: Flexibility on the Job and at Home." *American Journal of Sociology* 120(2):395–431.

Hirschman, Albert O. 1970. *Exit, Voice, and Loyalty: Responses to Declines in Firms, Organizations, and States*. Cambridge, MA: Harvard University Press.

Hirsh, C. Elizabeth and Sabino Kornrich. 2008. "The Context of Discrimination: Workplace Conditions, Institutional Environments, and Sex and Race Discrimination Charges." *American Journal of Sociology* 113(5):1394–432.

Hoffmann, Elizabeth A. 2006. "Exit and Voice: Organizational Loyalty and Dispute Resolution Strategies." *Social Forces* 84(4):2313–30.

2012. *Co-operative Workplace Dispute Resolution: Organizational Structure, Ownership, and Ideology*. New York: Routledge.

Trautner, Mary Nell, Erin Hatton, and Kelly E. Smith. 2013. "What Workers Want Depends: Legal Knowledge and the Desire for Workplace Change among Day Laborers." *Law & Policy* 35(4):319–40.

Williams, Joan C. 2000. *Unbending Gender: Why Work and Family Conflict and What to Do about It*. Oxford: Oxford University Press.

CHAPTER 4

Edelman, Lauren B. and Mark C. Suchman. 1997. "The Legal Environments of Organizations." *Annual Review of Sociology* 23:479–515.

McCann, Michael W. 1994. *Rights at Work: Pay Equity Reform and the Politics of Legal Mobilization*. Chicago: University Of Chicago Press.

Swidler, Ann. 1986. "Culture in Action: Symbols and Strategies." *American Sociological Review* 51(2):273–86.

CHAPTER 5

Albiston, Catherine R. 2005. "Bargaining in the Shadow of Social Institutions: Competing Discourses and Social Change in Workplace Mobilization of Civil Rights." *Law & Society Review* 39(1):11–49.

Barnes, Jeb and Thomas F. Burke. 2006. "The Diffusion of Rights: From Law on the Books to Organizational Rights Practices." *Law & Society Review* 40(3):493–523.

2012. "Making Way: Legal Mobilization, Organizational Response, and Wheelchair Access." *Law & Society Review* 46(1):167–98.

Bernstein, Mary, Anna-Maria Marshall, and Scott Barclay. 2009. "The Challenge of Law: Sexual Orientation, Gender Identity, and Social Movements," in *Queer Mobilizations: LBGT Activists Confront the Law*, edited by S. Barclay, M. Bernstein, and A.-M. Marshall. New York: NYU Press, pp. 1–20.

Broido, Ellen M. 1997. "The Development of Social Justice Allies during College: A Phenomenological Investigation." Doctor of Education, Counselor Education, The Pennsylvania State University, UMI.

Bumiller, Kristin. 1988. *The Civil Rights Society: The Social Construction of Victims*. Baltimore: The John Hopkins University Press.

DiMaggio, Paul. 1988. "Interest and Agency in Institutional Theory," in *Institutional Patterns and Organizations*, edited by L. Zucker. Cambridge, MA: Ballinger, pp. 3–22.

Edelman, Lauren B. and Mark C. Suchman. 1997. "The Legal Environments of Organizations." *Annual Review of Sociology* 23:479–515.

Engel, David M. and Frank W. Munger. 1996. "Rights, Remembrance, and the Reconciliation of Difference." *Law & Society Review* 30(1):7–53.

2003. *Rights of Inclusion: Law and Identity in the Life Stories of Americans with Disabilities*. Chicago: University of Chicago Press.

Fingerhut, Adam W. 2011. "Straight Allies: What Predicts Heterosexuals' Alliance with the LGBT Community?" *Journal of Applied Social Psychology* 41(9):2230–48.

Glass, Christy and Eva Fodor. 2018. "Managing Motherhood: Job Context and Employer Bias." *Work and Occupation* 45(2):202–34.

Glynn, Adam N. and Maya Sen. 2014. "Identifying Judicial Empathy: Does Having Daughters Cause Judges to Rule for Women's Issues?" *American Journal of Political Science* 59(1):37–54.

Gunningham, Neil A., Robert A. Kagan, and Dorothy Thornton. 2003. *Shades of Green: Business, Regulation, and Environment*. Berkeley, CA: Stanford University Press.

Kagan, Robert A., Neil Gunningham, and Dorothy Thornton. 2012. "Fear, Duty, and Regulatory Compliance: Lessons from Three Research Projects," in *Explaining Compliance: Business Responses to Regulation*, edited by C. Park and V. L. Nielsen. Northampton, MA: Edward Edgar, pp. 37–58.

Kokkonen, Andrej and David Karlsson. 2017. "That's What Friends Are For: How Intergroup Friendships Promote Historically Disadvantaged Groups' Substantive Political Representation." *British Journal of Sociology* 68(4):693–717.

Levitsky, Sandra R. 2008. "'What Rights?' The Construction of Political Claims to American Health Care Entitlements." *Law and Society Review* 42(3):551–90.

Madeira, Jody Lynee. 2006. "Recognizing Odysseus' Scar: Reconceptualizing Pain and Its Empathic Role in Civil Adjudication." *Florida State University Law Review* 34(1):41–97.

McAdams, Richard H. 2017. *The Expressive Powers of Law: Theories and Limits*. Cambridge, MA: Harvard University Press.

McCann, Michael W. 1994. *Rights at Work: Pay Equity Reform and the Politics of Legal Mobilization*. Chicago: University Of Chicago Press.

Phelan, Jessica. 2015. "These Are the Best Places to Be a Breastfeeding Mother." *Public Radio International*, vol. 2019.

Reason, Robert Dean, Elizabeth A. Roosa Millar, and Tara Scales. 2005. "Toward a Model of Racial Justice Ally Development." *Journal of College Student Development* 46(4):530–46.

Regala, Betty. 2006. "Mothers in Philippines Break Guinness World Record for Breastfeeding." *We're Building a New UNICEF.org*. May 16, 2006.

Russell, Glenda M. 2011. "Motives of Heterosexual Allies in Collective Action for Equality." *The Journal of Social Issues* 67(2):376–93.

Suchman, Mark C. and Lauren B. Edelman. 1996. "Legal Rational Myths: The New Institutionalism and the Law and Society Tradition." *Law & Social Inquiry* 21(4):903–41.

Trautner, Mary Nell, Erin Hatton, and Kelly E. Smith. 2013. "What Workers Want Depends: Legal Knowledge and the Desire for Workplace Change among Day Laborers." *Law & Policy* 35(4):319–40.

Young, Kathryne M. and Katie R. Billings. 2020. "Legal Consciousness and Cultural Capital." *Law & Society Review* 54(1):33–65.

CHAPTER 6

Abel, Richard L. 1982. "The Contradictions of Informal Justice," in *The Politics of Informal Justice*, edited by R. L. Abel. New York: Academic Press.

Albiston, Catherine R. 2005. "Bargaining in the Shadow of Social Institutions: Competing Discourses and Social Change in Workplace Mobilization of Civil Rights." *Law & Society Review* 39(1):11–49.

2010. *Institutional Inequality and the Mobilization of the Family and Medical Leave Act: Rights on Leave*. Cambridge: Cambridge University Press.

Apple, Rima. 2006. *Perfect Motherhood: Science and Childrearing in America*. New York: Rutgers University Press.

Barnes, Jeb and Thomas F. Burke. 2012. "Making Way: Legal Mobilization, Organizational Response, and Wheelchair Access." *Law & Society Review* 46(1):167–98.

Becker, Howard S. 1963. *Outsiders: Studies in the Sociology of Deviance*. New York: Free Press.

Boyle, Elizabeth H. and Amelia C. Corle. 2010. "Law and Culture in a Global Context: Interventions to Eradicate Genital Cutting." *Annual Review of Law and Social Science* 6(1):195–215.

Budig, Michelle J. and Paula England. 2001. "The Wage Penalty for Motherhood." *American Sociological Review* 66(2):204–25.

Bumiller, Kristin. 1988. *The Civil Rights Society: The Social Construction of Victims*. Baltimore: The John Hopkins University Press.

Chua, Lynette J. and David M. Engel. 2019. "Legal Consciousness Reconsidered." *Annual Review of Law & Social Science* 15:335–53.

Correll, Shelly J., Stephen Benard, and In Paik. 2007. "Getting a Job: Is There a Motherhood Penalty?" *American Journal of Sociology* 112(5):1297–338.

Crenshaw, Kimberle. 1988. "Race, Reform and Retrenchment: Transformation and Legitimation in Antidiscrimination Law." *Harvard Law Review* 101(7):1131–387.

Czarnecki, Danielle. 2015. "Moral Women, Immoral Technologies: How Devout Women Negotiate Gender, Religion, and Assisted Reproductive Technologies." *Gender & Society* 29(5):716–42.

Delgado, Richard, Chris Dunn, Pamela Brown, Helena Lee, and David Hubbert. 1985. "Fairness and Formality: Minimizing the Risk of Prejudice in Alternative Dispute Resolution." *Wisconsin Law Review* 1985:585–629.

DiMaggio, Paul. 1988. "Interest and Agency in Institutional Theory," in *Institutional Patterns and Organizations*, edited by L. Zucker. Cambridge, MA: Ballinger, pp. 3–22.

Edelman, Lauren B. 2005. "Law at Work: The Endogenous Construction of Civil Rights," in *Handbook of Employment Discrimination Research: Rights and Realities*, edited by R. L. Nelson and L. B. Nielsen. New York: Kluwer Academic Press, pp. 336–52.

2016. *Working Law: Courts, Corporations, and Symbolic Civil Rights*. Chicago: University of Chicago Press.

Edelman, Lauren B., Howard S. Erlanger, and John Lande. 1993. "Internal Dispute Resolution: The Transformation of Civil Rights in the Workplace." *Law and Society Review* 27(3):497–534.

Edelman, Lauren B., Sally Riggs Fuller, and Iona Mara-Ditra. 2001. "Diversity Rhetoric and the Managerialization of Law." *American Journal of Sociology* 106(6):1589–641.

Elliott, Sinikka and Sarah Bowen. 2018. "Defending Motherhood: Morality, Responsibility, and Double Binds in Feeding Children." *Journal of Marriage and the Family* 80(2):499–520.

Engel, David M. and Frank W. Munger. 2003. *Rights of Inclusion: Law and Identity in the Life Stories of Americans with Disabilities*. Chicago: University of Chicago Press.

Fraser, Nancy. 2016. "Feminism's Home Front: Contradictions of Capital and Care." *New Left Review*.

Galanter, Marc. 1974. "Why the 'Haves' Come out Ahead: Speculations on the Limits of Legal Change." *Law & Society Review* 9(1):95–127.

Gramsci, Antonio. 1971. *Prison Notebooks 5–23*. New York: Columbia University Press.

Gray, Garry C. and Susan S. Silbey. 2014. "Governing Inside the Organization: Interpreting Regulation and Compliance." *American Journal of Sociology* 120(1):96–145.

Grillo, Trina. 1991. "The Mediation Alternative: Process Dangers for Women." *Yale Law Journal* 100:1545–610.

Gwartney-Gibbs, Patricia A. and Denise H. Lach. 1992. "Workplace Dispute Resolution and Gender Inequality." *Sociological Practice* 10(2):79–96.

Hallden, Karin. 2015. "Taking Training to Task: Sex of the Immediate Supervisor and Men's and Women's Time in Initial On-the-Job Training." *Work and Occupations* 42(1):73–102.

Haveman, Heather A. and Lauren S. Beresford. 2012. "If You're So Smart, Why Aren't You the Boss? Explaining the Persistent Vertical Gender Gap in Management." *The Annals of the American Academy of Political and Social Science* 639(1):114–30.

Herring, Cedric. 2009. "Does Diversity Pay? Race, Gender, and the Business Case for Diversity." *American Sociological Review* 74(2):208–24.

Hodson, Randy and Vincent J. Roscigno. 2004. "Organizational Success and Worker Dignity: Complementary or Contradictory?" *American Journal of Sociology* 110(3):672–708.

Hoffmann, Elizabeth A. 2001. "Confrontations and Compromise: Dispute Resolution at a Worker Cooperative Coal Mine." *Law & Social Inquiry* 26(3):555–96.

2005. "Dispute Resolution in a Worker Cooperative: Formal Procedures and Procedural Justice." *Law & Society Review* 39(1):51–82.

2006. "Exit and Voice: Organizational Loyalty and Dispute Resolution Strategies." *Social Forces* 84(4):2313–30.

2009. "Dispute Resolution in the Homecare Industry: The Triangle of Patient, Worker, and Employer." *Sociological Focus* 42(1):57–78.

Kagan, Robert A., Neil Gunningham, and Dorothy Thornton. 2012. "Fear, Duty, and Regulatory Compliance: Lessons from Three Research Projects," in *Explaining Compliance: Business Responses to Regulation*, edited by C. Park and V. L. Nielsen. Northampton, MA: Edward Edgar, pp. 37–58.

Kelly, Erin L., Phyllis Moen, J. Michael Oakes, Wen Fan, Cassandra Okechukwu, Kelly D. Davis, Leslie B. Hammer, Ellen Ernst Kossek,

Rosalind Berkowitz King, Ginger C. Hanson, Frank Mierzwa, and Lynne M. Casper. 2014. "Changing Work and Work–Family Conflict: Evidence from the Work, Family, and Health Network." *American Sociological Review* 79(3):485–516.

Kirkland, Anna. 2014. "What Is Wellness Now." *Journal of Health Politics, Policy and Law* 39(5):957–70.

Kostiner, Idit. 2003. "Evaluating Legality: Toward a Cultural Approach to the Study of Law and Social Change." *Law and Society Review* 37(2):323–68.

Lazerson, Mark H. 1982. "In the Halls of Justice, the Only Justice Is in the Halls," in *The Politics of Informal Justice*, edited by R. L. Abel. New York: Academic Press, pp. 119–63

Lemaitre, Julieta and Kristin Bergtora Sandvik. 2015. "Shifting Frames, Vanishing Resources, and Dangerous Political Opportunities: Legal Mobilization among Displaced Women in Colombia." *Law & Society Review* 49(1):5–38.

Marshall, Anna Maria. 2003. "Injustice Frames, Legality, and the Everyday Construction of Sexual Harassment." *Law & Social Inquiry* 28(3):659–89.

2005. "Idle Rights: Employees' Rights Consciousness and the Construction of Sexual Harassment Policies." *Law & Society Review* 39(1):83.

McEwen, Craig A., Lynn Mather, and Richard J. Maiman. 1994. "Lawyers, Mediation, and the Management of Divorce Practice." *Law & Society Review* 28(1):149–86.

Moehling, Carolyn M. and Melissa A. Thomasson. 2012. "Mothers and Babies: The Politics of State Participation in the Sheppard-Towner Program." *The Journal of Economic History* 72(1):75–103.

Morris, Katy. 2017. "'More Reputation Than She Deserves': Remembering Suffrage in Wyoming." *Rethinking History: The Journal of Theory and Practice* 21(1):48–66.

O'Brien, Ruth. 2005. *Bodies in Revolt: Gender, Disability and a Workplace Ethic of Care*. New York: Routledge.

Plumm, Karyn M. and Cheryl A. Terrance. 2009. "Battered Women Who Kill: The Impact of Expert Testimony and Empathy Induction in the Courtroom." *Violence against Women* 15(1):186–205.

Roscigno, Vincent J. and George Wilson. 2014. "The Relational Foundations of Inequality at Work I: Status, Interaction, and Culture." *American Behavioral Scientist* 58(2):219–27.

Royster, Deirdre A. 2003. *Race and the Invisible Hand: How White Networks Exclude Black Men from Blue-Collar Jobs*. Berkeley: University of California Press.

Sarat, Austin. 1990. "'... The Law Is All Over': Power, Resistance and the Legal Consciousness of the Welfare Poor." *Yale Journal of Law & the Humanities* 2(343):343–79.

Shdaimah, Corey S. and Elizabeth Palley. 2010. "Children: Who Cares?" Paper presented at 2010 LSA.

Silbey, Susan and Austin Sarat. 1989. "Dispute Processing in Law and Legal Scholarship: From Institutional Critique to the Reconstruction of the Judicial Subject." *Denver University Law Review* 66:437–97.

Suchman, Mark C. and Lauren B. Edelman. 1996. "Legal Rational Myths: The New Institutionalism and the Law and Society Tradition." *Law & Social Inquiry* 21(4):903–41.

Trautner, Mary Nell, Erin Hatton, and Kelly E. Smith. 2013. "What Workers Want Depends: Legal Knowledge and the Desire for Workplace Change among Day Laborers." *Law & Policy* 35(4):319–40.

Williams, Joan C. 2000. *Unbending Gender: Why Work and Family Conflict and What to Do about It*. Oxford: Oxford University Press.

CHAPTER 7

Bobbitt-Zeher, Donna. 2011. "Gender Discrimination at Work: Connecting Gender Stereotypes, Institutional Policies, and Gender Composition of Workplace." *Gender & Society* 25(6):764–86.

Bumiller, Kristin. 1988. *The Civil Rights Society: The Social Construction of Victims*. Baltimore: The John Hopkins University Press.

DeCoster, Stacy, Sara Beth Estes, and Chalres W. Mueller. 1999. "Routine Activities and Sexual Harassment in the Workplace." *Work and Occupation* 26(1):21–49.

DiMaggio, Paul and Walter Powell. 1983. "The Iron Cage Revisited: Institutional Isomorphism and Collective Rationality in Organizational Fields." *American Sociological Review* 48(2):147–60.

DiMaggio, Paul. 1988. "Interest and Agency in Institutional Theory," in *Institutional Patterns and Organizations*, edited by L. Zucker. Cambridge, MA: Ballinger, pp. 3–22.

Engel, David M. and Frank W. Munger. 2003. *Rights of Inclusion: Law and Identity in the Life Stories of Americans with Disabilities*. Chicago: University of Chicago Press.

Fraser, Nancy. 2016. "Feminism's Home Front: Contradictions of Capital and Care." *New Left Review*.

Fraser, Nancy and Rahel Jaeggi. 2018. *Capitalism: A Conversation in Critical Theory*. New York: Polity.

Kellogg, Katherine C. 2009. "Operating Room: Relational Spaces and Microinstitutional Change in Surgery." *American Journal of Sociology* 115(3):657–711.

2011. "Hot Lights and Cold Steel: Cultural and Political Toolkits for Practice Change in Surgery." *Organizational Science* 22(2):482–502.

2014. "Brokerage Professions and Implementing Reform in an Age of Experts." *American Sociological Review* 79(5):912–14.

Kelly, Erin L., Samantha K. Ammons, Kelly Chermack, and Phyllis Moen. 2010. "Gendered Challenge, Gendered Response: Confronting the Ideal Worker Norm in a White-Collar Organization." *Gender & Society* 24(3):281–303.

Levitsky, Sandra R. 2014. *Caring for Our Own: Why There Is No Political Demand for New American Social Welfare Rights*. New York: Oxford University Press.

Meyerson, Debra and Joanne Martin. 1987. "Cultural Change: An Integration of Three Different Views." *Journal of Management Studies* 24(6):623–47.

Pedriana, Nicholas and Robin Stryker. 2017. "From Legal Doctrine to Social Transformation? Comparing U.S. Voting Rights, Equal Employment Opportunity, and Fair Housing Legislation." *American Journal of Sociology* 123(1):86–135.

Powell, Walter W. and Paul J. DiMaggio. 1991. *The New Institutionalism in Organizational Analysis*. Chicago: University of Chicago Press.

Stainback, Kevin, Thomas N. Ratliff, and Vincent J. Roscigno. 2011. "The Organizational Context of Sex Discrimination: Sex Composition, Workplace Culture, and Relative Power." *Social Forces* 89(3):1165–88.

Stryker, Robin. 2000. "Legitimacy Processes as Institutional Politics: Implications for Theory and Research in the Sociology of Organizations." *Research in the Sociology of Organizations* 17:179–223.

2007. "Half Empty, Half Full, or Neither: Law, Inequality, and Social Change in Capitalist Democracies." *Annual Review of Law & Social Science* 2007(3):69–97.

Suchman, Mark C. 1995. "Managing Legitimacy: Strategic and Institutional Approaches." *Academy of Management Review* 20(3): 571–610.

Wallace, Michael and Kevin Leicht. 2004. "Culture Wars in the Workplace? Cultural Antecedents of Workers' Job Entitlement." *Work and Occupations* 31(1):3–37.

Weisshaar, Katherine. 2017. "From Opt Out to Blocked Out: The Challenges for Labor Market Re-entry after Family-Related Employment Lapses." *American Sociological Review* 83(1):43–60.

APPENDIX

Hind, Christine. 2007. "Multi-Sited Ethnography as a Middle Range Methodology for Contemporary STS." *Science, Technology & Human Values* 32(6):652–71.

Hoffmann, Elizabeth A. 2008. "'Revenge' and 'Rescue': Workplace Deviance in the Taxicab Industry." *Sociological Inquiry* 78(3):270–89.

Lévi-Strauss, Claude. 1969. *The Elementary Structures of Kinship*. New York: Beacon Press.

INDEX

CAMBRIDGE STUDIES IN LAW AND SOCIETY

Books in the Series

Diseases of the Will: Alcohol and the Dilemmas of Freedom
Mariana Valverde

The Politics of Truth and Reconciliation in South Africa: Legitimizing the Post-Apartheid State
Richard A. Wilson

Modernism and the Grounds of Law
Peter Fitzpatrick

Unemployment and Government: Genealogies of the Social
William Walters

Autonomy and Ethnicity: Negotiating Competing Claims in Multi-Ethnic States
Yash Ghai

Constituting Democracy: Law, Globalism and South Africa's Political Reconstruction
Heinz Klug

The Ritual of Rights in Japan: Law, Society, and Health Policy
Eric A. Feldman

Governing Morals: A Social History of Moral Regulation
Alan Hunt

The Colonies of Law: Colonialism, Zionism and Law in Early Mandate Palestine
Ronen Shamir

Law and Nature
David Delaney

Social Citizenship and Workfare in the United States and Western Europe: The Paradox of Inclusion
Joel F. Handler

Law, Anthropology, and the Constitution of the Social: Making Persons and Things
Edited by Alain Pottage and Martha Mundy

Judicial Review and Bureaucratic Impact: International and Interdisciplinary Perspectives
Edited by Marc Hertogh and Simon Halliday

Immigrants at the Margins: Law, Race, and Exclusion in Southern Europe
Kitty Calavita

Lawyers and Regulation: The Politics of the Administrative Process
Patrick Schmidt

Law and Globalization from Below: Towards a Cosmopolitan Legality
Edited by Boaventura de Sousa Santos and
César A. Rodríguez-Garavito

Public Accountability: Designs, Dilemmas and Experiences
Edited by Michael W. Dowdle

Law, Violence and Sovereignty among West Bank Palestinians
Tobias Kelly

Legal Reform and Administrative Detention Powers in China
Sarah Biddulph

The Practice of Human Rights: Tracking Law between the Global and the Local
Edited by Mark Goodale and Sally Engle Merry

Judges beyond Politics in Democracy and Dictatorship: Lessons from Chile
Lisa Hilbink

Paths to International Justice: Social and Legal Perspectives
Edited by Marie-Bénédicte Dembour and Tobias Kelly

Law and Society in Vietnam: The Transition from Socialism in Comparative Perspective
Mark Sidel

Constitutionalizing Economic Globalization: Investment Rules and Democracy's Promise
David Schneiderman

The New World Trade Organization Knowledge Agreements, Second Edition
Christopher Arup

Justice and Reconciliation in Post-Apartheid South Africa
Edited by François du Bois and Antje du Bois-Pedain

Militarization and Violence against Women in Conflict Zones in the Middle East: A Palestinian Case-Study
Nadera Shalhoub-Kevorkian

Child Pornography and Sexual Grooming: Legal and Societal Responses
Suzanne Ost

Darfur and the Crime of Genocide
John Hagan and Wenona Rymond-Richmond

Fictions of Justice: The International Criminal Court and the Challenge of Legal Pluralism in Sub-Saharan Africa
Kamari Maxine Clarke

Conducting Law and Society Research: Reflections on Methods and Practices
Simon Halliday and Patrick Schmidt

Planted Flags: Trees, Land, and Law in Israel/Palestine
Irus Braverman

Culture under Cross-Examination: International Justice and the Special Court for Sierra Leone
Tim Kelsall

Cultures of Legality: Judicialization and Political Activism in Latin America
Javier Couso, Alexandra Huneeus, and Rachel Sieder

Courting Democracy in Bosnia and Herzegovina: The Hague Tribunal's Impact in a Postwar State
Lara J. Nettelfield

The Gacaca Courts, Post-Genocide Justice and Reconciliation in Rwanda: Justice without Lawyers
Phil Clark

Law, Society, and History: Themes in the Legal Sociology and Legal History of Lawrence M. Friedman
Edited by Robert W. Gordon and Morton J. Horwitz

After Abu Ghraib: Exploring Human Rights in America and the Middle East
Shadi Mokhtari

Adjudication in Religious Family Laws: Cultural Accommodation, Legal Pluralism, and Gender Equality in India
Gopika Solanki

Water on Tap: Rights and Regulation in the Transnational Governance of Urban Water Services
Bronwen Morgan

Elements of Moral Cognition: Rawls' Linguistic Analogy and the Cognitive Science of Moral and Legal Judgment
John Mikhail

Mitigation and Aggravation at Sentencing
Edited by Julian V. Roberts

Institutional Inequality and the Mobilization of the Family and Medical Leave Act: Rights on Leave
Catherine R. Albiston

Authoritarian Rule of Law: Legislation, Discourse and Legitimacy in Singapore
Jothie Rajah

Law and Development and the Global Discourses of Legal Transfers
Edited by John Gillespie and Pip Nicholson

Law against the State: Ethnographic Forays into Law's Transformations
Edited by Julia Eckert, Brian Donahoe, Christian Strümpell, and Zerrin Özlem Biner

Transnational Legal Ordering and State Change
Edited by Gregory C. Shaffer

Legal Mobilization under Authoritarianism: The Case of Post-Colonial Hong Kong
Waikeung Tam

Complementarity in the Line of Fire: The Catalysing Effect of the International Criminal Court in Uganda and Sudan
Sarah M. H. Nouwen

Political and Legal Transformations of an Indonesian Polity: The Nagari from Colonisation to Decentralisation
Franz von Benda-Beckmann and Keebet von Benda-Beckmann

Pakistan's Experience with Formal Law: An Alien Justice
Osama Siddique

Human Rights under State-Enforced Religious Family Laws in Israel, Egypt, and India
Yüksel Sezgin

Why Prison?
Edited by David Scott

Law's Fragile State: Colonial, Authoritarian, and Humanitarian Legacies in Sudan
Mark Fathi Massoud

Rights for Others: The Slow Home-Coming of Human Rights in the Netherlands
Barbara Oomen

European States and Their Muslim Citizens: The Impact of Institutions on Perceptions and Boundaries
Edited by John R. Bowen, Christophe Bertossi, Jan Willem Duyvendak, and Mona Lena Krook

Environmental Litigation in China: A Study in Political Ambivalence
Rachel E. Stern

Indigeneity and Legal Pluralism in India: Claims, Histories, Meanings
Pooja Parmar

Paper Tiger: Law, Bureaucracy and the Developmental State in Himalayan India
Nayanika Mathur

Religion, Law and Society
Russell Sandberg

The Experiences of Face Veil Wearers in Europe and the Law
Edited by Eva Brems

The Contentious History of the International Bill of Human Rights
Christopher N. J. Roberts

Transnational Legal Orders
Edited by Terence C. Halliday and Gregory Shaffer

Lost in China? Law, Culture and Society in Post-1997 Hong Kong
Carol A. G. Jones

Security Theology, Surveillance and the Politics of Fear
Nadera Shalhoub-Kevorkian

Opposing the Rule of Law: How Myanmar's Courts Make Law and Order
Nick Cheesman

Ironies of Colonial Governance: Law, Custom and Justice in Colonial India
James Jaffe

The Clinic and the Court: Law, Medicine and Anthropology
Edited by Ian Harper, Tobias Kelly, and Akshay Khanna

The World of Indicators: The Making of Government Knowledge through Quantification
Edited by Richard Rottenburg, Sally E. Merry, Sung-Joon Park, and Johanna Mugler

Contesting Immigration Policy in Court: Legal Activism and Its Radiating Effects in the United States and France
Leila Kawar

The Quiet Power of Indicators: Measuring Governance, Corruption, and Rule of Law Edited by
Sally Engle Merry, Kevin E. Davis, and Benedict Kingsbury

Investing in Authoritarian Rule: Punishment and Patronage in Rwanda's Gacaca Courts for Genocide Crimes
Anuradha Chakravarty

Contractual Knowledge: One Hundred Years of Legal Experimentation in Global Markets
Edited by Grégoire Mallard and Jérôme Sgard

Iraq and the Crimes of Aggressive War: The Legal Cynicism of Criminal Militarism
John Hagan, Joshua Kaiser, and Anna Hanson

Culture in the Domains of Law
Edited by René Provost

China and Islam: The Prophet, the Party, and Law
Matthew S. Erie

Diversity in Practice: Race, Gender, and Class in Legal and Professional Careers
Edited by Spencer Headworth, Robert L. Nelson, Ronit Dinovitzer, and David B. Wilkins

A Sociology of Constitutions: Constitutions and State Legitimacy in Historical-Sociological Perspective
Chris Thornhill

A Sociology of Transnational Constitutions: Social Foundations of the Post-National Legal Structure
Chris Thornhill

Genocide Never Sleeps: Living Law at the International Criminal Tribunal for Rwanda
Nigel Eltringham

Shifting Legal Visions: Judicial Change and Human Rights Trials in Latin America
Ezequiel A. González-Ocantos

The Demographic Transformations of Citizenship
Heli Askola

Criminal Defense in China: The Politics of Lawyers at Work
Sida Liu and Terence C. Halliday

Contesting Economic and Social Rights in Ireland: Constitution, State and Society, 1848–2016
Thomas Murray

Buried in the Heart: Women, Complex Victimhood and the War in Northern Uganda
Erin Baines

Palaces of Hope: The Anthropology of Global Organizations
Edited by Ronald Niezen and Maria Sapignoli

The Politics of Bureaucratic Corruption in Post-Transitional Eastern Europe
Marina Zaloznaya

Revisiting the Law and Governance of Trafficking, Forced Labor and Modern Slavery
Edited by Prabha Kotiswaran

Incitement on Trial: Prosecuting International Speech Crimes
Richard Ashby Wilson

Criminalizing Children: Welfare and the State in Australia
David McCallum

Global Lawmakers: International Organizations in the Crafting of World Markets
Susan Block-Lieb and Terence C. Halliday

Duties to Care: Dementia, Relationality and Law
Rosie Harding

Insiders, Outsiders, Injuries, and Law: Revisiting "The Oven Bird's Song"
Edited by Mary Nell Trautner

Hunting Justice: Displacement, Law, and Activism in the Kalahari
Maria Sapignoli

Injury and Injustice: The Cultural Politics of Harm and Redress
Edited by Anne Bloom, David M. Engel, and Michael McCann

Ruling Before the Law: The Politics of Legal Regimes in China and Indonesia
William Hurst

The Powers of Law: A Comparative Analysis of Sociopolitical Legal Studies
Mauricio García-Villegas

A Sociology of Justice in Russia
Edited by Marina Kurkchiyan and Agnieszka Kubal

Constituting Religion: Islam, Liberal Rights, and the Malaysian State
Tamir Moustafa

The Invention of the Passport: Surveillance, Citizenship and the State, Second Edition
John C. Torpey

Law's Trials: The Performance of Legal Institutions in the US "War on Terror"
Richard L. Abel

Law's Wars: The Fate of the Rule of Law in the US "War on Terror"
Richard L. Abel

Transforming Gender Citizenship: The Irresistible Rise of Gender Quotas in Europe
Edited by Eléonore Lépinard and Ruth Rubio-Marín

Muslim Women's Quest for Justice: Gender, Law and Activism in India
Mengia Hong Tschalaer

Children as "Risk": Sexual Exploitation and Abuse by Children and Young People
Anne-Marie McAlinden

The Legal Process and the Promise of Justice: Studies Inspired by the Work of Malcolm Feeley
Jonathan Simon, Rosann Greenspan, Hadar Aviram

Gift Exchanges: The Transnational History of a Political Idea
Grégoire Mallard

Measuring Justice: Quantitative Accountability and the National Prosecuting Authority in South Africa
Johanna Mugler

Negotiating the Power of NGOs: Women's Legal Rights in South Africa
Reem Wael

Indigenous Water Rights in Law and Regulation: Lessons from Comparative Experience
Elizabeth Jane Macpherson

The Edge of Law: Legal Geographies of a War Crimes Court
Alex Jeffrey

Everyday Justice: Law, Ethnography, and Injustice
Sandra Brunnegger

The Uncounted: Politics of Data in Global Health
Sara L. M. Davis

Transnational Legal Ordering of Criminal Justice
Gregory Shaffer and Ely Aaronson

Five Republics and One Tradition
Pablo Ruiz-Tagle

The Law Multiple: Judgment and Knowledge in Practice
Irene van Oorschot

Health as a Human Right: The Politics and Judicialisation of Health in Brazil
Octávio Luiz Motta Ferraz

Shari'a, Inshallah: Finding God in Somali Legal Politics
Mark Fathi Massoud

Policing for Peace: Institutions, Expectations, and Security in Divided Societies
Matthew Nanes

Rule of Law Intermediaries: Brokering Influence in Myanmar
Kristina Simion

CPSIA information can be obtained
at www.ICGtesting.com
Printed in the USA
LVHW081231260821
695979LV00022B/201

9 781108 488549